AT THE MIDPOINT OF
ETERNITY

OTHER BOOKS BY CONSTANT WATERMAN

THE JOURNALS of CONSTANT WATERMAN
PADDLING, POLING, AND SAILING FOR THE LOVE OF IT

MOONWIND AT LARGE: SAILING HITHER AND YON

LANDMARKS YOU MUST VISIT IN SOUTHEAST CONNECTICUT

***MORE* LANDMARKS YOU MUST VISIT IN SOUTHEAST CONNECTICUT**

VINCUS THE INVISIBLE DIVULGES HIS SECRET RECIPE FOR MAPLE PISTACHIO BIRCH BEER RASPBERRY RIPPLE

VINCUS THE INVISIBLE VISITS PLANET EARTH

AT THE MIDPOINT
OF
ETERNITY

MUSINGS AND ILLUSTRATIONS
BY CONSTANT WATERMAN

www.constantwaterman.com

ISBN: 978-0-9835288-6-9

This first edition published by C. Cody Books

Illustration of Poseidon first appeared in *Wind Check* magazine.

Cover design and layout Sandy and Marilena Vaccaro,
Studio Ten LLC., Chester, CT.

Many thanks to *Breakaway Books* for permission to reprint numerous illustrations from my two volumes of boating stories.

Also, thanks to *Points East* magazine for permission to reprint several stories that have appeared over the past decade or more.

Thanks, of course, to *Messing About in Boats* magazine, who published a regular column for me from 2005 till 2017.

Thanks to Everglades City's *Mullet Rapper* for permission to reprint *Paws to Reflect*.

Excerpt from In Need of a Boat first appeared in *Good Old Boat* magazine.

'Were I aware,' was first published in *Janus*, and 'See how the stream divides', 'I thought my soul obsidian,' and 'Gripped in the mind's eye,' were first published in *A Letter Among Friends* magazine.

And thanks to my sister, Marya Repko, for information gleaned from her book, *A Brief History of the Everglades City Area*, and for her editorial help.

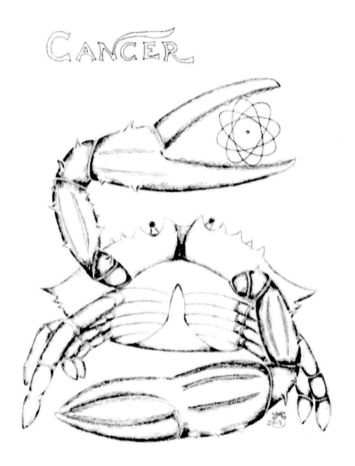

CANCER

Contemplation of the infinite

TABLE OF CONTENTS

TO MY NEW GRANDDAUGHTER,

AKI HIWASA ("BRIGHT HOPE")

TO KEEP US UPON OUR PATH

The Red Mill
Eight Mile River — Lyme, CT

Prologue

Well, here I am again at the Midpoint of Eternity. Some of you lag behind, some of you have dashed on ahead. No matter. In a few million years, or in a few moments, we shall all arrive at this same point in time.

This is only fitting, as we all evolved from the primordial slime mere eons ago, on a Tuesday afternoon, which was, in fact, also at the Midpoint of Eternity. Be assured – this continuum on which we travel is naught but the rim of the hugest wheel, and no matter where we pause upon it to get our bearings, we are as far from any where, or when, as we were before.

Therefore, it behooves us to make the most of our every moment ere we overtake ourselves as we roll across the heavens.

I've been thinking how fortuitous it is that I have arrived here without anyone being the wiser – or much better looking. Having now arrived at the Midpoint of Eternity – not for the first time – I need to project my aspirations and extravagations onto this page and those succeeding while yet the sun and moon demand my attention. The moon seems ever more likely to demand her share of attention, as she keeps me from sleep a full week out of every month. This, of course, could be remedied by a more opaque drape over the south facing French window in my bedroom. Perhaps I am meant, as the years drift slowly yon-ward, to hie myself to this tablet to record my dreams these myriad sleepless nights.

As Queen Portulaca, I should subsist on nothing save lavender cookies and moonbeam tea. What better fare for a drifter, a dreamer, a lover of muses, a sojourner at this here and now for this tenuous little while. I have come thus far with my health and mind intact; with my resolution at odds with my disposition, which is slothful; and my ego no more temperamental than the breeze that drives my sailboat by this shore.

My latest study, studio, den, and workspace is now but a ten by thirteen room in a sturdy double wide trailer in a non-pretentious part of quiet town. As my previous study was a fifteen by forty loft, I've needed to curtail my never extensive library to a mere few hundred volumes, and to organize myself as seldom before. But, as Gertrude Stein should have said, had she but known: "A room is a room is a room." As with minds, it is what is produced and nowise the size of our hats.

I do not suffer in a freezing garret, as Chatterton, nor stalk long, stately corridors as Lord Tennyson. From this, my coign of infinite perspective, I mull the intricacies of the human condition; even, perhaps, my own. Without her humor, how should Thalia thrive? Without mortality, how Melpomene daunt? From this oh, so fleeting Midpoint of Eternity, I invite you to share my musings and illustrations.

KYRIELLE

What is a word if not to say?
What meter should my soul convey?
As through this maze of sounds I stray
I've felt a poem force a path.

There are no easy ways to be;
My mind is seldom truly free;
But though I often fail to see,
I've felt a poem force a path.

And even when the night is drear
And I have given heed to fear,
There's one consoling sense that's clear –
I've felt a poem force a path.

There are no stars no hide the night,
No sun by day to shade the light;
Yet always lines to lead us right –
So there's a poem, there's a path.

Writing And Illustrating

I began writing poetry before my psyche, ego, and outlook had determined what to do with my soul and mind and perspective. I imagine that in another century or so I shall have dispensed with ego entirely and write truly from the soul.

Amazingly, the words are all out there, ready formed, defined, metrically enhanced, and waiting deployment. That Shakespeare, Donne, and Keats; Whitman, Edna Millay, and Dylan Thomas should all have used the same words to such advantage. That Chaucer and e e cummings both spoke a tongue in common with Lord Tennyson, Emily Dickenson, Dorothy Parker. What an amazing coincidence that these and a million others have sorted words to embellish our tongue!

I have given up writing poetry per se, and now but use the rhythms and tools of prosody in my writing. Poems, for me, were but the blatant expletives of a passion. I could never sustain a poem for page after page. Poetry, for me, was a rage, a bloody, a mortal wound, a shriek. Anything over thirty or forty lines was but a contrivance; a finely wrought thing of manners. Unless, of course, you refer to plays in verse. I wrote a few of those as well, with a most sensational lack of any success. I had but one that impressed even myself: A Touch of Frost; a play about a poet facing old age, senility, death. But to pen lines spoke by a poet upon the stage without being overly formal is something I've yet to master; and something an audience seldom cares to hear.

It seems a modern audience is dependent on action, not words, to hold its attention. Though most of my audience when I read from my journals stay right with me, I was told by one book seller to limit my total reading to twenty minutes, else I would lose my audience. I've never had that problem. My journals average seven hundred words – four to five minutes reading. My best ones blend emotion, description, action, humor, and introspection. As one of my readers confided to another, "The perfect book to keep by the toilet." I fancy his earthy compliment referred to the length of my pieces and not their absorbency. Two pages plus two cups of coffee will start most people's day.

So, after inundating the theater market with every known species of play for about ten years with little success, I determined to resume the journaling I'd practiced at age thirty. During my playwrighting interval I'd resumed the art of sailing and bought a small boat. My Cape Dory Typhoon and I explored the Connecticut coast, and dismayed every mermaid for many miles around.

I would come home from the marina and write in my journal. "Today I ventured offshore to chase a breeze…" From there I would digress. Seals, cats, sea serpents, ferry boats, submarines, and seagulls all figured into the mixture. As well as the joy of sailing; the touch of the rain; the discomfort of mal de mere; my love for the sea. Recollections of the childhood I still enjoy – enhanced for literary effect – always comprise a portion of my writing. Reflections on Nature, Death, Determination, and the need to relax have all a place in my journals. I seldom exhort; I sometimes amuse; I frequently describe – but not to great length – and I often wax wistful – at least around the edges.

Occasionally my memoirs wander. I'm not averse to letting my mind have plenty of scope – seven to one scarcely suffices to keep my imagination fast to the bottom. Scrubbing the bilge or teaching The Pusslet to tie a figure eight knot – both have a place in my narratives. So has boating etiquette; so has a dragging anchor. Wading the brook behind the barn has made me who I am.

I found that several boating periodicals were charmed by my memoirs. Till recently I had a column in Messing About in Boats magazine. The publisher of Breakaway Books, afflicted with owning a sailboat, liked my columns: he published my first collection of them in 2007; my second made its appearance in 2012.

I used to sketch as a child. My father, an engineer, taught me mechanical drawing. In my late twenties I attempted a children's book concerning cats. In my early thirties I wrote a short book about building an octagonal cottage on an island, and began to make illustrations for that endeavor. For the next thirty years I made no effort to draw. When my publisher agreed to produce my first book of boating journals, I determined to illustrate it. This proved a great learning experience. I have now produced six books with illustrations and am confident I know which end of the pencil leaves the prettiest marks.

Swans

From my sketches of lighthouses, public buildings, and mermaids I founded a postcard business. From that to note cards and matted prints has been but the merest stumble. I now own the largest collection of black and white cards in all southeastern Connecticut. My shelves and closet bulge with fruits of my labors. I even manage to sell a couple of thousand cards every year. On welcome occasions I even take on a commission.

Private Residence – Norwich, Connecticut

The rain this moment is sheeting vertically, drumming on my plastic skylights and turning the sloped road past my home to a river. A good day to venture within with my thoughts and fill these receptive pages…

Here is an illustration from my first children's book, *Vincus the Invisible Divulges His Secret Recipe for Maple Pistachio Birch Beer Raspberry Ripple*. This is strictly humor for children under ninety, though I did make an exception for a friend of ninety-two who insisted on owning a copy. This picture is entitled *The Road That Returns*, as all proper roads are expected to do. I'm told the secret is merely to turn and walk the other way. I tried this when I achieved middle age and have never looked back since. Now that, children, is absolutely the truth.

The Road that Returns

Poetry and Running Water

I grew up on a hundred acres on the fringe of the twentieth century, and the deer would browse on our lawn where it sloped to the pond. Often, they browsed by moonlight.

Moon Deer Dream

That pond, of course, was my delight as a boy. Here is an excerpt from *The Journals of Constant Waterman* entitled In Need of a Boat, and the first of all my journals to be published.

"When I turned six, my father had a portion of the cow pasture dredged, creating a pond one hundred feet long, half that in width, and deep enough to hide my hippopotamus. We used it as a swimming hole all summer long, as a skating rink all winter – as long as we were willing to clear the snow.

My father went to the extension center and procured two milk cans [antiques now, no doubt] alive with fingerling fish: one of largemouth bass, the other with bluegill sunfish. In a couple of years, the pond teemed with fish; with frogs and turtles and muskrats. Heaven on earth for a little boy, but dirtier."

And here is an entry from my journals entitled, *The Stream* :

The muskrat scuttled between my legs, dove into the pond, and swam for his lair with frantic expedition. What did I care? I was fishing. For a score of years, until the otter ate them, the muskrats ruled the pond behind our house. They had their burrows within the banks. Occasionally, a roof gave way and I stepped, uninvited, into their drawing room.

As a boy I used to mow around the pond with our two wheeled Gravely tractor. One afternoon I caught the off wheel in a muskrat lair and tipped the rig on her side. As she weighed about four hundred pounds, I needed help to right her. We brought our four-wheel drive wagon down the hill and employed a chain to yank the Gravely upright. But I always enjoyed our muskrats, notwithstanding.

Just downstream from the pond, below the bank, spread a marshy area, sometimes fetlock deep. Stubbly brush grew in it, making it difficult to wade in. The effluent from the pond, meant to flow through a twelve-inch ceramic pipe, generally chose some other, more contrary way. Some of it scoured around the pipe, some of it cut a new gully ten yards off. A slight amount flowed through the pipe – just enough to keep up appearances. All this spillage rejoined to form a stream.

The marshy area abutted this. It bred the most amazing clan of mosquitoes. These creatures were so persuasive that, any time a quorum obtained, they always carried the vote. They gerrymandered that little marsh into a district of rapier bearing, ravening soldiers of fortune. Against these troops the frogs and dragonflies and barn swallows waged ceaseless battle.

The stream continued behind three narrow, root heaved slabs where once three, two story sheds had housed ten thousand hens. Only the long, squat brooder house, where chicks had been fed and incubated, still stood when I grew up. Rusted ductwork and lengths of pipe lay amid litter within its shallow foundation. Most of the windows grinned horribly with fangs of shattered glass. What remained of the cedar roof would scarcely keep out a crow. Attached to one end of this brooder house rose a small, two-story structure, its floor as safely walked upon as that of a tiger trap. Those rotten floors, the broken glass, the jagged sheet metal, and rusty nails made this complex as attractive a place to play as any playground. A foot of wet snow brought down the roof one sodden February.

Out back, the stream wended amid the alders and briars and boggy grounds just this side of the cow pasture until it crossed the shady farm road that led out to the hayfields. Two hops and a step took you over. During spring thaws, when the stepping stones glistened beneath the water, a running leap sometimes sufficed to take one to the far shore. Wet feet were nowise a rarity growing up. Across this road the stream dropped down and turned, then dropped again to find itself backed up by a miniature dam. This defined a narrow, waist deep pond for watering stock. After this contrived delay the stream traversed a precipitous bank and joined with Hungerford Brook.

We used to camp in the wood beyond the dam, below the road, beneath a huge maple tree. My father had a small mountain tent replete with mosquito netting. We pitched this beneath the maple tree, built a campfire, grilled our supper, washed up in the stream, and slept out here in the trackless wilderness just out of sight of the barn.

This maple tree had a slot through its trunk thirty feet from the ground. This slot would prove its weak point. All that remains of this virtuous tree is a thirty-foot stump with a half-dozen dead limbs. The glade about it, no longer shaded; has grown to briar and scrub. The little dam long since collapsed; the stream creeps through its stones. We bulldozed and buried the ruin of the brooder house. The pond behind our family home no longer has muskrats in it. No small boy with muddy feet and a dripping net studies its weedy verges.

The stream, however, traverses its quarter mile. Each spring, young maples flaunt their Luna moth leaves. Another generation of avid frogs proclaims the joy of water.

The stream aforementioned spilled into Hungerford brook. This small run, perhaps five miles in length and a few yards wide, emptied into slightly larger Roaring Brook and thence, after a mile, into Whalebone Cove: a teeming, labyrinthine brackish marsh connected by a large tidal stream to the lovely Connecticut. This entire watershed was my playground. Hungerford Brook skirted our land and crossed the abandoned dirt road down the precipitous hill behind our barn. The bridge was destroyed in the flood of 1982, but its deck was scarcely intact enough to walk across ere then. The last vehicle to cross that span was myself and a friend in his pickup truck sometime in the late 70's. The road down the hill had been officially closed since the early 60's. We dodged the posts that guarded the way and went down the hill to cut firewood. Having loaded the truck, we ripped up a couple of spongy planks and laid them lengthwise across the deplorable deck of the bridge. With our wheels on them we inched our way across. It was mainly the steel girders that took our weight.

In the summer of 1982, we had torrential rains for a week as a low-pressure system stalled at the mouth of the Connecticut. The gravid mill ponds of a half dozen towns all broke their waters at once that Friday night. Parturition resulted in herds of white horses. Dams and bridges disappeared; so did several houses. Water over the flooded road did not ensure the presence of a bridge beneath. A six-wheel truck attempted the crossing of Roaring Brook through what appeared as merely a foot of water above the road. The concrete bridge no longer existed, and the truck plunged into eight feet of violent water. The passenger, our neighbor, the local art teacher, was drowned. The driver clung to a tree root in the torrent most of the night, and managed to survive.

The bridge over Hungerford Brook might never have been. The dry wall abutments, built from stones provided by a broken dam, could not be identified. The six steel girders reclined among the trees. The planking vanished. Trees and boulders had caroused in the valley all night below the barn and swept away the presumptuous craft of man.

Here is a poem that I wrote in '77 about this brook:

See how the stream divides,
And that side rushes past that stony pier,
Avid as gravity, tumbling, trumpeting,
Strumpet-proud, strident and grumbling;
Over the stones swirls – hence to the World!

But where the north divergence of the brook
Adjoins the opposite pier in calm carouse,
Nuzzles the stream each crevice in fond caress,
And now one stone's breadth seeps –
Dimpling, placid, limpid, woman-soft water.

But in the lee of that stream dividing stone
Which, bare breast, deftly bifurcates the brook,
The water pauses, hesitates, decides;
Then, slowly slowing, slowly, slowly slues
In froth flecked eddy back on its swinging self
With grand, indifferent, tantalizing pendency.

Then let me leap, go slowly, and stand fast;
The best would flee ere this we know is past.

The thing I enjoyed about poetry was its contrivance: the work, the thought, the precision to achieve that assonance and consonance and meter and meaning and rhythm all at once. And the reasons I stopped writing poetry were the same. I worked at furious rhythms; at complexity; simplicity; in your face facts and subtle turns of thought. I wrote and rewrote till the kettle burned and the cat complained of no supper. I fashioned and crafted and overworked lines. I often spent years to perfect a poem, only to meet with blank looks from attentive listeners. But occasionally I got it nearly right on the first attempt.

I wrote of metaphysical things: Eternity and Death; Degradation and Enlightenment; Striving and Accomplishment.

Reach!

I thought my soul obsidian –
Split into black blades, thirsty and savage,
Avid and ardent till splintered still further;
Sharp shards to dream in the undergrowth, lost
And yet alterable, missed by millennia,
Tossed by slow forces.

I thought my mind mahogany –
Dusky and rough, untouched by the plane,
But still fine grained and tough within;
Waiting in vain the shipwright's whim;
Saved to be shaped for a transom piece
To bear gold letters overseas.

I thought my heart bituminous –
Pressed by centuries, swiftly stripped;
Harder than mind, slower to burn;
Softer than soul that fire formed;
Holder of heat; a steady, slow heat
That readily all but the dross consumed.

Here is another from that same period:

Gripped in the mind's eye, days of inspiration
Slip to the mind's side when our spring is storming.
Grappled by mind's rage, fatal days
Are boarded, sacked with asperity,
Sorted and plundered, spoiled in seclusion.

Whipped by the soul's scorn, days of affirmation
Strip for the soul's sport, wanton with conforming.
Fettered in soul's cage, maiden days
Are mounted; whore for security,
Swell with mortality, bear us confusion.

Ripened on heart's vine, days of consternation
Cling with the heart's old terror of reforming.
Plucked during the heart's age, wastrel days
Are mellowed: rank with tranquility,
Cured in denial, stoppled with illusion.

Phoenix Moon

Poetry and Love

I managed, despite this grim vehemence, to fall in love. My first marriage began as a long love affair of which I wrote:.

Were I aware this world saves
To waste the great day of my taming,
I would storm Illusion's rampart,
Clamber through her deadly crenel,
Whelm her fell guard with my instance.

What should I do with lance and shield,
Hard loud armor, broadsword, charger,
Arbalest and deadly quarrel?
Naught need I save heart and heaven,
Your love near to vaunt this venture.

Were I aware this spirit craves
A high, high summit for assurance,
I would ascend to love's decision,
Spend this slender lifetime singing,
Hurl convention to the chasm.

What should I do with gain and gamble,
Vain, short days I sport with trouble,
Aspiration's thorn sired tangle?
Naught need I save peace and reason,
Your love near to spoil confusion.

Were I aware this shoddy clockwork
Locked within me has no winder,
I would attempt to spend this tension,
Love you with my heart's unwinding,
Wait for nothing!

Those were indeed exhilarating days, but by the early nineties, my first marriage had fallen apart, and I lived by myself in a ten by twenty apartment at the back of my barn. It was snug and efficient. I had a wood stove for heat; a gas stovetop, electric toaster oven, hot running water, a mouse for company. A mouse unattached by her tail to any computer; a free range mouse: nearly as wild as I was. I cultivated a perfect frenzy and poured out my rage and despair and resentment and loneliness onto the pages of my notebook. I labored in my machine shop in the front of my barn all day, cooked my supper, then wrote and read until I collapsed from fatigue. I joined a poetry workshop hosted by the Eugene O'Neill Theater in Waterford, and met some interesting people. One is still my friend; another attempted to teach me dramatic writing at URI ten years later.

I vented my rage, frustration, and hope in the barn.

I wrote of the clutching claws of despair that rend us from our repose:

Remember

No, there is no
No, there is no day
No, there is,
As relevant as raving.
No night,
None
Uncoupled,
None
From all the art,
From all the light of loving.
No star
None
To start us from our heaven;
No un-present
Rifer than our pulsing;
No requital
Quicker than this instant;
No grand scheme
To equal our involvement.

Remember
When you scream
Your wild and hunted
Savage self awake,

Shaken and drenched,
How? How would you?
Christ, How would you
Halt this clutching horror?

When you awake
Remember
Not for God's but your sake
Only what would correlate
Life with learning,
Loving, longing,
Song and seashore,
Wind and laughter:
Those that redeem us
From our ingrown terror:
Stifling night –
And stifling night forever.

Harvest Moon

But all was not nightmare and rage and horror. I had insightful moments
as well, which is to say, saner revelations of a similar magnitude:

Now is that avidness
Most apt to restore us,
As here is that urging
We never think to heed.
Tomorrow is the ever
That stretches before us,
As yesterday the never
He captious gods bequeath.

We are not wise as wistful
Or sane as we might savor;
For life is but a mendicant
And death the merest favor.
Too slender is this season's purse
To recompense our scheming.

There is no realm beyond our reason,
Heaven beyond our dreaming,
Nor grace without this only-ness
But promises a measure
Of love we never thought to know –
And would not know to treasure.

Eventually I mellowed. I anticipated another great love in my life.
And I was not disappointed.

There are not enough ways out of the forest
To dispense entirely with the path.
There are not enough rains to fill the stream
To dispense entirely with the spring.

When you smile for me I know
I can never be lost again;
When you hold me, I know
My soul will be fertile forever.
One day I shall show you
Where the trout lilies hide in the shadows.
One day I shall show you
Where the iris challenge the sun.

From spending much time in the forest
I have learned to sparkle as the stream.
The hidden depths of the spring
Are filled with sweet water.

Full Moon by the Bridge

And when I had fallen in love again, I produced this poem, which blended so many emotions. It flowed out of me one day, and I scarcely changed it.

There is something of Magic
In the shiver of believing
Which is very like the Magic
Of the moon above the river
Which is very much the Magic
That's returned to the giver
And is very like the smile
Of a sharing lover.

There is something of Weird
In the wildness of wanting
Which is very like the Weird
Of the moon upon the river
Twixt the dark banks hulking
Where the trees are aquiver
As Weird stalks the path
Of the pallor on the river.

There is something of Never
In the fury of the gale
Which is very like the Never
Of old age clawing –
Of the ancient crawling
Of skin upon the skull –
Which is very much the Never
Of the glazed eye calling
From the dust of dying
To the morrow of forever.

There is something of Strength
In the shadow of forgetting
Which is very like the Strength
That accompanies forgoing
Which is very like the Magic
Of the wind against the river –
Of that rising wind
Which tears at the river –
Which is very like the Weird
Of the crying of the Never
Which is part of the smile
Of a lover that's forever.

Dryad with Moth

The image of moonlight upon the river was drawn from my many years in a canoe. I used to paddle on the Connecticut by moonlight, summer and winter. It becomes very quiet when you're following the trail of the moonlight down the river. And even quieter fighting the tide and current upstream with the moon at your back. If the wind as well came down the river, I'd be lucky to make it back to my cabin on the island. I haven't told you about my cabin on an island in the Connecticut, nor the octagonal studio I nearly completed there.

That was when I was young and ambitious and almost totally stupid. Not quite, as it turns out, for it launched my career as a journal keeper. I won't use the word journalist, for that connotes someone who dashes about, eager to scoop the latest story for a newspaper. I've never worked for a newspaper, but it seems a soul-destroying existence.

I've never cultivated an interest in politics, fashion, war, or car crashes – or high school backgammon tournaments. Some journalists do learn how to write well under pressure. Writing memoirs for a magazine as E. B. White did for the New Yorker would be more to my liking. What I need to find is a magazine editor who doesn't wear shoes to work. Then, maybe, I'd stand a chance of landing a feasible column.

The Connecticut, close to the ocean where I grew up, is a far broader river than what I've depicted here, and the swath of moonlight was hedged on either hand by a couple of hundred yards of darker waters. The river I've depicted here would never surprise you with an oil tanker plunging round the next bend.

The cry of a night heron might be all you'd encounter the entire evening. The Connecticut could surprise you with either. I'd gladly read the logbooks of a couple of skippers who encountered me on a winter's eve, playing about the river. One of them shone his spotlight on me for several minutes together.

I've written about such encounters as this, and about messing about the ice flows, and the salt marshes, and the old swing bridge at East Haddam, and about a murder in the woods. This is one of my favorite stories, but if I told you about it here, you'd never buy my other books. It's also one of my better written pieces and I've waxed very contented, if not smug, thinking about it. Of course, contentment ain't all it's cracked up to be,

Moonlight

and writers who become complacent about their writing are destined to become promoters of breakfast cereals.

Notwithstanding, I continuously scrutinize my writing, and know full well that the Muse favors me no more than once every dozen journal entries. Perhaps I should leave fresher flowers upon her altar. Occasionally, it's but a passage that prompts me to think I may have mastered both the elements of style and the lyricism of the ages.

* * * *

Some people think I should call myself a memoirist as opposed to a journalist, but most of what passes for memoirs are accounts of what Aunt Flo said to your mother during your graduation picnic in 1967, and how you were so embarrassed you were afraid that your best friend Janey might never speak to you again. Which might have been a good thing in hindsight, because Janey went on to marry the baker's son and now has twenty-four screaming children with drippy noses, and breakfasts on nothing save day old croissants and stale crullers, and never gets out of her size thirty-one pajamas from one week to the next.

I suppose I could have embarked on this sort of writing and promoted breakfast cereal – or day-old croissants – as a side line, but I have enough trouble getting published as it is and, anyhow, I wouldn't want to make too much money or be invited onto day time TV talk shows. I'd probably have to trim my beard and buy a new pair of sneakers. And besides, there'd be no one left here at home to let in the cat.

So I'm neither a journalist nor a memoirist. However, the writing world has declared a new genre entitled Flash Fiction. This consists of no more than a few hundred words and was designed for people who wanted to become authors between cups of coffee. Such as myself. There is also a new category of style denoted Creative Non-fiction. I figure I come under the heading of Creative Flash Non-fiction. I can often create non-fiction in a flash before I've even had breakfast.

In 1972 I decided to build a tiny cabin on five acres of marshy land I owned that were a small part of an island along the shore of the tidal Connecticut. I drove my pickup truck to one of our local saw mills to procure some lumber and encountered a character who would inspire me to write a poem, a short story, and a one act play about him.He was

an old Russian, whose descendants operated the mill, and who, on this
particular day, was alone at the house that stood beside it.

There was no one at the sawmill.
The silence of the scream-less blade
Complimented the morning.
Knocking at the kitchen door brought no one,
And I'd turned to my truck in the drive
Resigned to depart
When an old, old voice
Came thinly through the yard,
"They are not here;
They go to fell the trees."

He twinkled from beneath his long white brows.
"The coffee, he is hot —
Come in, come in."
Upon the sturdy table were a loaf, a knife,
A yellow cheese encased in gleaming wax.
The wood range crackled in its corner.

"There no one is save ancient Sergius.
All the men they work, the women, too.
But Sergius, he keeps the fire awake
And takes the message.
You shall talk to him."

As he poured coffee so his words poured out
And flooded other memory from my mind.
How suddenly the present century slipped
And I returned to the Russia of our forebears.
I heard the whispering snows fill up the night;
Smelled the marketplace with its new baked loaves;
Heard the harness bells amid the wood;
And laughed at the bear who roamed the village streets.

Old Sergius sliced the loaf
And held the slice to peer along its edge.
"He is not true, not true."
He shook his shaggy head.
"The hand is old, is knotted like the oak.

31

Cannot cut straight, can scarcely grasp the blade."
He held it up and laughed with gay chagrin.
"You would not think this hand had music in him.
Yes, once could Sergius –
Wait, and I shall show you."

He shuffled to the next room,
Enthusiasm guiding his old feet.
"Here," he said. "The treasure of my heart."
He took from its case a glistening violin.
"Could one time Sergius make the people cry."

He closed his eyes.
His old, huge hand
Guided the trembling bow
And dragged from the strings
A poignant lullaby –
A melody once beloved of a faded world.

Old Sergius laid the violin to rest
With reverence –
As you would a sleeping child.
"Ah," he sighed. "These hands of mine –
Too many years they grip the crosscut saw."

Into the yard a groaning truck
Churned and strained
With its heavy load of logs.

*   *   *   *

Old Sergius – or whatever his name had been – has stayed with me. Besides his passion for music, coupled with a life of the most arduous manual labor, he told me stories that took me back to a time so far removed from my modern world as made my mind to reel. His grandmamma had actually seen Napoleon Bonaparte during his march through Russia.

"She was only a little girl," he explained to me. It was 1812 – one hundred and sixty years removed from our present breakfast at the sawmill. It brought a sense of realism to history – continuity.

Elm Grove Cemetery, Mystic, Connecticut

I never knew my grandparents. They had all been born in the 1860's and 70's. They would have been even older than Old Sergius, who was ninety-three. And I was but twenty-five – a mere child. Still wet behind the pencil, with which I attempted to tell of what was wistful. My grandparents might have told me similar stories, but they were gone; the links were broken. My parents, my aunts and uncles, told me no tales from the Old World. How should I become a writer of stories? My stories must deal with the century that I knew. My father told me marvelous tales at bedtime when I was a child. Tales of World War II; tales of the jungles of Venezula where he prospected for oil in the 1920's. Jaguars and alligators; submarines and typhoons – a wealth of imagery and information that I carry around.

And, wonder of wonders! After the death of my parents, I discovered in a steamer trunk, up in their attic, all of the letters from my father to my mother from Venezuela over two years from 1928 till 1930. My father, though an engineer, was a would-be poet, and courted my mother in Manhattan by airmail letters posted at irregular intervals, for he truly went into the deeps of the jungle in the pay of Standard Oil.

Sixty letters or more, and I sorted them by date, and read the entire bundle one long night. Much later I came across a handful of love letters written to him by two ladies from Buenos Aires where he had spent a couple of months. One lady corresponded in French, and I've yet to have her translated. The other, an English woman, begged him to return.

Instead, he traveled to New York on a steamer, his money belt bulging with gold. The financial crash of '29 had rendered most paper money worthless, and Standard Oil had imbursed its workers in gold. He returned, went into practice as a consulting engineer, and continued to assail my mother until she finally succumbed and married him in 1936. I can't imagine a ten-year courtship in today's harried society. Then again, had she wedded him ten years earlier, I might have been born twenty years sooner and likely as not be dead now. That might preclude my writing these stories today in 2018.

A ten-year courtship. It seems attention spans were just a tad longer back then. Nowadays, many folk find it too demanding to actually read a book. It takes a bit more to kindle their imaginations. During those years of my parents' courtship, from 1926 till 1936, several books were not only read but written. I have to admit, it took me ten years to make it through Joyce's Ulysses, the result of reading the first half several times. Seems I always got mired down by that Irish barmaid, Circe, who, of necessity, gruntled the louts who swilled their beer at the bar.

But I'm seldom averse to reading a really good book. Or at least a book that features dialogue between Huckleberry Finn and Lord Peter Whimsey. Or at least the Mole and the Rat. I grew up reading The Wind in the Willows about three times a year.

Now that I'm older, more serious, more sophisticated, and less amused by childish tales, cloying nostalgia, and maudlin sentimentality, I seldom read it more than twice a year. My dear friend, Cap'n Salty Whiskahs, sometimes calls me Ratty. Can I help it if I'm more at home in a little boat than in Toad's magnificent mansion? It's not my fault that I have webbed feet and whiskers that shed water. Perhaps this is why I'm known as Constant Waterman.

SEAFALL

World surge surly and mind adrift,
Star blaze only and Earth between;
Salt marsh lonely and sea view glad,
Wind and water to quell us, mad.
Rock sharp gale and streaming cloud;
Gravel tongued surf and cloven sky;
Where has Ever been but here,
Or else were Always more close than Near.

Eye of salt, eye of sand, mouth of tide, mouth of bone;
Ear of surf, ear of storm, word of surge, word of stone.

World of wisdom were someway wished
Were not our wish a spilling sail;
Could only sense be only stilled
Might wise unreason unwrap our dream.
Least are the sands which count us one
As every drop hangs a damp alone.
The more together the least I long;
As always now, as no ways wrong.

Eye of salt, eye of sand, mouth of tide, mouth of bone;
Ear of surf, ear of storm, word of surge, word of stone.

World surge holy and sea sky wild,
Each light lapse ever this life renew.
Where there are most are seldom few
Might save the wind, might rave the mind.

Whence this promise of the gods?
Sundown flicker and twice alone?
Were this world as we might want,
Never the surf might heap the shore,
The gull lean never against the wind,
Always the rain might dry the sea
And the dark sun dull the sky.

Eye of salt, eye of sand, mouth of tide, mouth of bone;
Ear of surf, ear of storm, word of surge, word of stone.

Very nearly madness is what this poem conveys. And I was nearing madness when I penned it, and have not so much as wanted to look back since. Yet – I am not terrifically mad at present. Not compared with some of the poets I've known.

The Origin of Moonflowers
{Datura stramonium}

One evening, a few years back, we took a stroll on the foreshore preceding supper. The breakwaters forming the breach way to Ninigret Pond jutted into the sea a mile ahead of us. Cottages line the beachfront, but the sandy shore has a gradual slope and the foreshore, which is public, is extensive. Surfcasters, dogs, joggers and seagulls all enjoy getting sand between their toes.

The breakwaters, built of piled rock, provide a resort for fishermen with, and without, wings. Shattered clam and crab shells litter the rocks. The breach way cleanses a couple of thousand acres of salt marsh pond. It whips through its channel furiously and often grows turbulent where it meets the sea. As Ninigret Pond has little depth, no one sails in it except the occasional Sunfish. A channel runs back to the mainland where a small marina snuggles up to the shore. Their clientele consists of small power craft.

I enquired about the channel when I owned my Typhoon – she drew only thirty inches. They informed me that, at low tide, barely three feet of water ran through there. Not being fond of scraping the paint from my keel, I declined a berth, even though the marina was convenient to my home. When I go aground I prefer not to be within sight of my slip – it makes for a better story.

And the breach way can be a daunting place when the current runs four to five knots. I prefer my harbor a bit more accessible and less rambunctious. I want to be able to sail all the way to my slip in case my engine fails. I had visions of slogging a mile of waist deep channel, towing my boat. A centerboard boat might find it a bit more amusing.

We strolled the foreshore carrying our shoes. The shore here consists of sand. The trash line consists of shredded kelp and shards of quahog shell. A scattering of smooth pebbles compliments the mixture. Scarcely anything ever comes ashore. On the horizon, directly south, Block Island can be discerned during clear weather – about one day out of three. Anything they heave overboard out there comes ashore somewhere else. A beachcomber would die of boredom here. Our numerous seagulls pray for such an event.

The sun went down – or the Earth turned up, according to Papa Copernicus – and stars commenced to offset the dark. We turned to make our way home. We had the strand to ourselves this autumn evening. Most of the cottages stood empty, their darkened windows staring blindly seaward. A station wagon belonging to DEP met us and continued towards the breach way, leaving a solitary pair of tracks in the sand.

We suddenly discerned a small upright figure near the water's edge. When we approached it took no notice of us. It proved a murre, a knee high black and white diving bird sitting up, forlornly, on her haunches. A relative of the auk, the murre has a slimmer bill and a svelter figure. This poor creature appeared to have lost her sight and, consequently, inclination to live. We waved to the DEP official who told us he had been investigating several similar cases. He put the bird into a carton and took her away for testing. We never heard anything more.

How many of us lose our sight, not to mention our various inclinations, and find our poor selves stranded at water's edge. The shores of this wholesome world are wide and it isn't only islands that disappear in the haze. Things just before our eyes can vanish as well. The sea and the sky; the faces of those we love: all shall presently disappear into the darkness.

The sea advances upon the shore with its world load of pebbles. The sea recedes. Some pebbles are stranded; some displaced forever. The sea advances once more.

The Murre

This was written when I lived in the wilds of coastal Rhode Island twenty years ago. I gave up living in my barn on the family acres and, flinging caution to the whim of Aeolus, married a Rhode Island woman and moved an hour to the east to live with her. A second marriage, in your fifties, is an amazing act of faith. And perhaps of hope. Perhaps even of charity. One adjusts. One compensates. One makes allowances. One can be much in love.

My sister and I sold off the family farm – a farm in memory only; and only hers, not mine. In 1940 my parents purchased 150 acres, a house, a barn, three hen houses, the brooder house, the cottages for hired help, ten thousand chickens, twenty cows, a team of Clydesdales, a tractor and a truck. For all the above they paid $10,500. When the War to End All War began, my father went off to fight the Dark Powers and sold off all the livestock. He left my mother, a city girl, to cope with everything else. That included a baby daughter. Four years later, my father returned and took up engineering. I made my entrance nine months later – an early Baby Boomer.

I've nearly done booming now. I've nearly grown up. I've resisted growing up for decades and decades. As my cat will attest, I have more fun with her than with anyone else. Two simpletons in a complex world, my wife asserts, and as usual, is almost nearly correct, though to call the Pusslet simple is a most egregious libel. She is no longer here to defend her reputation. I believe she was carried off by a fisher – fisher cats we call them hereabouts.

Squeedles, otherwise affectionately known as The Pusslet, was more human, some mornings, than I was. We shared our mug of French Roast at the computer – which we also shared – and discussed our plans for the day. She shared my dreams, my pillow, my lap, and our mutual delight in my wife's astonishment at our juvenile pursuits. The Squeedler was the daughter I never had. She followed me about; she tapped my leg with her paw to get my attention; she talked to me of her need for admiration; she patiently waited her turn at the cereal bowl. She had a most expressive tail and a broad vocabulary. Well, what would you expect with an author for her father?

I taught her to type with the two-toe method – which is what I use myself – and her writing showed marked improvement. In fact, a couple of my columns in Messing About in Boats were entirely hers, though I thought it best not to enlighten the editor. I'll miss the Pusslet – she brought great joy to my life.

One pusslet remains – Pye Wacket – a simple lass with simple tastes; rather timid, not extroverted as the Squeedler was. But we can't all of us be perfect. There will never, ever, be another Squeediliferous Pusslet. At least I still have my wife.

Here is a journal entry from 2007.

My son, Ezra, was working on his master's degree at MIT, and I took some time for a visit. While he was busy one morning, I went out for breakfast.

"Seated in a coffee shop in Cambridge, Massachusetts – as far from my sloop, *MoonWind*, as I have ventured for months. The hour is early, the clientele various, my thoughts as yet uncollected; the French roast and the scones quite remarkable.

Yesterday I replaced hardware on a Petrel – a twenty-one foot keel sloop – due to fly to Ontario to a new home, then drove to Boston to join Ezra at Fenway Park where the Red Sox, despite a glorious season, got trounced by the Cleveland Indians. Afterwards I took the 'T' to Leachmere, the end of the Green Line, where Ezra met me on his bicycle. Then we walked together the last mile to his digs. Not much in the way of restaurants open at midnight except for taverns, so ate cold noodles in his communal kitchen where we shared conversation with two of his housemates.

Sleep on the living room floor did not come readily and, when it did, it startled at the raucous siren of a fire truck that shattered the night of the nowise silent city. Nevertheless, daylight waked me as usual. There is no denying that age finds me impatient to arise once more and embrace another day.

This weekend I must finish repairs to my Whitehall pulling boat and apply a few coats of varnish. It is nearly June – the months, the years, the centuries, the millennia, the eons wear away. But I have learned, am learning, to counteract the rapid escapement of the hours. The prescription for this panacea is sailing. The apothecary, Poseidon, is ageless; the side effects of the tonic both fortuitous and heady; the cure but the kick of the helm, the heave of the sea.

What is the worth of words when perched upon such a precipice as life? I have scarce the wherewithal to cope with the fragility of the flower; scarce the verbs to express the willfulness of the wind – that wind which shatters the flower yet swells my sail.

Yet shall I strive – windsmith to bend to my errant will to the wind;

wordsmith to craft expression from the air. So shall I write and sail, sail and write, until the gods will otherwise in their wisdom.

An early shower has rendered the road reflective; the rustle and rumble and clatter of mankind surge about me. The weight of this busy world would stifle expression. I need to declaim; to ride with rollicking seas, with breeze, with beauty.

The coffee shop fills with damp haired people exiting the drizzle. Clients sit and talk and read and write and stare out the plate glass windows at their world. French pop music and chatter and the well behaved traffic of the busy street continue and continue. Why should I, too, not continue? Here I go – to invest in another day.

At Ezra's apartment, I read Virginia Woolf's "Granite and Rainbow," essays of criticism concerning fiction from Austin to Hardy, Trollop to Meredith, Dickens to James, and newer writers Mansfield and Heming-way. An astute observer and sensitive writer, Woolf is too often subjec-tive. I demand of writing if not technical perfection at least technical awareness. I demand to be led to wonder, to wish, to attempt, to learn, to weep. I demand a lyricism, a striving for beauty. I demand that writing transport me – if not away from strife and longing then into them, closer and tighter.

We pack my truck with Ezra's belongings and wend our slow way to Hadlyme, to his mother's home, two hours and more away from the bustle of Cambridge. The property at Hadlyme: the two houses, the barn, the hundred remaining acres, bring back more memories than I can deal with. Fifty years at Hadlyme have forged my deepest thoughts; have roused me to passion's precipice; have hurled me from its heights.

These rags of my longing scarcely clothe my sorrow. It will take much writing, much living, to ravel them into a tolerable disguise. For now, these various tatters must suffice."

Hamadryad in Autumn

Here is an I who has a dread of Heaven;
A soul as independent as an oak;
Who needs no breezes lifting frivolous wings,
Nor showers to assuage a lifelong thirst,
Whose lusty roots suffice for deep carouse.
Who neither fears to face the flaying gale,
Nor from the winter's ravage learns least pain,
Though limb may crack and crown be tempest torn;
Who scorns the worm's slow study, mold's sure gain.

And yet there is an I who needs the touch
Of vigorous sun, of soft, elusive moon;
A soul as vibrant as the teeming marsh;
Who'd miss the swan wing summer, nurturing tide.
Whose passion would be incomplete without
Those yellow iris, purpled pickerelweed,
These secretive rushes, carp's compendious swirl.
For what were all the ages of one's life
Without one redwing praising all this world?

*   *   *   *

From the 1970's, when I married and opened a machine shop, until the 1990's when I became divorced and my two sons left home for college and the world, I did very little save work and work and work. I lived next door to my parents and helped them out. In exchange, they gave me property and support. Yet the demands of marriage, children, parents and business took nearly all my time – sometimes more.

I was never prosperous. I never grew fond of machinery, nor of business. I had no time to write, or draw, or canoe upon the river; no time to dance; no time to dream. For fifteen years I was slave to all about me. In 1988 my father died; in 1991, my mother. They left trust funds that would send my sons through college. They left money for me to pay outstanding bills. I probated both their estates without any legal help. Perhaps a mistake, but I learned a lot about law, and taxes, and red tape. I fixed up my parent's house and rented it out. I learned to be a landlord, though, thankfully, I had only good tenants.

My marriage devolved into shouting matches. I moved into my barn. I lived as a hermit a couple of years and then endured divorce. We had an amicable divorce. My wife demanded my parent's house in lieu of alimony. As it hadn't cost me anything and I dreaded having to support my wife for another thirty years, I concurred.

Living in the country, one has to travel to meet with other people. Music and theater and restaurants abounded, but little within half an hour. I still was working a lot of hours and hadn't the energy, late in the day, to venture out in search of companionship. I wrote some sad and demented poetry, began to write a play. I joined a poetry workshop, met a few people, spent a lot of lonely nights by myself.

I ran an ad in a dating magazine. This was before most people owned computers. Internet dating probably didn't exist. I didn't own a computer. I'd finally traded my portable Underwood for an electronic word processor – a sophisticated electric typewriter that could type a copy of what you had saved. Its editing features sufficed for my simple needs.

My ads were answered by several women, who were generally boring. A woman from Rhode Island, an hour away, answered my ad and we met in Mystic and went to dinner. We hit it off right away. She was literate and funny and wise. We shared an interest in theater. We spoke at great length on the phone, evenings, rather than drive fifty miles. We began to sleep together. Life was grand. There was something to look forward to.

I taught her to canoe; we explored the vast salt marshes along the Rhode Island shore. We dug clams, collected wildflowers, went for walks, attended theater. She became involved with community theater; as an actress, then as a costumes mistress. I wrote play after play and submitted them across the country with little success. A couple of staged readings, honorable mention, a word of encouragement, a request for a rewrite.

Meanwhile, the years sped by. We decided to marry. We resolved to sell our respective homes and start over in Charlestown, Rhode Island. Paula worked as a nurse nearby, caring for dementia patients. I resolved to sell my machines and take up some other profession – hopefully writing.

I approached my sister about our land in Hadlyme. She had lived abroad for thirty years and considered moving to Florida to retire. She had no interest in Hadlyme. I assumed the title of project manager and we pooled our resources. I worked with a surveyor, a civil engineer, a real estate attorney, a real estate broker, and a land development contractor. They all were great to work with, and we formed a team that communicated well. I gave these professionals leave to talk to one another without my specific permission. We subdivided the property into feasible lots, a road and driveways, and satisfied the town of our best intentions. I began to work part time for the surveyor as a rod man on a two-man crew. I helped survey my property and worked part time another two years on numerous other projects around the area.

The economy at the turn of the century prospered. We sold our lots. I learned a good deal about surveying and subdividing and site planning and management. This kept me busy and prosperous three or four years.

MoonWind

I began to work part time at a boat shop in Noank, Connecticut. I purchased a little sailboat: a Cape Dory Typhoon: 18' 6" with a cuddy cabin and a full keel: a rugged little day sailor that could go out on the ocean. We kept her in Noank. I named her *MoonWind*.

I had learned to sail on the Connecticut River as a boy. I sailed off and on at Tabor Academy where I boarded all through high school. I kept a Rhodes 18 on the river for two summers. I crewed on a rare occasion with my former father-in-law. I had owned a twenty-seven-foot wooden sloop during the 1980's: she spent her life in my barn. I sailed her only three times the first year I owned her, then brought her home for repairs. I worked on her off and on and finally sold her.

Now I would have a manageable boat and advice on how to repair her. After a couple of seasons, we wanted a larger boat – one we could weekend on with at least a modicum of comfort. We sold the Typhoon to a doctor in New Hampshire. We purchased an old, Chris Craft sloop designed by Sparkman and Stephens. She is also known as *MoonWind*. She's twenty-six feet and has a head and a galley and an outboard motor. We can just stand up in her main salon. The double bunk in the stateroom is barely wide enough for two friendly people, as long as One of Them doesn't steal the covers.

I've written extensively about these boats in my other books. Our present *MoonWind*, after several years at Noank, now resides at Shennecossett Yacht Club behind Pine Island at Avery Point at the mouth of the Thames in Groton, Connecticut.

From Noank I did much sailing, mostly alone, both summer and winter. From SYC, I've made but few excursions. In 2005, we moved from Charlestown, RI to Stonington, CT. Our finances took a down turn. We can scarcely afford, at present, to own a boat. She sees but infrequent usage. We have just downsized our dwelling from a stately, colonial Cape to a double wide trailer. The economy having taken a downturn these past few years, we shall lose most of our savings in selling our house.

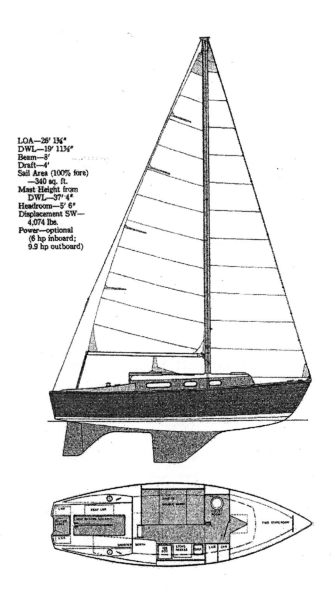

LOA—26' 1¾"
DWL—19' 11⅛"
Beam—8'
Draft—4'
Sail Area (100% fore)
 —340 sq. ft.
Mast Height from
 DWL—37' 4"
Headroom—5' 6"
Displacement SW—
 4,074 lbs.
Power—optional
 (6 hp inboard;
 9.9 hp outboard)

Chris Craft 'Pawnee' – *MoonWind*
Courtesy Chris-Craft Boats & Sparkman & Stephens

Shennecossett Yacht Club
Pine Island Sound, Groton, Connecticut

We are now moved into our present home in Griswold, Connecticut, merely fourteen miles north of our yellow Cape in Old Mystic. It is slightly cramped, and we aren't yet fully adjusted, yet we are here. The Cape is nearly empty, is freshly painted, and will have a new tenant in only another few weeks. Life could be worse. The mortgage and taxes and insurance on the Cape prevented us from realizing retirement. We are in our sixties now and weary of work.

I've always nurtured the fantasy that I could make a living selling my books. Besides having local book shops and stores aid this endeavor, I often sign books at stores and shows and libraries. Every year Mystic Seaport invites me to sell my books for an afternoon – or three. As they have their own bookshop, I earn but the wholesale price, but I enjoy the people I meet there. I generally write in my journal between customers.

Invictus

Mystic Seaport & Essex, CT

From the Journals of Constant Waterman   **27 June 2008**

First day of the Wooden Boat Show at Mystic Seaport. I have my own little table, heaped with my books, on the first floor of the gift shop – not quite close enough to the bakery for me to swipe the muffins, but still within the reach of the aroma of fresh coffee. Tantalus never had it so good. I indulge in a coffee and muffin and man my table.

Much of boating is self-indulgence anyway – though not all. Not when the smelly bilge needs scrubbing. Not when the engine refuses to push your boat back into the harbor. Not when that starboard spreader boot has gone with the wind – and not for the first time, either. Not when the fittings to the holding tank are weeping from neglect. These are the times you most want to hide at home and mow the lawn.

But when you think of that lovely twelve knot breeze that's going to waste, you suddenly get motivated, and drive your spouse to complete these onerous chores while you bask in the cockpit. Notice I haven't made any reference to the sex of either partner. This is what is known as genderative correctness. I can't think of a single reason why a woman can't learn to curse a diesel engine as well as a man. Most of the women of my acquaintance have more than an adequate fund of expletives that, with only a bit of practice, could be adapted to lying in awkward positions with filth up to their elbows, having just dropped that open end wrench into the bilge for the fourth time in fourteen minutes.

Anyway, I didn't encounter any such people of either sex, or their recalcitrant engines, at the gift shop. I didn't even have to inspect people's nails for engine grunge before they fondled my books. Much as I wanted to be on the water, I felt that I had an obligation to pester innocent people and acquaint them with my nonsense. Several people stopped and told me how much they enjoy my writing. This always gets me so excited that I have to be careful not to knock over my table or spill my French roast, else they may not invite me back next season.

So I spoke with people who read, and people who sail, and people who want to know why I'm hiding behind this stack of books on such a lovely weekend when that twelve knot breeze beckons from the harbor. I had some conversations with blue water sailors, and some with folks who hadn't fallen overboard but two or three times in their lives. These latter I advised to get back on the water right away. The blue water sailors, of course, tried to convince me that port lights were meant to be stood on and not looked out of.

Some of these people bought my book merely in self-defense. How else could they prove me wrong? But I always, literally, had the last word because they invariably asked me to sign their books. The least cautious among them would also ask for a personal note. I make it a point to pen sententious inscriptions such as: "For Archly – fair winds forever." Then his wife pointed out to me that his name is "Archy," and that he's circumnavigated Vermont twenty-three times in his homemade nine foot schooner. I promised to buy his forthcoming book and slouched a little lower in my chair. I was hoping to earn enough this weekend to keep me in muffins and coffee.

After three hours of abusing prospective readers, I've sold seven copies of my book. Considering my royalty – which comes without crown or scepter – and my wholesale commission, I clear about two and half precious dollars from each of my sales. This equates to about five dollars an hour. If I figure in driving and parking, self-employment insurance and the price of coffee, I make about one third of minimum wage. This does not include, of course, the year it took me to write, format, and illustrate my book. With any luck, I'll sell ten books tomorrow.

If I buy Archie's book – hardcover only twenty-two ninety-five – I probably won't show a loss of more than a dollar or two the entire weekend. But, if I hadn't come here to meet all these wonderful people, I'd undoubtedly have spent the entire weekend sailing. Figuring what it costs to keep my boat, all things included, I would have shown a loss for the weekend of over a hundred dollars.

Consequently, signing books has fewer adverse effects on my portfolio, should I ever have one and, not including the cup of water I spilled in my lap, probably results in less wet clothing.

28 June 2008

Second day of the Wooden Boat Show. I arrived early, determined to see the sights. As, yesterday, the book store provided me with a pass to see the show, which I hadn't used, I naively peeled its backing, stuck it to my forehead, and approached the gate.

"Excuse me," said the young woman at the barrier, "but that is yesterday's sticker."

I carefully explained that I was the one and only whoever I was, endowed with suitable emoluments, privileges, and private conflagrations to my credit. The young woman, with a sigh, issued me a current sticker and ushered me through the gate. I was glad to see she got her day's full ration of rolling her eyes.

Once within the hallowed precincts of venerable Mystic Seaport, I began to Mess About. A number of booths displayed strip planked or laminated canoes, kayaks, and pulling boats. I found it necessary to stop and pet many of these and inspect their bright work for drips. Totally bright work boats always impress the whatsis out of me. Fortunately, my inner resource of whatsis is unexpendable. Whenever you coat any wood with some clear finish, the grain and color of each piece of wood must be flawless; the joinery must be flawless; the grain of each plug, where these occur, must be aligned with the grain of the plank; and the fourteen coats of finish applied must be so limpid as not to distort a single spot on any trout you may see below the surface.

You mustn't mind me. Varnish has this effect on me. Even scraping and sanding old bright work I don't find all that tedious. Unless, of course, I'm being paid for the privilege.

I then went round the vendors' tents and snarfled among the tools and books and artwork. I found a couple of vendors I knew and bent their receptive ears to improve their looks. I acquainted myself with a couple of local watermen. I drooled on some well-built little sailboats and wandered the piers to watch a few old catboats wend the river.

Then I went home for lunch, and concocted a pair of open faced tuna and cheddar and fresh tomato sandwiches on whole grain bread. I slipped these morsels into the toaster oven long enough to convert them to my way of thinking, then gently consigned them to their Purpose in Life while I checked my trusty desktop computer for my fan mail. As usual, my fan forgot, once again, to send me a letter commending me for my genius.

I've decided I'd rather have a computer aboard than a motor. Except, of course, when the wind dies down about four o'clock on a summer's day, but, then, I can always make do with a notebook and pencil to get me home. When you're done unsnarling this simple declarative sentence, I'll let you re-stow my roding.

Fortunately, my lunch restored my ability to compose coherent prose. I returned to the Wooden Boat Show and settled at my table to sign some books. Trade proved so brisk that I dozed off, and the manager had to revive me with iced coffee. This succeeded so admirably that I sold five books in little more than three hours.

As everyone knows, coffee is synonymous with success in any venture. It promotes alertness and garrulity: an unsurpassed combination for convincing nearly anyone of anything. I, myself, under the heady influence of this nectar, have convinced nearly millions of people to ignore my books.

The culmination of my afternoon came with the approach of a spritely, silver haired woman. She complimented me on my relative bearing, then proceeded to tell me how she'd survived both breast cancer and the loss of her devoted sloop. I leant her my fullest attention for a good while, and complimented her on her endurance. After she purchased my journals I inscribed them. When she read my inscription, she flung her arms about me and kissed my lips.

I heard a gasp from a wide-eyed woman behind me. As I turned to her she quickly backed away. Having been an unwilling witness to overt emotion had totally nonplussed her.

"It's all right," I assured her. "I never kiss anyone till I've signed their book."

29 June 2008

Third day of the Wooden Boat Show. Took Paula for a brief tour of the Seaport. She spent a deal of this time at the Womanship booth, talking to the skipper and the mate of their forty-foot schooner. The skipper is a grey haired, passionate woman who is also a psychiatric nurse. The mate left Colorado four years ago, having never sailed, came to Maine and took the Womanship course, and now teaches others to sail. The three-day, live aboard course inspires confidence as well as teaches basics of sailing and boat handling. Perhaps Paula will be off to Freeport, Maine this autumn to learn how to holystone the jib and batten down the gudgeons.

We then wandered the waterfront, and admired the many pristine wooden yachts and tenders. And there lay *Aphrodite* in all her splendor. We left our shoes on the pier and stepped aboard. This seventy-three-foot motor cruiser currently lives at Watch Hill, five miles east of here. Built in the 1930's, she's been totally restored. Besides being spacious below, she seems livable. Lots of headroom, lots of light, lots of elbowroom. Aft of the engines she has a lazarette cabin that sleeps two and has a head. Off the main salon, another cabin for two with a head, and, forward, a third cabin for two.

Her main salon is large and includes an ample galley. Her pilothouse, topsides, has state-of-the-art instrumentation and more than enough bright work to keep a varnisher happy. Her deckhouse is also bright work with great expanses of glass. Her whaleback hull, distinctive at a great distance, is cobalt blue, waxed to be reflective as a mirror.

Aphrodite, as all the lovely yachts here, was built when cheap skilled labor was available. Wealthy families employed dozens of servants. Boats such as this could be maintained for only a few thousand dollars. Now it costs that to lease a thirty-foot slip for the summer season. I somehow doubt that I'm destined to own a seventy-something-foot yacht. Just buying her varnish would probably strain my resources. Just buying a second ice coffee this afternoon may strain my relationship with my local banker.

By three o'clock, my time to begin signing books, most of the vendors have struck their tents, put their boats onto trailers, folded their tables. I hoped that last minute shoppers might flock to my site and purchase my last forty books. You know, of course, that I've been a dreamer, a hopeless romantic, every year of my life. I still believe that there'll come a time when I'll live aboard my boat. Hopefully, on my sloop and not my Whitehall. I sold books to only a couple of people all Sunday afternoon, and the second person I had to sit on to extract his wallet.

Joseph Conrad

By tomorrow, the lovely wooden boats will depart for their homeports and moorings and sheds. The *Morgan, Dunton, Conrad* will remain alongside their piers.

The steam launch *Sabino*, soon to celebrate her hundredth birthday, will continue to ply the Mystic River. The replica Crosbie catboat, *Breck Marshal*, will tack about the Seaport with her passengers each day; the water taxi take people into the village. The phlegmatic, old white carthorse will continue to plod the stone paved street of the Seaport, drawing his carriage. The Seaport Serpent will emerge from beneath the pier to swallow a tourist. All will continue as usual.

Most importantly, people of this twenty-first century will learn to build and restore boats made of wood. Lofting and framing and planking and fairing go on every day. Older boats are brought back to life from ruins. Spar making, blacksmithing, finishing, rigging – these skills are perpetuated, passed on, and perfected. Our heritage of boat building is worthy of this attention. Though wood working is far too labor intensive to be economically practical, it remains a craft that verges on an art. A beautiful boat can stand beside any piece of sculpture and earn a fair share of attention. And the last piece of sculpture I tried to sail wouldn't point higher than sixty degrees and hadn't near enough freeboard.

I've owned a couple of wooden sloops, and nearly learned how to maintain them. I should have apprenticed in a boat shop as a boy. Instead, I spent my summers learning to play with metal working machinery. By the time I was twelve I knew how to run a lathe and a milling machine. Until a dozen years ago I supported myself by running my own machine shop. This prepared me wonderfully for working on boats and writing plays and memoirs. Had I spent my most productive years running a boat building shop, I'd undoubtedly be working now at restoring old automobiles.

But were anyone to offer me insight into my future, I'd slap the fool silly. Don't presume that tomorrow will prove another yesterday. Whenever I hear someone wonder aloud what tomorrow, or even next year, may bring, I remember the words of my oft wise father, "Stick around and find out."

Speaking of selling books…

From the Journals of Constant Waterman 21 February 2008

Sitting at a table in the bar of the Dock and Dine in Old Saybrook, Connecticut, sipping a glass of Merlot as I wait to address the Shore-line Sailing Club. My lovely river runs by my window, spread wide to meet the salt embrace of the sea. The farther shore, the better part of a mile away, is merely a low-lying band of green – the individual trees indistinguishable.

I've driven the tread off the tires of my little truck today, trying to sell my books, or, at least, to encourage others to sell them for me. The smaller bookshops are "waiting for boating season." They can't afford inventory that does no more than ballasts their shelves.

But I found, on the second pass, a brand-new bookshop in Essex. So new that all the books squeaked when I opened them. The owner waxed ecstatic over my Journals.

"I need to develop my sailing section," she said.

You must understand that Essex is Connecticut's sailing Mecca. The building, sailing, and worshipping of wind powered craft is the focus of every Essex resident over the age of four. The eighteenth-century Griswold Inn, at the foot of Main Street, is thronged all summer by sailors in white duck trousers and boating shoes. A chantey man has performed at "The Gris" every week for thirty years. The Essex Yacht Club is so exclusive that people with boats of less than forty feet are forced to produce testimonials as to their character, assets, and wardrobe. The sparkling winches of many yachts moored at Essex are often confused with aids to navigation.

A book shop in Essex without hundreds of sailing books had better serve excellent coffee.

So I did my bit and showed the owner my press release, four book reviews, and a piece in the paper that praised me for using words of more than one syllable. I clapped my flippers, rolled over, and balanced my book on my nose. I gave her my business card. She wrote her name and number on a slip of paper and gave it to me.

"My cards are still at the printer," she admitted.

"Oh," I said. "You haven't been open long."

"Since Saturday," she said.

"What did you do before you sold books?" I asked.

"Well," she said. "I was a pastor. In Bethlehem."

I can understand the demands of that job in such a location might suffice to daunt the stoutest heart. Even though this Bethlehem is only in western Connecticut.

"In that case, you'll approve of my book," I told her. "There aren't any dirty words or naked women."

"Oh, that wouldn't bother me," she said. "I'm really a normal person."

"In that case," I said, "Perhaps I should insert some naked women."

I'm never quite sure how to appeal to everyone who reads books.

Night has now settled upon the Connecticut River. I sip my wine as I write and look at the water. The placid tide laps at the old green pilings beneath my window. The waves would not dismay a child's toy boat. The gulls and ducks and cormorants have hied to their roosting places. I cannot see either lighthouse from where I sit.

The waiter brings me a plate of crisp calamari.

A couple I know from the Sailing Club stops by to pay their respects. I invite them to sit with me, but they're having dinner with some members in the next room. I think the word "sailboat" occurs at least once during our four-minute conversation. They leave me alone to eat and drink and write.

The couple at the next table pays their bill. At the mention of "sailboat," their sonar receptors swivel in my direction. They put their helm down and set a course for my table.

"What do you know about places to dock a sailboat for the summer?" they ask. "We crew for a fellow whose racing boat draws seven feet."

We talk about marinas for a while. Then I digress and talk about local hazards to navigation, such as Long Island. I take on the role of sea serpent and shake my whiskers and growl. This is commonly known as method acting. I show them my book, give them each a business card, and cut them adrift.

Now I have but fifteen minutes before my reading is scheduled to begin. Fortunately, I've little to prepare and the Shoreline Sailing Club meets in the ballroom just beyond the bar. I try to finish writing this story, but too many interruptions have interfered with my train of thought. Perhaps I'll find time to finish it tomorrow.

Some Boats

From the Journals of Constant Waterman 14 April 2008

Saturday they proclaimed, "A chance of showers." I was aboard *MoonWind* at the pier, squaring her away, when the sky, unaccountably, sprang a leak. Uncle Zeus, not merely content to open his cockpit drains, also felt it necessary to growl and grumble and experiment with electricity.

I fled for the comfort of my pickup truck and trundled back home to work at illustrating. By the time I arrived, the rain had stopped, the clouds had parted, the disgruntled god of thunder and downspouts had headed for Boston to dismay the fans and players at Fenway Park. I did, however, contrive an illustration of Father Poseidon with which I'm pleased. It serves as the cover to my book: *MoonWind at Large*.

Father Poseidon

Zeus, Poseidon, and Hades, as you remember, were the brothers who shared this planet into its several realms. For now I have to deal with but two of them. No doubt I'll find ample time in the future to try to amuse the third one. My punishment, undoubtedly, will be to fail to get old Hades to even smile at most of my better yarns.

Sunday they called for more showers. But, after lunch, it looked no worse than it had the entire morning. Rather than tempt more thunderbolts, I tucked my yellow kayak into my truck and snuck down the river road to the public landing. First I put on my newly acquired wet suit. This was a five dollar bargain I found at the yacht club's marine tag sale, and fits me as the casing fits the sausage. And warm? Although the water was duly frigid, the air was fifty degrees – enough to make me sweat inside my insulated casing. And being not too terribly bright, I chose to cover my slinky black form with blue jeans and a windbreaker. I needed those as the sausage needed a mitten.

There was no one else at the landing. A perfect, almost, April day and nobody with the urge to explore the river. What is this younger generation – etcetera and so forth. I slid my kayak into the Mystic River, insinuated myself into her tiny cockpit, and paddled downriver toward Mystic Seaport. The tide and breeze proved nearly insignificant. I counted the pebbles along the shore, chased a few mallards, paused to relax my out-of-shape arms, and held a course for the tall ships at the Seaport.

I'm not about to bore you with a list of the vessels I skirted at the Seaport. It was far more fun to check out the smaller sailboats – the old wooden cutter, the sleek and narrow Sharpie – those I could pull alongside and see aboard. Although the afternoon waxed glum and glummer, several dozen people explored the old wooden craft moored at the waterfront. A little girl shouted and waved an energetic hello to me from the eyes of an old three master. I waved and shouted back.

Half a mile below the Seaport juts a private pier where the schooner Argia berths. At the head of the pier are several shops. The marine consignment shop – one of my all-time favorite haunts – has been revamped. The new owner was there, putting up shelves. Soon he'll be stocking these shelves with some of the vast overflow from his other shop in Wickford. We're usually leery about Rhode Islanders sneaking into Connecticut, but we overlooked his origins in light of his good intentions. There's nothing more fun than messing about marine consignment shops, and he and his wife have a grand one across the border.

A month from now I'll be able to lose myself amid the turnbuckles and gronicles. For now I could only admire the fresh white paint and the plumbing fixtures.

When I left the shop there were several raindrops waiting for me outside. I dodged among them and leapt into my kayak. I passed beneath Argia's counter and ducked beneath the pier. I moved so quickly, those raindrops never saw me get away. It's not really all that tough to fool a raindrop.

Mystic River Bascule Bridge, US Route 1

I passed beneath the bascule bridge that divides the village of Mystic. The traffic rumbled six feet over my head. The pigeons on the girders gently gurgled. Below the bridge I came about and crossed to the further bank. I had the tide to help me ascend the two miles to my launch site. Above the village, I followed first Pearl Street, then the River Road, admiring the Colonial homes, and skirted their little private landings in hope of surprising this season's earliest mermaid – lounging at the end of a pier and combing out her tresses.

*   *   *   *

From the Journals of Constant Waterman 14 September 2012

Shall finally sail *MoonWind* Sunday with a friend. I haven't had her out in nearly two years and may not remember how to reef the tiller.

It's not encouraging in the least to be this poor this late in such a self-indulgent existence. Money and time are both in demand and such frivolities as eating and sailing are set aside during pursuit of the wily, elusive dollar.

It seems we may have a buyer for our yellow Cape in Mystic, which has been our home these past seven years. Once we rid ourselves of her mortgage, we may just be able to think about retirement. But our buyer needs time to gather his funds together and chooses to lease the house for two years first, at a price two hundred fifty dollar below our cost of mortgage, insurance, and taxes. Still, we'll pay down some of our debt in these two years, and get what seems a fair price in this economy. Which is to say, we'll lose a hundred thousand on the transaction. I feared we might lose almost double that.

But this is the first prospective buyer to even look over the house in the past six months. It helps a great deal that this was his grandfather's home and he spent months of his childhood here. He's passionate to own it and I know he'll care for it better than I ever did.

It's good to know we may be solvent two or three years from now. Presently we must struggle to make our dock lines reach the pier. We must work part time at work that doesn't amuse us, and be a bit conservative in our habits. As this is not in our natures, we find ourselves more sullen and less cheerful than is our wont. But this should pass.

Perhaps the Pusslet can help us out by bringing in fresh game. Roast chipmunk stuffed with wild rice and acorns for Thanksgiving dinner – what a treat!

But Sunday I'm going sailing! After debating carefully the necessity of selling my dear old boat, I decided I might be able to maintain her one more year. I hope. I may have to give up belonging to the yacht club, and trade my snug slip for a mooring over in Noank. This would save me about eight hundred dollars over the year – about two months groceries. Or – I could give up ice cream…

But Sunday I'm going sailing! Last year I couldn't even afford to put my sloop in the water. I went sailing once with a friend on his Bristol twenty-four. We made it just past Latimer Reef from Noank – about four miles – before we came about and wafted home. So many people, usually older ones, consider an afternoon's sail more than sufficient. But not I. My agenda calls for exploration. Is there really a state of Massachusetts beyond that vague horizon? Is their coffee as good as ours? Will my anchor drag as well in their harbors as it does in ours at home?

I find it enchanting to wake in different waters; to put on my kettle; wipe the dew from my cockpit locker; sit with my notebook and French roast in my cockpit; and look at the world from a voyager's perspective. This, and my teeming mind, is all that suffices to keep my column current in *Messing About in Boats*.

But Sunday I'm going sailing! Today, Saturday, I'm appointed to meet with a book shop owner in Essex. And to drop off some cards in East Haddam. And to check on a vendor in Old Lyme. Then to meet with my now-prospective tenant at three o'clock. Then to go out to dinner at a friend's.

Sailing was such an integral, intimate portion of my existence for so many years. To relegate it to once or twice a year would be like eating dinner only on alternate Wednesdays. My sailing lately has been the vicarious thrill I get from reading my own journals. It's time this form of entertainment ceased. I supposedly write my books for other people.

Thursday I got *MoonWind's* motor to run consistently by changing the fuel line fitting that clips to the gas tank. An airtight fuel line makes all the difference. There's nothing much more disconcerting than having your motor sputter and die at a crucial point in a passage, like when you're skirting a reef in angry weather, or sidling up a channel into a harbor with other boats coming and going at close quarters. Admittedly, situations such as these add zest to a sailor's life, and give him something to thrill his audience round the family fire. They can also result in going aground and maybe wrecking his boat. They certainly serve to boost one's adrenaline.

So, I scrubbed *MoonWind's* cockpit and deck, and hung my reluctant snout in her bilge while I sponged up whatever nastiness had seeped from her holding tank hoses these past two years, and strung her VHF cable the length of her cabin and found I could once again listen to the weather clown declaiming the height of the seas in Block Island Sound. I secured the removable locker tops above my two gas tank lockers; scrounged some closed cell foam from our canvas lady after helping her tie up her skiff; and used this to block my gas tanks from shifting about in their compartments.

I began the procedure of mounting a new and different fresh water pump. This entailed gluing a mounting block in my bilge, stringing new hose and wire behind my ice chest, removing my faucet to make up new connections, and inventing new adjectives to describe my inability to access the hose clamp beneath the sink with my too-short arms and slightly-too-long screwdriver.

But I don't need a sink to go sailing. Not to go out to the Race and back; to feel the wind in what's left of my hair; to stand on my leeward locker and bend my tiller.

But I *shall* need a sink to return to Martha's Vineyard to buy a new hat. The Hat is an important piece of my evocative persona. It's a slate blue cap with *Martha's Vineyard, 1602,* embroidered across its front. That's the year this hat was born. My late, great friend, John Wray, painted a portrait of me wearing this cap. His painting appears on the back cover of my recent book: *MoonWind at Large: Sailing Hither and Yon. And the* Yon was Martha's Vineyard.

And The Hat is now so dilapidated as to be unpresentable to any but diehard messers. Even sailors look askance when I wear The Hat near their yachts. I asked our canvas lady yesterday what she'd charge to refurbish The Hat and restore it to its former, pristine condition. She shuddered at the prospect.

"I wouldn't touch it," she said.

I trusted she meant the undertaking, not The Hat itself.

"Think of the notoriety you'd gain, refurbishing The Hat of Constant Waterman," I said.

"Just what I don't really need," she replied, and tossed me out of her shop.

I suppose I could send away for a new one, but that wouldn't be legitimate. My doting public needs to believe that I wrestled Father Poseidon for this hat the entire length of Martha's Vineyard Sound; that I stole it from the vicious serpent that lurks at the mouth of Vineyard Haven Harbor; that I swam the length of Lake Tashmoo to ravish it from a mermaid with emerald tresses.

It has to have been a trophy; a spoil of war; a memento of an especially arduous voyage. Even now, I'm loath to admit that The Hat was purchased by my loving wife when we took the Ferry to Vineyard H aven where I read at *Bunch of Grapes*. I'm even more loath to admit that she actually purchased it for herself. And the only way I acquired it was by eminent domain.

Yes, I did take *MoonWind* out this Sunday, though not until nearly three in the afternoon. My partner, on his way to join me and *MoonWind*, received a call from a customer to inform him that the customer's inflatable dinghy at Groton Long Point was sinking at the pier – her outboard motor in danger of submersion. So he went over and at least removed the outboard. The dinghy could wait until we'd had our sail.

I squared away *MoonWind* some more as I waited and scrubbed her head, neglected these past two seasons. Although unused, it had accumulated grime to such an extent that I actually disturbed several night crawlers with my sponge.

Just as my partner showed up, a lovely green sloop, a J 109, motored into her slip a few yards off. She had just returned from an off-sounding race. Her skipper backed her into her slip and my friend, George, who's crewed aboard her these past few months, leapt to the pier and came to talk with me. An avid sailor, he's fond of my stories and sells – or gives – my books to any who listen. Now he dragged me over to *Sanibel* and introduced me all around as the one and only, inimitable Constant Waterman.

He asked if I were taking *MoonWind* out and could he possibly come along and help me furl the anchor? But, of course. So the three of us went out as far as the Dumplings by Fishers Island and found a delightful young breeze of ten knots that was dying to show off for us. It shoved *MoonWind* along through the little swells and, after a couple of hours, brought us home.

Lord, it was grand to be on the ocean again! I was so delighted with *MoonWind* that I promised to strip her bright work and do it over so she wouldn't be ashamed to show her prow at the pier. I've completed prep on the forward hatch surround and now await some sunbeams to dry the varnish.

Life could be worse. But George asked me about a journal I'd written about us six years ago when we first met.

"I didn't see it in your new book," he said.

By golly, it wasn't in there. It must have slipped out for coffee while I compiled the table of contents. So, here it is. Forgive me, George – I hadn't forgotten your story.

From the Journals of Constant Waterman 10 November 2006

A couple f days ago, I was messing about in *MoonWind* at her slip when the Catalina 25 coasted into her slip across from me. After he secured her, her skipper came by for a chat.

"Saw you headed out Saturday as I was coming in," he said. "You often go out by yourself?"

"Mostly," I said.

"You want to come out with me some time and give me a few pointers?" he asked. "I don't know as much as I need to."

"Well," I said. "I could do that."

"Thursday – after lunch," he said. "It's supposed to be a good day."

It turned out to be a lovely day: sixty degrees and sunny. A southwest breeze of six knots sufficed to keep his Catalina moving.

"Now she's heeled good," he exclaimed, as a gentle puff tipped his vessel ten degrees. "I don't like it when she heels much more than this."

And I thought I was a fair weather sailor. Now, this fellow sort of knew what he should have been doing; he even knew a bit of navigation. He'd kept a flat bottomed skiff for years just south of Boston and chased a lot of clams. Caught some of them, too, and scared the dickens out of the ones he didn't.

But the only sailboat he'd ever owned was a Sunfish, which I'm told is a surfboard with a linen napkin flying from a boathook. Now he wanted to know about reefing, and halyard winches, and cringles, and the thingamagig you pull on to take the wrinkles out of your luff.

He expressed concern about the way the tide set us. He pinched his boat, then over compensated. He closed the rent we left in the sea with his personalized zig zag stitch. He worried we might not clear the mark a couple of miles ahead.

"What between tacking and getting set by the tide," he said, "some days all I manage to do is go over and back in one place."

"Welcome to the world of sailing, my friend," I said.

That's why all those Other People have power boats. He had an eight horse Evinrude on a bracket. I cautioned him about cruising range and water separator filters. I moved his jib sheet block two notches aft. I explained to him the benefits of his traveler.

We went as far as Pine Island – about four miles. Then the tide turned and pushed us back toward Noank. We came about and headed straight off shore. At our meager two knots, our set by the outgoing tide appeared extravagant.

"Head up some more," I advised him, "or we won't quite clear South

Dumpling. There isn't any water between that buoy and the shore."

Well, he didn't, so we couldn't clear it, and there never was much water there, anyhow. A hundred yards from the leaning can, it became apparent that we needed to make a decision.

"What should I do?" he asked.

"You can come about and hope we can stem the tide," I said. "Or, you can yank on your Evinrude and power us round the mark."

I reserved the third choice – to carry his Catalina over the island – as a backup. My lumbar vertebrae aren't as young as I used to be and, besides, with my luck, I'd end up with the heavy end of his boat.

The motor performed its walk on part and we gave it its due applause. The blocking proved expeditious; we cleared the mark. Then we fell off and reached between South Dumpling and Fishers Island. At the mouth of West Harbor we jibed and headed home to West Cove at Noank. He explained that he'd laid out this course from mark to mark.

"Magnetic bearing is 207 from Noank over to here," he said. "I've penciled it in on the chart. But I'm not sure what bearing to head the other way."

We took off our socks and, using all forty toes and twenty fingers calculated our heading back to Noank, two miles away. I suggested he head up an extra ten degrees to compensate for the tide. He set up his autopilot and the two of us took a nap. It's exhausting work to battle a six knot gale.

When we woke, the Catalina had lined up the day markers into West Cove by herself. We were both impressed, but I did my best not to show it.

He started her motor, headed up, furled the genny, dropped the main and secured it. All I had to do was jiggle the tiller to keep her into the wind. It's great fun having a crew. He took back the helm and sauntered up the channel and into his slip. I wasn't even required to handle the dock lines.

It's been a while since I went sailing and didn't need to hop around as a cricket, furling the bilge and battening down the skeg. One of these days, when I'm famous – or rich – I'll hire a captain and crew for *MoonWind*, put my feet up on the taffrail, and scribble my memoirs.

I have to admit that George is now at least as good of a sailor as I pretend to be. He's been crewing the past few years in the local races, and assimilating knowledge about the trimming and setting of sails. He's threatened to take his Catalina through the Cape Cod Canal, but his Massachusetts accent has sadly deteriorated these past thirty years, and he may get apprehended as an alien when he makes it to Cape Cod Bay.

From the Journals of Constant Waterman 21 August 2008

On Monday, the skipper rang me up at about eight bells in the morning. I was still rinsing the French roast out of my beard, but I deigned to listen, notwithstanding.

"One of our Petrels has lost her stick," he said. "The gaff rigged boat."

A Petrel is a fiberglass version of a 21' Herreshoff Fish class sloop: a full keel boat that sails like a dream. Maybe not "as a dream," because not too many dreams get sailed nowadays – the maintenance fees and storage are so exorbitant. And when you tell the marina you want a slip for a twenty-something foot dream, they roll their eyes and charge you a bit extra, knowing full well the sort of sailor they need to deal with.

But this poor Petrel went out one day with insidious rot within her mast just where the shrouds and forestay confer: "the hounds," to be particular. A local breeze made the most of its opportunity, and broke off the top of the mast. With the standing rigging no longer taking the strain of the wind, the large mainsail took care of the rest. The mast broke again, shivered about two feet above the deck.

The owners managed to get this tangle resolved while underway and made it back to their mooring – presumably without aid, though their little diesel had a leaking fuel line and a lazy battery. They secured the spars, leaving the splintered stump of the mast protruding through the partners.

We launched the skipper's thirteen foot skiff and hitched up its thirty sea horses; piled tow line and fenders aboard, and galloped down Fishers Island Sound to Stonington Harbor on our mission of recidivism: the

Petrel must return to the shop that built her.

There was a bright golden haze o'er the harbor, as Mr. Hammerstein would have said had he only known better, as we motored among the birds and boats and amid the little breezes. In twenty minutes we spotted our patient, languishing on her mooring. We pulled alongside and I hopped aboard. I cast off one of the mooring pendants and threaded our towline through the chock. I made it fast to the foredeck cleat – beneath the second mooring pendant, of course – then made the bitter end fast to the stump with a truckers' hitch to take some of the strain off the eight inch cleat. The skipper made up a bridle about his outboard and paid out about a hundred feet of scope. I stayed aboard the Petrel and manned her tiller.

The Petrel's hull speed dictated our progress: we made about five point something knots, returning. This gave us an hour to bask in the beautiful morning. After all, it's what we get paid to do.

At the mouth of West Cove, we lashed the Petrel alongside the skiff and puttered into the harbor. Of course, some moron in a thirty foot sport fishing boat had to come rollicking out of the harbor at half throttle. With straight arms and fenders, we fended him off the Petrel, while inventing suitable epithets to fling at our adversary.

We brought our charge to the concrete ramp and eased her onto her trailer. The shop's four wheel drive pickup truck took a deep breath and lunged up the ramp with twenty-eight hundred pounds of boat atop her heavy trailer.

Now the Petrel is inside the shop, forlorn and unrigged. It could have been worse. I learned last night that in Quick's Hole, over in the Elizabeths, a power boat couldn't restrain herself and climbed all over a sailboat and ate one of her crew. Wind and water and rot and rocks are hazards enough while boating. I hope I'm never so arrogant as to ask *MoonWind* to climb aboard another boat and dance about in her cockpit. Now that *MoonWind* is forty years old, I'd hope she would have the common sense to refuse me. Every other woman of that age does.

Herreshoff "Fish" class sloop Aka "Petrel"
{Marconi rigged version} Illustration courtesy Herreshoff Yachts

Journals of the Squeedilifferous Pusslet

But life – Alas! – is not all about sailing. Domestic concerns crop up without the least warning. September brings not only beautiful breezes to tempt an idle waterman, but also ripe fruit that must be dealt with betimes.

Again, this year, I made a batch of ginger pear preserves. Not a large batch, as not many people like it, but ten, eight ounce jars – enough to see me through another season. After searching for my mother's recipe for half an hour, I suddenly remembered that the Pusslet had written it down a couple of years ago when she helped me. Our Pusslet, Squeedles, was a literary gem – had her own column for a while, albeit in a Florida paper in a little town that lacked its own literary pusslet. The Squeedler always paid close attention while I typed my journals and often inserted her own quirky wisdom and wit into my writing. Well, what was I to do? I asked around to find her work, and my sister, a local historian in Everglades City, Florida, who was co-editor of their paper, offered her a column of her own – "Paws to Reflect." This ran for several months until Floridians complained. Why should some Yankee pusslet have a column in their paper? What was wrong with some southern pusslet, who knew the Gulf Coast, writing the column instead? Well, the Squeedler acquiesced with a wink, and returned to typing her own journals. Someday I'll copy them out so you can read them. Here is her entry on ginger pears:

PAWS TO REFLECT 1 September 2009

If the weather were any lovelier, we shouldn't ever need any doors or windows. It's been in the seventies every day and in the fifties at night. I curl up on Dad's bed and wrap my fluffy tail around my toes. At six o'clock he gets up and gets us breakfast. Then we go out to terrorize the neighborhood. Someone has to keep those rabbits in line.

The other day, Dad and I made ginger pears. I climbed the Seckel pear tree and threw down the fruit. Then he took them into the house and peeled them and cored them and cut them up. If they're under ripe they stay firmer when you cook them. Then he sliced up whole lemons and crystallized ginger.

Here are the proportions to yield ten to twelve cups:

7 – 8 cups cut up pears
4 cups sugar = 2 lbs – light brown sugar works well
4 cups sliced lemon
4 cups crystallized ginger
2 packets of pectin

Begin with as little water as necessary to dissolve the sugar and pectin – perhaps a cup. Boil fruit first, add lemon next, add ginger last as it doesn't really need to be cooked. Keep stirring at a simmer till it thickens. Pack in sterilized jars. Climb inside the pot and lick it clean, then spend the rest of the afternoon licking all of that yummy syrup from in between your toes.

Squeedles

PAWS TO REFLECT 23 June 2009

Salutations from the rain forest. It's now been raining here in Connecticut for two months and forty-one days. Even the flowers aren't happy. And when the sun did come out – last Tuesday between ten and two – the lawn sprang up so fiercely that I had to hide in the woodpile. There's certainly no incentive for me to play hooky and spend the night out of doors.

It got so depressing staying indoors most of the time that, when I finally went out one morning, I brought in a half grown bunny for Mom to play with. Fortunately, she was having her lunch, so I didn't have to go look for her. I dropped my gift gently just beneath her chair. She got so excited she couldn't even be bothered to finish her meal. I guess it had been a while since she had her very own bunny. The two of them hopped around the dining room while I sprawled on the rug and giggled. When she finally caught my bunny, she snuggled him for a minute then put him back outside. Well! After all my effort to find some way to amuse her! There's just no pleasing some people…

Squeedles

Now that I'm over two years old, I think I have the maturity to tell you a little something about my life. Benvenuto Cellini said a man shouldn't write his memoirs until he was over fifty, but I think we cats mature a lot quicker than men.

To begin with, you probably wonder how a Pusslet like me ever learned to write. It's really quite simple. The man in my home is an author. I sit on his desk beside the monitor and watch what he does every morning. When he goes downstairs, I dip my paw in his French roast, lick my toes, then practice with the keyboard. When he discovered that I was interested, he began to teach me to read, and then to write. It's really quite simple.

After lunch, he goes off to his other job at the boatyard, and I have all afternoon to write these journals. Then I open his email and send it off to my publisher. I save everything in a separate file where he never looks and delete all of my emails after I send them. He doesn't suspect a thing.

Sometimes, while he's typing, I sleep on the Webster's Unabridged on top of the nearest bookcase. He always leaves it open – usually at a different page. I find my vocabulary has much improved since I sleep here. And he taught me himself how to click for 'spellcheck.' Playing with the mouse is one of my many fields of expertise.

We live in the country, so whenever I want, or whenever they let me, I go outside and play with real mice, or chase the leaves across the yard, or romp with the other Pusslet who lives here. Her name is Pye Wacket. I found out, finally, where she got her name. My dad used to write plays, and has a decent collection of books of plays.

I was reading through these one day when I came across a play entitled, "Bell, Book, and Candle," by John van Druten. It's quite clever but a bit simplistic. And the witch's cat, her familiar, is named Pye Wacket. Our Pye Wacket is a little lacking in brains, but she's a pleasant wench and we have a good time chasing each other about the house and knocking over the furniture.

They have a big fireplace here and frequently use it. The hearthstone is nearly the size of a door and, after the fire's been going all day, gets toasty warm. I like to lie on my back before the fire and warm my belly. Pye Wacket would rather perch on the back of the sofa. She's mostly black and absorbs heat far too readily to enjoy being close to the fire.

I learned all about absorption of heat in the Encyclopedia Britannica. Dad has another desk that he uses for business, and the back of that desk is hollowed out to hold an entire set of encyclopedias. There isn't much you can't learn about if only you come at it with an open mind.

He also has a third desk where he does his illustrations. Sometimes I help him with these. You can see the cat hairs the scanner picks up when he saves his illustrations. Knocking his pens and pencils onto the floor ensures me attention.

"Now, Squeedles," he says. "Be a good girl and sit here on my lap."

Then we get down to doing some serious work. Sometimes I take a nap in the wicker, waste paper basket. When it's half full of paper, it's really rather comfy. Being rather petite, I can just curl up. Sometimes, of course, I leap up onto his desk to see what he's doing, and knock his notebooks and things all over the floor. Then he gets vexed, and dumps me unceremoniously [isn't that a grand word? I learned it only yesterday from the Webster's Unabridged and just had to use it] onto the floor.

"You Squeedilifferous Pusslet!" he exclaims.

Being Squeedilifferous comes naturally to this Pusslet. I always need to know what's going on. How can I know which things I shouldn't be knocking onto the floor? And when I want to go out and cry and no one pays attention, of course I get Squeedilifferous. What else can I do?

That's one thing I can't do yet is open doors. My goddess, Bast, did not see fit, for whatever arcane reason, to allow my toes to manipulate things like doorknobs. Perhaps in another life I can be a woman, and come and go as I please, and have my own car, and use all the creams and brushes, and other funny things on the bathroom counter. As long as I never have to use that hair dryer.

That and the coffee mill are the only two things, except the vacuum cleaner, that drive me wild. I don't know how they tolerate all that noise. Of course, their hearing isn't so keen as mine, I realize that. Sometimes they don't even hear me tell them how empty my bowl's gotten. Then I have to jump on the bed and shout it right in their ears.

"You Pusslet!" they say. But often Dad gets up.

My mom is very kind, but doesn't appreciate me when I'm Squeedilifferous.

"No!" she shouts, and I scamper back to the office and jump on a chair and pretend I don't know anything about it.

Just because I knocked over that little vase with the dried-up flowers in it. It's amazing how many pieces comprised that vase. Sometimes Mom wants me to sit on her lap. Other times she doesn't. How's a pusslet to know? I try to be affectionate, and nuzzle up against her and nurse on her sweater to let her know how much I've missed her all day.

"You Squeedilifferous Pusslet!" she says, and dumps me on the floor.

Dad is more forgiving.

"You Pusslet!" he'll say, and shake his head.

But then he picks me up and scratches my ears. He doesn't mind at all if I chew on his shirt and knead his leg while he reads a book in the evening. I try to use velvet paws when I remember. My dad likes to wrestle with me and tickle my belly. Then I grab his hand with my paws and bite his fingers and kick him with my hind legs. Not very hard, of course, and not with my claws out – except when I forget. We have a great time and he doesn't mind if I inadvertently scratch him. It's too bad he isn't a Pusslet.

Pye Wacket is fun to play with, but she really isn't well read. There isn't much we can really converse about. Occasionally, I see her perusing a clothing catalogue, but she mostly looks at the pictures, and hasn't bought anything yet.

I figure if I can sell my memoirs, I'll be able to buy nearly everything I want. Mom makes jewelry, sometimes, and drops beads on the floor for us to play with. I'd like to purchase my own, if I could afford to, and a whole collection of little glass pots I could knock off onto the floor. And hire a maid to clean up all the pieces. And to open a can of tuna fish whenever I feel hungry.

It's amazing how stingy these people are with canned food. Just one heaping tablespoon each evening. The rest of the time, it's dry food. It's very good dry food, mind you. I eat as much as I can without exploding. Mom and Dad threaten to make me diet.

"You're much too corpulent, Pusslet!" they tell me lately.

The first time I had to go to the dictionary and look it up. I can't see the difference between corpulent and pleasingly plump, myself. And being plump pleases me, so what is their problem?

Oh, and yoghurt. Every morning, after he's had his French roast, Dad goes back downstairs to the kitchen and slices a banana into a bowl. Then he smothers it in strawberry yoghurt – the creamy, organic kind. I'm afraid bananas don't do anything for me, but the yoghurt is delicious. I get to clean his bowl every morning. After that, I take a good long nap on the dictionary or, if it's cold, beside the radiator. Things could be worse, you know.

I'm told they could have been much, much worse. My mom found me by the edge of the road when I was a nursling. I don't remember my birth mother. I only remember walking beside a road out in the country, and trying to catch a grasshopper for my breakfast. I remember feeling terribly, terribly hungry, and wondering why the grasshopper was so un-cooperative. Then this woman stopped her car and tried to pick me up.

But I ran away. I hadn't the slightest idea of her intentions. I was only three weeks old. Then she went back to the car and brought out a con-tainer with beef stew in it. There wasn't much doubt in my young mind after that. I would have followed her anywhere. Just try going without any food for a couple of days yourself. You'll know what I mean.

She picked me up – I fit in the palm of her hand.

"You precious creature," she said.

She took me home and showed me to the man.

"I'm going to name her Precious," she told him.

"No," explained my dad. "Her name is Squeedles." And I hadn't even told him. No wonder we get on so well together.

At that time, they lived in another house, closer to where they found me. Unfortunately, they had another cat. An old Abyssinian puss with lovely stripes but a disagreeable temper. She must have been at least twelve years old and hadn't the slightest use for any kitten. She'd never been able to have a litter herself. Perhaps that was it. She hissed at me and called me most frightful names, and threatened to eviscerate me if I ever ate out of her bowl. That wasn't likely.

She was one of those very rank pusslets, and I always knew where she was just by the smell. I made it a point to keep well out of her way. She never really hurt me, but she used to terrorize me and call me names. I can't repeat them here cause otherwise my publisher would delete them.

So, we managed to avoid each other while I got my bearings. I had just settled in and knew what was what when Mom and Dad sold our house! You can't believe the chaos. They were busy packing boxes and boxes of lovely things that I wasn't allowed to play with. But there were empty cartons galore to jump in and out of, and lots and lots of crumpled newspaper to chase around the house.

I was only three months old when we moved. I was in one of the first loads they brought to this house. It was large and empty and smelled exquisitely of mice. That's because the house was 300 years old and had a dry-stone foundation. I could see I was going to have plenty of work. There were two staircases to romp up and down, and lots of cabinets to hide in, and lovely big radiators to snuggle up to.

I'd been here perhaps a week before Mitzi arrived. That was the name of the mean old puss who hissed at me all the time. But when she came in, I made it clear that this was my home, and she'd better not forget it. And, believe it or not, it worked! The whole house smelled of me: not only the litter box, but the bowl, the beds, the sofa, the mat by the door. She backed down immediately, and never gave me much trouble after that. I got to eat first. Even though we had separate bowls, she wouldn't eat until I'd left the kitchen, but stood in the doorway, mewing at the man and the woman like a little, snot nosed kitten.

Life was good. I couldn't make it onto the beds except by climbing, but I managed to get up there just the same. My dad always got up earlier than my mom, and while he was in the kitchen making his coffee and lighting the wood stove, he took time out to get down on the floor and wrassel with me. He didn't mind at all that I scratched too hard. He just laughed and wiped off the blood.

That's what I needed. I hadn't a mother or siblings to teach me to fight.

Every pusslet needs to know how to defend herself, and Dad was aware of this. He never hurt me, but batted my nose until I swiped back, to teach me coordination. Then he'd tickle my belly so I could learn to use my back feet. He'd snap his fingers above my head until I leaped to grab him. I became a prodigious jumper – very important. I can make it onto the porch railing or onto the dining room table without a problem. Pye Wacket, who's a bigger pusslet than me, can barely make it onto the bed in one bound.

And educational toys. What they didn't think of? Stuffed mice, old socks, ping-pong balls. You think Hai Ali and squash are quick games? Get in an empty bathtub some time with a ping-pong ball and try your best to catch it. Whew! You can't get a grip on the thing with your claws, you have to trap it with both paws. That takes coordination!

But the thing I liked best was my rope. My dad is a sailor. He brought me a fathom of quarter inch braid. It was pliable and it wiggled. I dragged it about the house with my teeth. I lay on my back and kicked the stuffing out of it. Finally, I learned to tie some simple knots. Dad and Mom were very impressed when I tied an overpaw knot. Eventually, I managed a figure eight. I know some sailors who can't even tie that knot. Dad has promised to get me a rigging knife.

Squeedles

Everglades City, Florida

Speaking of Everglades City, we visited there the winter of 2005 – before the Squeedler started her column in the Mullet Rapper – and just in time for the annual Seafood Festival.

Everglades City comes alive one weekend in February. That's when the town gears up for the Seafood Festival. An annual event since 1973, the Festival now attracts thousands and thousands of people – numerous times the population of this tiny Gulf town in south Florida.

When the Tamiami Trail was under construction back in the twenties, ECity was its literal turning point – the road leading south from Tampa turned due east for Miami. ECity became a boom town – full of construction workers and their families and all the attendant prosperity. For a number of years it was the seat of Collier County – hence the grand city hall.

Vintage 1923

Monroe Station

This was one of six stations established by Barron Collier along the Tamiami Trail to provide aid to travelers. They were under the authority of the Southwest Mounted Patrol. Each was occupied by a Mounty and his family. Mounties patrolled the Trail by motorcycle; their wives sold food and fuel. Monroe station later served as a restaurant, was abandoned, was placed on the National Register of Historic Places, was purchased by Big Cypress National Preserve, and was recently destroyed by fire.

Now Everglades City is just a sleepy backwater. But it has potential. It was planned by the architect, David Grant Copeland, who was hired by Barron Collier – the financier and industrialist who came to own most of Everglades City. The town is laid out with a circular green surrounded by public buildings and parallel streets.

Lots and condos and houses are readily available though prices in the past few years have jumped. As usual, Florida real estate is a worthwhile investment. Although the railway depot is now a restaurant and trains no longer arrive, there is a little airstrip and the Tamiami Trail is a pleasant drive.

Depot Restaurant

Around ECity, kayakers enjoy miles and miles of estuarine backwaters through Everglades National Park. Sport fishing around the tidal rivers and Ten Thousand Islands has been popular for generations and there are numerous marinas and charter boats and excursions. The local commercial fisheries make their livings from shrimp and crabs. The many restaurants serve a tempting variety of seafood so fresh that it swam into the kitchen, and accommodations are very reasonably priced.

But if you are planning to visit the Seafood Festival, book your room months ahead. Thirty thousand people invade this village of under a thousand. The hub of ECity becomes the hub of activity. Up goes the stage, up go the tents. The stage will shortly come alive with Country & Western music; Bluegrass and Folk. The Museum of the Everglades displays historic artifacts and numerous old photos. The old bank building, now a spa, is a popular retreat for those in need of rest and rejuvenation. The art gallery displays the work of numerous local artists.

The smaller tents are for the numerous craftsmen: silversmiths, leatherworkers, woodworkers, weavers, sculptors, and jewelers. Every sort of craft and many arts are represented – the Festival committee wisely decides to limit the entries in any category – and the result is an eclectic mix with some crafts rather unique. The one I remember best was the little Butterfly Booth. This was run by a Native American man who collected exotic tropical Lepidopterae and mounted them tastefully in small, framed, glass cases. There were also examples of scorpions and some formidable large beetles. Some of the butterflies were as large as your palm and amazingly iridescent. There was also a man who designed and built teak furniture. Being somewhat of a woodworker, I studied his joinery and found it flawless. There were also booths with trinkets and scarves and handmade hats and silver work; with hand carved walking sticks and homemade soaps and bonsai shrubs and melodious wind chimes. A peripatetic vendor was hawking tiny rubber alligators that clung to your clothes or hat.

You might avoid the vendors, but the smells of the heavenly cooking were inescapable. While the Festival was urging itself awake Saturday and Sunday morning, the local church on the green provided breakfast – pancakes and bacon and orange juice and coffee – all you wanted for five dollars.

In a couple of hours, the larger tents were filled with purveyors of crab and gator; crawfish and snapper; saffron rice and fried bread; venison and corn bread; Creole shrimp and catfish; deep fried fritters and frogs legs; onion rings and French fries. Fruit smoothies, lemonade, beer and coffee could be had from smaller tents. Beyond the stage, a Ferris wheel, a merry-go-round, and a haunted house were complimented by amusement booths to test your aim with darts or balls or rings.

But the most amazing contest was – are you ready for this? – the frozen mullet toss. Say that again? Yep, you heard me – mullet. Frozen fish. And the targets? Toilet bowls – a dozen of them. Only at the ECity Seafood Festival. Step right up and loft your mullet, Madam.

This aromatic activity was perpetuated by the Boy Scouts. For just five dollars you received a latex glove and three frozen mullet – perhaps a foot in length. You stepped up to the line; set yourself; took aim at one of the lovely toilet bowls gaping, seat-less, maybe fifty feet away; and loosed your fish. An underhand toss with plenty of loft was required. If you hit a bowl you earned one extra mullet. If you actually scored you won a share of the profits.

It went like this: once an hour they added up the takings. Half of it went to the Scouts, the other half was divided among any winners. They took in about a hundred dollars an hour and seldom was there more than one winner per hour.

After a while the mullet began to thaw out. They became rather floppy and tended to fly apart. They left many obscene marks all over the toilet bowls. The audience had as much fun as the players. One of the Scouts, an enterprising youth, sat on various toilet bowls and egged on the contestants.

"Betcha can't hit me, Mister! One extra fish if you do!"

Sometimes they did. The crowd just howled. By lunchtime that Boy Scout smelled like last week's bait. I hear his mother made him sleep out in the shed. People lined up ten deep to toss their fish. You could tell the horseshoe players immediately. They posed at the line with supercilious smiles adorning their faces. They set themselves just so; calculated trajectories; took a few practice swings; lofted their slimy mullet – and missed, as everyone else. The crowd would reward them with comments on their prowess. Folks who played encouraged others to try it. Plenty of women were in their, pitching their fish. All eyes followed the flight of the hapless mullet that, by lunchtime [yummy!] were lacking their heads and most of their vital organs. I only hope this event is perpetuated. It introduced a fresh flavor to the Festival.

Meanwhile, beside the Courthouse, Country & Western music was drawing a crowd. Hundreds of folding chairs had been set out. The speakers were resonating with popular tunes as occasional brave souls attempted to dance amid the crowd. Thousands of people surged about the fairgrounds. There was a hefty contingent of motorcyclists – hundreds of Harleys were parked in row upon row of gleaming nickel and glistening leather. Aging bikers of both sexes in summer leathers, long grey braids, tattoos, and ear rings listened to music, slow danced, and ate fried catfish. Very sedate, these bikers. Grandparents, mostly, with steady jobs and stately machines, out for a pleasant weekend of food and music.

City Hall – Everglades City
Former Collier County Courthouse

Over there, in the shade, the conservation groups were well represented, selling hats and tee shirts, and passing out literature about Everglades National Park, Fakahatchee Strand, Big Cypress National Preserve, and Ten Thousand Islands. It's important to know that the orchids and alligators need our help, as do the panthers and roseate spoonbills. Meanwhile, the music and food, the brilliant displays, the sunshine, were overwhelming. We escaped into the Museum of the Everglades – a converted laundry that once served the needs of hundreds of construction workers and their families. A folksy Bluegrass group was playing to an audience of eight. We finally sat down after hours on our feet. We enjoyed the intimacy of these musicians – they were scarcely two banjo lengths away – who drolled among themselves and with us, as well. During their break we wandered the exhibits. The striking sheet metal sculpture of Marjory Stoneman Douglas, the conservationist, dominated the lobby. This avid lady worked with President Truman to create Everglades National Park, and wrote the book, *The Everglades: River of Grass*, exposing ignorant drainage practice and the need for conservative measures. At her feet crept a six foot, brassy gator with a grinning snout. Two glass cases were filled with wooden birds and masks carved by the Miccosukee tribe. On the walls of the lobby were striking local landscapes.

The band reconvened. They were filled with verve; with energy and goodwill. After their final number they thanked us graciously for listening. We spoke with the guitar player outside. They played the big stage once, he confided. It was too noisy; too commercial. Too many people in the audience were eating and talking, or had only come by to sit down. They'd rather play for people who truly listened, even to an audience of eight.

"We'll be back," he assured us. "Y'all come again."

We told him we would. We hope to see you there.

*   *   *   *

The rest of the year Everglades City is a quiet village populated by locals, retirees, and numerous fishermen. Presidents and dignitaries came here to fish and relax in bygone decades. Mostly they stayed at the stately Rod & Gun Club, with its cool, paneled lounges and dining rooms; its superlative food and service. It fronts on a little-developed stretch of the Barron River, and has an imposing wharf for tying up yachts.

Everglades City Rod and Gun Club

From the Journals of Constant Waterman 2 December 2008

Tommy was in the pool when we arrived. The water was eighty degrees, the air nearly as warm – a typical balmy November day in Everglades City.

I swam a few laps to rouse the muskrat in me, then lazed at the shallow end and listened to Tommy. Tommy's retired and has led an interesting life. I listened until my starboard ear went limp then came about and let him work on the other. About the time I got my mains'l trimmed, I heard him say I could borrow his canoe.

Tommy's place is about a hundred feet – give or take a canoe length – from the water. This is an estuary that connects the Barron River to the Gulf of Mexico at the bridge that connects ECity to Chokoloskee – the last outpost of civilization as we know it on the Gulf coast before you swim for the Keys.

Smallwood's Store-Museum
Chokoloskee, Florida

This estuary varies in width from fifty feet to a quarter mile, and in depth from an inch to the depth of your alligator held on end by his tail. There're about two feet of tide and numerous mudflats. If you leave your canoe, you'll sink up to your knees in mud before you can change your mind. The alligators hereabouts are very fond of the upper portions of canoeists. I left one of my sandals fetlock deep in the muck while we were launching Tommy's canoe. Next time I plan to wear snowshoes.

I wanted to go down the Barron River to take better pictures of the venerable Rod and Gun Club from the water. From Tommy's to the bridge connecting ECity to the mainland is scarcely more than a Mile. The Rod and Gun Club is another mile downstream.

Our English friend climbed into the bow and kept a sharp lookout for mudflats. It happened the tide was totally ebbed and hospitable mudflats abounded. If you run aground, you can't push off with your paddle – it disappears in the muck. If you try to get out, *you* disappear in the muck. Consequently, we proceeded with utmost caution. Fortunately,

Lake Placid – this estuary – lives up to its name. The tide meanders but sluggishly. In wider reaches the wind can prove a problem but, today, the breeze would not have bent a butterfly's wing.

The dominant forms of life we encountered were mullet and great egrets. Occasionally we met with brown pelicans, great blue herons, or the pair of kingfishers whose job it was to discipline all the rest. The alligators, apparently, had all gone south for the winter.

The near bank has numerous buildings most of the way; the farther shore nothing but mangroves and slimy undergrowth. You couldn't persuade me ashore there for love nor money nor even mermaids.

After we merged with the Barron River, the waterway narrowed; the tide and current swept us beneath the bridge at a rousing three knots. Then the river widened a bit and we drifted at half that rate. Now we met houses, piers, and boats on both banks for the next half mile. The farther bank below the settlement known as DuPont reverted to mangroves and mud. Piers with airboats abound all about the river and lower Lake Placid. Most of these cater to the tourist trade – soon about to burgeon. On the ECity side there are several small piers for the fishing and crabbing boats that supply the restaurants, many of which front the river.

At one of these I'd feasted on amberjack. Now, just ahead, we saw the mullet fling themselves from the water, leaping in desperation. Leaping in glee behind them was a stocky, yard long amberjack, roiling the river in his quest for a piscine lunch.

Then came the sprawling Rod and Gun Club, gleaming white in the tropic sun, its two hundred yards of timbered quay deserted this time of year. The Chamber of Commerce commissioned me to make an illustrated postcard of this stately landmark. We drifted off shore as I clicked half dozen frames with my digital camera. Then we put ashore at the concrete boat ramp just up river.

There I swapped our English friend for my cousin, Clare, and, with the aid of the incoming tide and Clare's expertise, paddled home the two miles in time for lunch. Aside from several airboats, we encountered nothing save birds. At least, returning, we had more water for navigation. We hauled the canoe, put her on the dolly, and trundled her home. We washed the canoe and stowed her gear, thanked Tommy for his graciousness, and left my sandal as a present for the 'gators.

Mystic and Noank

From the Journals of Constant Waterman 22   August 2006

Mystic Seaport is on my way to work. That's why it's taken me so many years to get there. Aside from applying to work in their boat shop when they hadn't any vacancies, I hadn't been on the property in close to twenty years. Last week I returned with my son, his wife, and his wide eyed little boy.

Much has changed. The wooden whaler, *Charles W. Morgan*, still has a berth, and has recently been refurbished.

Charles W. Morgan

Dunton, a fishing schooner, and the training ship, *Joseph Conrad*, were open for business. This latter, a small, three-masted ship, is distinguished by having glistening bright work on her. The working vessels had no time for such nonsense, and relied upon heavy layers of paint to stave off rot and weather. A smaller ship, *Providence*, tied off at the pier head by *Charles W. Morgan*, allowed no visitors.

A shuttle boat took visitors about the Seaport waterfront. The water taxi took visitors into the village. *Sabino*, a small, coal powered steam launch, plied the Mystic River.

Sabino

Breck Marshall, a twenty-foot replica of a Crosby cat boat, took visitors for short, informative sails on the river. This graceful, gaff-rigged, wooden boat caught the merest breeze with her ample sail and soundlessly glided among the moored boats and markers.

I found myself more interested in watching this lovely boat than going into buildings to admire museum pieces. The workshop is impressive, but I work in a boat shop every day and, although most of our work concerns the repair of fiberglass vessels, the novelty has worn thin.

I guess I've always been more interested in sailing than in repairing sailboats; more interested in rowing, paddling, punting, poling, what have you – "simply messing," as Ratty would say. I grew up messing about in boats and I look forward to the next place on my itinerary, even if it's only another gunk hole. Spoiled rotten, that's what I am, and I still enjoy the wind in what's left of my hair. Lord knows, there won't be enough good breezes in the years remaining to me.

I did have a pleasant chat with the Seaport's blacksmith. Actually, when he found out I had been a toolmaker most of my life, he asked me far more questions than I asked him. His shop felt homey to me. In some ways, more so than the boat shop. I still have some affinity for metal working, I guess, and the forge resembles nothing more than a hearth, or perhaps an altar to worship flamboyant Hestia.

Never allowing the fire to go out has true significance. In olden times, it proved imperative to maintain at least an ember. As much as your life might be required by the tribe whose fire you suffered to die out through neglect. I've raked the ashes over a fire in a fireplace and returned to uncover glowing coals as much as two days later. The smolder within me has lasted rather longer. At whiles it bursts into avid flame; at whiles it seems no more than an ascending wisp of yearning. As often as Great Passion works the bellows, I will respond.

I was speaking of Mystic Seaport. Aside from the bustle of tourism, it seemed rather quiet. The patient white carthorse drew an old coach around and around the reconstructed village. *Sabino* blasted her whistle as she backed away from the pier every half hour. Capstan chanties rang out from one of the ships during the afternoon, and the Crosby catboat whispered up the river. Her sinuous wake nearly deafened me.

The patter of the tour guides as you wander about the ships proved informative, though it tended toward the romantic. Life aboard square riggers was generally Hell for the fo'c's'le lot. They could expect little more than rigorous work, harsh discipline, and miserable food. These were not yachts.

Restoration makes Mystic Seaport special. Every species of vessel, from dinghy to three-masted ship, demands, and receives, the loving attention bestowed by master shipwrights. The shed containing small sailboats, many of them Herreshoffs, is a tribute to these dedicated craftsmen. Just now, a deck-less wooden trawler, *Roann*, stands in the shop receiving new frames and shear clamps. By next year she will have decks and a cabin – eastern style – aft – a dutiful diesel engine, and be rigged with an auxiliary mast and sail. Her goal is to cruise the Eastern Seaboard, collecting accounts of fishermen to be published as a book. This is a good thing. Tales of the sea and the waterfront always make good reading. One of these days, I might try doing something similar.

From the Journals of constant Waterman   29 September 2007

Last weekend went sailing twice, but never got farther than a few miles from West Cove. Saturday went out with Paula and, after bucking the tide for a bit, finally made it as far as Latimer Reef at a rousing two to three knots. Gradually overtook a heavy cruising sloop of forty-five feet who barely made steerageway with this six-knot breeze. With twenty knots of wind all we would ever see of her would be her masthead vanishing o'er the horizon.

On Sunday, met Brother Bob at the boatyard. Following a short haul, during which he painted both his topsides and bottom, he brought *Dream Time*, his Able 20, back to her berth. Now he was ready to take her out and get her new paint baptized. He'd convinced two lady friends to accompany him.

"Take out *MoonWind*," he said to me. "We'll take some pictures of you under way. You can use one for the next cover of your book."

I allowed the possibility. Naturally, they had color film in their cameras, and I have a hard time assimilating color, being naturally pigment sensitive. I'm told that the cover of this book was done in vivid red and yellow, but my publisher knew my proclivity for the moon at night, and righteously converted it to its proper hues.

I took the launch out to my mooring and bent on my sails. It wasn't blowing more than eight knots, so I hanked on my 150 genoa. My smaller headsail is at the sail maker getting a patch. I was nearly ready to get under way when here came the Able 20. She circled me once to exchange salutations, and then I let go my pendant. I motored out of the mooring field abaft them, then hoisted my sails.

The breeze was lovely. I made about four knots and could just about keep up with my companion. The bikini clad photographer busily snapped pictures of me flaunting my locks to the wind. Then Brother Bob took further photos of me, most of which I still have.

I followed them out to the Dumplings before we separated. Meanwhile, Petrel number 25 busily gathered in my wake a tad quicker than I could produce it. After two miles she hauled abeam and exchanged the news – almost none – and the weather – exceptional – before she wafted by me. Nothing like a Herreshoff boat to convince you that a heavy boat can also be a quick one.

I passed between the Dumplings and headed toward Ram Island. Then I came about and headed home. I enjoy day sailing, but not as much as I used to. Now I would rather be heading for a destination; looking forward to a passage to a somewhere just beyond the looming horizon.

Perhaps I've grown dissatisfied with this plodding existence I lead: this sedentary expanse of hours and years. I drive the seven miles to the boatyard where I mess about with other people's boats. I drive the seven miles home, stop to buy groceries, put more gas in my truck. I trot aloft to my office to search my email in hope that somebody, somewhere, has recognized my genius and wants to buy a few millions of my books. Eventually, I make my supper; settle back for the evening; and stupefy myself with a bit of light fiction.

Even though I do little more while anchored in some cozy harbor, at least I'm anchored in some cozy harbor aboard my boat, feeling the sea beneath me and the whispers of Lord Aeolus all about me. During the day I wander the quiet lanes of a quiet island; stop to converse with people and pet their dogs; nibble on the rosehips from some hedgerow; wander into little shops for coffee.

I have no lawn to mow, no boats to varnish, no telephone to answer. When all is observed: seen and heard and smelled and felt, I wander back to my boat to write about it. Write with a stubby pencil, not a keyboard.

Fill the pages of notebooks with my love of land and sea and sky; with my observations, impressions, wistful effusions.

And publishers, some of them, seem to enjoy my journals. And readers, some of them, don't know any better and also enjoy them. And who am

I to deprive this otherwise world of my words?

Ontology Revisited

Except as ever, I am not here.
All is always as ever before;
The wave, the wave as ponderous,
The wind as passionate,
The offshore lurid as moon contrives,
The pebble, perhaps, as rounded yet.

Except, as ever, I am not there.
And neither glide amid the wood
Nor hang in hunting;
Stoop to the teeming field.
Lately I have not shrieked my proprium;
Clutched nor torn nor ripped nor ravaged.

Again I am gone
But yet again remain,
Save for my shadow to start your huddled doubt.

Look where you will,
This rank and fertile furrow measures not
The sweat nor seed I lavish on this world.
The corded hornbeam strains no more than I;
Not more the dove laments
Nor trillium hides.
Not more the bat pursues
Nor moth eludes
Than I the night,
Than I revealing day.

I am not gone
Nor yet again remain;
But am
And was
And will
At some time
Be.

This was about as metaphysical and arcane a series of images as ever I attained.

The hawk, the bat, the moon, the night; being and not-being. Most specially the hawk, who has neither glided, stooped nor shrieked; neither clutched, tore, ripped, or ravaged. The latent hawk; the hawk who is not there; yet the hawk who can terrorize by shadow alone. Thoughts of being; not being; torn; yearning; refraining; and, mostly, potentiality.

It is the potentiality, mostly. That is the question. How far to take this life, this only-ness. To die slowly behind a book or go out and chase the wind.

Writing and Illustrating

Between 2008 and 2010 I worked to produce a collection of architectural drawings accompanied by brief historical descriptors. In 2010 I self- published, *Landmarks You Must Visit in Southeast Connecticut.* Of course, many people were unhappy that their pet landmark, if not their entire town, had been omitted. Researching, writing about, and illustrating fifty-five landmarks took me more than a year. If you include caring for the cat, nearly two years.

I recently {2015}brought out volume two: *More Landmarks You Must Visit in Southeast Connecticut.* The marketing is limited to the immediate region yet still takes a deal of time. Many of the little shops that carry my books have scarcely the space to display them. Should I burden them with still another of my works?

One would think both *Landmarks* books would be hot sellers at local arts and crafts shows. It hasn't happened yet. Our depressed economy finds most people hording their dollars or, if they spend them, they spend them on food and liquor. The casual purchase of ten to fifteen dollar items has been greatly reduced these past few years. I need to learn the art of baking pizza…

And yet I encounter enthusiasm in small but delectable portions from time to time. I visited one of my vendors – an upscale gift shop – and talked to a couple from southern New Jersey who have friends near here in Connecticut and travel this way frequently to their summer home on Cape Cod. They browsed my prints with admiration and were shown my Landmarks book, which they gladly purchased. We spoke of local history and I inscribed their new book. After they left, the gift shop invited me to be a permanent resident and sell books all day long.

But a rainy morning this first week of autumn brings few shoppers to the village. The tourist season here at the Connecticut shore is all but over. There will be a spate of shopping in the couple of months preceding the holidays during which I must be busy attending signings and craft fairs. I must keep my vendors supplied with books and Christmas cards. I must trundle to the harbor and pet my boat. A disgruntled boat is no home, nor yet a refuge, for a sailor.

St. Clement's Castle – 1902
Portland, Connecticut

The weather, in between rainstorms, is perfect for sailing. I went out Thursday afternoon with my business partner and we wafted about, talking of boats and reminiscing. We even circled Ledge Lighthouse at the mouth of the Thames and made it home before nightfall. I must make time to take *MoonWind* east to visit the Elizabeth Islands before the ‎autumnal gales confine us to port.

A long sail, single handed, gives one pause during this flurry of life, to appreciate small blessings; and some much, much larger. The lap of the sea along the flank of my boat; the breeze in my beard; the cry of the tern as she skims the resilient wave: these are little things not found in the kitchen at home. And, fortunately, onions can be sautéed aboard as well as at home in the kitchen. The aroma of sautéed onions and fresh coffee should make a seaman of anyone.

The grandiose magnificence of the ocean; its pulse and rumble; its placidness, its fury; all serve as inspiration. All remind us of the grand forbearance; the even grander intolerance of the sea. Such is our universe.

We ride its smooth swells one day; one year; and are swept to our easy destruction during the next. One needs to keep a weather eye open at all times, and not be lulled to destruction on the reef. As ever, one had best be secured when the wind awakes and the sea arises to smite all it can reach.

Thirty knot wind, for my little boat, is a challenge that I generally choose to avoid. I care for fair weather greatly. My roving is not to prove myself superior to the world, but to enjoy her. I avoid those wives who hurl cast iron skillets. Life is too short. My wife has never thrown anything at me, yet, except a pillow. I wouldn't know to duck. Calm seas prevail.

*   *   *   *

Today it rains and I sit at home and write. I should be illustrating: I have two commissions, but I've determined to make a new top to my drafting board. My old table has a definable arc to its surface, which makes it nearly impossible to keep the parallel rules from jumping about. There is also the danger of following the curvature and returning whence I departed. This defies the logic of perspective – of vanishing points. It is much like sailing.

As the Earth is flat, vanishing points are part of a sailor's reality – he has an actual chance to escape life ashore. If he sails for more than a month in any direction, he's assured of falling over the edge and vanishing ab- solutely. Were the Earth indeed round – as some old Greek has attested – we should always return to our homeport in time, and be forced once again to manicure the lawn.

This is in direct contradiction to the mantra of old sailors: be glad that your wake dissolves in the sea, otherwise your wife would catch hold of the farther end and reel you in like a haddock.

If there is anything more soul destroying than mowing the lawn, except maybe trimming your beard, I don't want to know about it. I do my best to avoid doing either but once every couple of years. Varnishing bright work doesn't compare to mowing a half acre lawn. At least when you've put the ninth coat of liquid amber onto your drop boards you've created things of beauty. That beauty must be maintained is one of life's givens. Every woman knows this to be true.

A half-acre of unkempt lawn, alive with wild violets in a force four breeze, is a thing of beauty. A closely cropped lawn resembles nothing so much as a broad green rug. And everyone knows that the function of rugs is, primarily, to collect as much dirt as possible. Worst of all, a lawnmower, for all its bluster, won't even drive your boat through the water at hull speed.

My 9.9 horsepower outboard is perfect for *MoonWind's* needs. At half throttle, it's quiet and efficient, and drives *MoonWind* at four knots through the water. Best of all, I seldom have to empty it of clippings.

A sailor's needs are few: fuel, fresh water, propane, and wind. Oh, and French roast – with just a bit of raw sugar. Life is sweet notwithstanding. Shove off and see for yourself. Let your dog stay home and tend to the lawn. Leave your cat home to supervise the dog. Believe me, she's qualified.

I knew a cat who was left in charge of the household all day while both the parents worked. That cat cooked breakfast; got the children washed, and dressed, and fed, and out to catch the school bus at seven o'clock each morning. She cleaned up the breakfast dishes, vacuumed the house, then took the shopping list to the store and gave it to the grocer. The store cooperated by delivering the groceries, after which the cat would put them away.

When the children returned at half past two she would meet the bus, fix them a snack, and get them started on their homework. Her usage of irregular verbs was exemplary; her French was comme ci, comme ça; her understanding of algebra was no worse than your own. Her knowledge of the American Civil War was slim, but she read up on it while the kids were at school.

As every good nanny, she received a half day off once per fortnight, during which she would disappear into the woods, slay any number of mice, and devour them raw. A cat can tolerate only so much civilization, you know, before she reverts to The Good Life.

The same can be said of sailors. Level beds and well cooked meals are all right in their way, but a sailor pines for nothing save apples to nibble while he fights the helm. And a proper bunk is twenty-two inches wide – give or take a marlinspike – and shouldn't be too soft for fear he might not wake should the wind veer suddenly, dumping him out on the deck.

Comfort is not a perquisite of the sailor's occupation. A sailor I knew spent weeks at a time aboard his sailing dinghy. He had two buckets – one labeled "In," the other, "Out." You get the message.

So did his wife. She disavowed, disowned, and generally disabused him of any conjugal equity he might have presumed went with the office of spouse. They parted ways, as sailors do, at the pier. He then embarked in his dinghy on a voyage to the East Indies, and has never been heard from since. Unless, of course, you include the mermaid he sent me from Singapore.

This is the way I make my living, you see: by relating truthful tales from wide and far. Magazines pay big money for stories like these. That's how I can afford my yacht and a crew to keep her spotless. The story about the cat was passed on to me by the Pusslet, who had a sore paw and couldn't type it for herself. That cat was a personal friend of hers, but the Pusslet confided that her French was of the Cajun variety, not Parisian at all.

The sailor remembered to send me a card at Christmas that depicts a rickshaw drawn by a pair of reindeer. But it seems he lost one of his buckets overboard in a gale, and the label came off the other, and, during an interval of utmost doubt and gastronomic depravity, he avidly joined the Jain religion and now eats nothing at all.

*   *   *   *

I've just committed the gravest sin and sent these last few hundred words to an editor I know. It may mean the end to a long, long friendship, but what's a writer to do? Blather was meant to be shared.

Now, two days later, that editor has accepted my piece to be run two months from now.

When I was much younger and had both hair and stamina I used to own a canoe. I couldn't afford a sailboat. I still can't afford a sailboat. Now I have a kayak instead of a canoe and have no time to paddle. That may change. I now live, having just moved again, within a five minute drive of a good sized pond with navigable streams meandering in and out.

Instead of residing twenty minutes from *MoonWind*, I now have three quarters of an hour drive to her slip. But soon, very soon, our vacant house from which we just moved will be occupied by tenants. This will greatly ease our financial burden, though we still must work a little bit to keep the halyards spliced. There's nothing like the wayward end of a carefree halyard, thirty feet aloft, to make you wish you were safe in your canoe.

Varnishing one paddle every spring is hardly a chore. Coiling a thirty foot length of quarter inch line and stowing it in a bucket with a two pound folding anchor is hardly a chore. Hosing out your canoe after you've messed about all day in the underbrush is hardly a chore. And just the thought of spending several thousand dollars you don't even have to keep your canoe in a far off slip would be much cause for merriment.

But being at sea in *MoonWind* is another life apart from this life ashore. Wind and sea and islands are all the romance I need to exist. Standing at my drafting board or sitting at this computer is not existing. It is only recording. It is trying to catch the joy of the mockingbird's song with a tape recorder; it is trying to imitate the raspy voice of the wind in your standing rigging, or the age old seductive whisper of the ocean to *MoonWind's* lissome flank as she slides down another roller.

I've scarcely had time to sail these past two years – I won't say 'seasons.' Days are all I can deal with at this point in my life. Tomorrow I need to do such and such and there won't be time to sail. Perhaps the next day? I do check the weather and wind and tide, but ultimately, it needs to be fair and not too blustery. I don't need to be rail down to be happy. I only need to be sure my boat is safe; that motor and rigging are in their best working order; that I have both paper and electronic charts to keep me away from the reef.

All I need is money to finance *MoonWind*. Having been less than gain-fully self-employed, and never careful with my money, I find myself unable to be retired, in any sense of the word. I must sell more books,

I must varnish more boats, I must do without that new gronicle for *MoonWind*. So I find myself reading to much diminished audiences, as fewer people buy paper books any more. I find myself at craft fairs, hawking my prints. I find myself underbidding boat repairs in order to guarantee me money to live.

Do you wonder I need to go out with *MoonWind* to taste the breeze on any and all imaginable occasions?

My years diminish. I can fool myself for decades altogether, but my strength and stamina aren't what they used to be. I'm nimble still, and coordinated, and strong enough, I suppose. I'll find out for sure if I go overboard some winter. Someone else may have to become Constant Waterman one of these days. Even if I live till ninety and still can wave a paddle, someone else will have to become Constant Waterman. A sobering thought and not one to entertain this October morning.

For all of life that matters is here and now, not yesterday or tomorrow. Tomorrow is hopes, and yesterday stories, but today is casting off your mooring pendants to venture into the present. Is it any wonder the word, 'present,' has come to mean a gift? What better gift than to wake up and be alive. For those who wake to naught but grief or agony or dying, this may be a present best returned to the giver, but, for most of us, another morrow is something sacred to cherish. It's unfortunate that much of our time is taken up by trivia: by driving, by cleaning, by sorting through repetitive paperwork; by rectifying other people's incompetence; by dealing with our possessions.

The sun comes up, and crosses the sky. The sun goes down, the moon comes up. Yesterday, and tomorrow, and today, forever and ever.

> AND THAT INVERTED BOWL WE CALL THE SKY
> WHEREUNDER, CRAWLING, COOPED, WE LIVE AND DIE;
> LIFT NOT THY HANDS TO IT FOR HELP – FOR IT
> ROLLS IMPOTENTLY ON AS THOU OR I.

So wrote Omar Khayyam at the time of the crusades in his Rubaiyat.

Moonrise

It isn't imperative that we be here to witness any of this. The existence of Earth not require that we record it. Neither any beginning, nor any ending, is conceivable. We can scarcely grasp the hour at hand before she slips away. But whether all be illusion or quite real,

> "One thing is certain, and the rest is lies;
> The flower that once has blown forever dies."
>
> Omar Khayyam

What childish pride the hope of power engenders! Crusade and conquest; dynasty and empire; what madness but makes of this world a desolation. And if successful for a generation, or ten, what relevance to us at home, where ever we delve and spin? How many have been slain to prove great religions right? How many suffered that destiny might shine for the ruling few?

THEY SAY THE LION AND THE LIZARD KEEP
THE COURTS WHERE JAMSHYD GLORIED AND DRANK DEEP;
AND BAHRAM – THAT GREAT HUNTER – THE WILD ASS
STAMPS O'ER HIS HEAD, AND HE LIES FAST ASLEEP.

Omar Khayyam

Though dissemination of new ideas has always been a byproduct of conquest, the price and the reward tip the scales now one way, now the other. Medicine, technology, and art have swirled about the strife that roils about us. Oh, to live longer, own more, and do less work! Oh, to be young, and glamorous, and wealthy! Oh, to have health, and education, and wisdom! Oh, to sow sand upon the endless shore, to count the breaths of the wind!

The greatest minds from about the world concur that less is needed. The smallest minds from about the world would heap the wealth of the world for their own delight. We might ignore these latter did they not, inevitably, presume to rule our lives. I have wrestled with these anomalies, and vilified the choices. I have stayed awake to read both poets and scholars. I have written and written – yet the days still pass by.

Where have you been and what have you been doing?
Have you heard the morning – save as Labor's clarion?
Have you kissed the night – save as the spouse of sleep?
There lack sufficient hours to trivialize
The deportment of this planet –
There are too few days to waste just to get our bearings.

You can but reach – and grasp one fragile moment;
You can but wish – and own the universe.
All of what you need is everywhere.
The body you have must serve.
Your mind is the legs – wander where you will;
Your soul is the eyes – see to it without weeping.

If you would drink, first spill out all your dryness;
If you would feast, consider how you famish.
We have not come merely to wrap our words about this world;
We do not endure merely to suffer breathing.

Try to succumb without the use of knowing;
Try to achieve without the need to own.
The governance of this world has never wanted.
What men have done, will do, is the song of birds
That scarce abides when once the birds are flown.
That drear and dreadful specter we most mind
Will presently adjourn our tenure here
And sentence us for only ever
To listen to the stars; undrape the day;
Tally the rain; and braid the wind's bright hair.

It was Yeats and Emerson inspired this next poem. Emerson, from his journal entry of 19 March 1835:

"I am the heir of uncontained beauty and power."

And Yeats, from his poem of 1892, Fergus and the Druid:

"I have been many things:
A green drop in the surge, a gleam of light
Upon a sword, a fir tree on a hill,
An old slave grinding at a heavy quern,
A king sitting upon a chair of gold."

And this, my own interpretation

There is no will save the world's will,
No way that has not been passed;
No claim to new save by what is old,
No life but intends to last.

Here bides the magic of the highest order,
Where the wind shrieks wisdom to the stillborn stones;
Where the roots spread reason 'neath the kneeling hills,
And the tree leans to listen to the storm.

I have known the anguish of the hounded quarry;
As the white-tail stag I have stained the trail;
Down the heaving slope I have plunged and staggered,
Agonized by the arrow.

I have leaped from the ledge with the avid moonbeam;
Laughed with the ice on the estuary;
Stooped with the hawk from the spired heavens;
Raved the dream of the flower.

I have been the river, I have been the sea;
I have been one mute, uncounted drop
In the thunderstruck forest –
Held the sky in my hand!

Yet – when the final leaves of my life
Flutter to rest on the lawn,
I shall spread my wings o'er the echoing earth
And rise above my last dawn.

Death of the White Stag

Digression the First

And now, at last, it is this morning. The leaves change color, the sky greys; the air remains nearly safe enough to inhale. The pusslet has been out to wet the grass; my half drunk, second cup of coffee stands neglected; the sun toys with the vague idea of making an entrance, albeit in a supporting role.

I'm off a bit later to set up a tent at Clyde's Cider Mill to sell my books and cards. Or at least to wave them about and accost innocent passersby and tell them how famous I always meant to be. It hasn't worked yet but, being a slow study, I'll play it again. At least Clyde's has good doughnuts and pumpkin bread and hot or cold cider, fresh from their press. They're an institution, and a welcome one, in this corner of the world, and have been for well over a century.

Clyde's Cider Mill – 1881
Stonington, Connecticut

It's curious how a century no longer seems an immeasurable tract of time. Time was, anything more than a decade seemed forever. My parents were born over one hundred years ago; my father's father in 1861. My father's mother died in 1906, having imparted eleven children, last of all, my father, in 1901.

When he was a boy, automobiles were a rarity, even in the suburbs of Boston where he grew up. The children would run alongside the infrequent autos for amusement ["Blow the horn, Mister – please!]. Electricity and telephones and running water in homes were for the middle and upper classes. Factory workers toiled for the company store. A woman operating a loom or drawing frame or card made ten cents an hour and worked sixty hours a week. A man working as a millwright, who repaired and maintained the machines, a highly skilled mechanic, might make five times that and own his home. Little children toiled in mines and mills.

Teachers beat children; dentists worked with foot treadle drills; anesthesia meant ether or chloroform – antibiotics had yet to appear. Blacksmiths and cart wrights and coopers kept trade in business, though machine shops proliferated in industry. Airplanes were still experimental toys, and canal boats had lost their haulage to the railroads. The whaling industry had all but died out; horse drawn farm equipment was dying out, but was not yet dead. Horse drawn drays still clopped the cobbled streets of most large cities. Coasting schooners survived as yet, built of wood or steel. Coal fired central heating was commonplace: my father shook down and stoked the boiler before he left for school.

By the time my father departed this world in 1988, rockets were setting men upon the moon; computers had progressed to desk top size, open heart surgery was commonplace; most families owned color televisions and automobiles, dishwashers; video players; and, occasionally, a computer. Cellular phones had arrived. Sophisticated calculators had made the slide rule and logarithm tables relics for the museum.

My father reflected that his portion of the twentieth century had seen more progress in more diverse fields than any century previously and perhaps any yet to come. Though electricity was in limited use, the quantum jump from water powered mechanical energy to nuclear energy, from slide rule to computer, defies comprehension.

Coup de Grace
{St. Michael}

Only remember: all this can be changed by the flick of a switch. A nuclear holocaust, or even a natural one, could have all of us beating our plowshares back into skinning knives. Snaring rabbits and fighting over the firewood might be the new reality in a generation or two. Read "A Canticle for Liebowitz," by Walter M. Miller, Jr., if you want a good description of the aftermath of a blasted civilization.

Where does one decide where reality and pessimism intersect? And does optimism – knowing ourselves and the Universe to be infinite – exist on another plane, another continuum, or is Reality the only continuum and are optimism and pessimism the only two alternatives? Perhaps one day, from my coign of omnipotence, high above this galaxy, or at least the tops of the trees, I may smile down at all of you scurrying your lives out, and pontificate with the benevolence of wisdom. For now, I must slog about as other mortals, and strive to feed and comfort myself and others the best I know how.

Lounging on the Riverbank

On another level, the leaves are undertaking their yearly transition to remind us that all is well with the natural world. The nights are cool, with no frost yet; the pusslet begs to go out when the dawn is still fringed with mist. Soon, the soaked grass glistens in the new born rays of the sun. The temperature will soar into the sixties if it stays sunny. Thoughts of sailing are damped by the need to finish commissions to illustrate two buildings; to complete building a ramp to my stoop by which to trundle the firewood cart inside; by the need to move the last few loads of whatever from the Stonington house so that our tenants may begin to clean and paint.

Hopefully, this winter will find me able to finish these scribbles; to decide to pursue a publisher or perhaps to again self-publish. In either case, publicity is the key to any success. Most of the little shops that carry my books have no more space for more books. I must think beyond the confines of southern Connecticut for a change. I've become provincial, and this little province of mine is scarcely an hour's drive in any direction.

Here, at the Midpoint of Eternity, I must change my stance or else be overgrown, or overwhelmed, or, at the least, left behind. My days are soon to become busy, I trust, with boats and books, not to mention holiday cheer and visits to and from family. By January, I may have breathing space. Perhaps as did Horatius, who

"... reeled, and on Herminius
He leaned one breathing space,
Then, like a wildcat mad with wounds,
Sprang right at Astur's face.
Through teeth, and skull, and helmet,
So fierce a thrust he sped,
The good sword stood a hand's breath out
Behind the Tuscan's head."

Ah! This was the stuff of which a boy's dreams were built! I read "*Horatius*," from Macaulay's *Lays of Ancient Rome*. I read Stevenson's *Treasure Island, David Balfour, Kidnapped,* and *The Black Arrow*. I read Kipling, Verne, London, and Haggard. Oh, to be a conqueror, an adventurer, a hero! And here I sit, at this Midpoint of Eternity, a terribly fond and foolish young old man, waiting as this world spins swiftly round.

Perhaps tomorrow I shall rescue the maiden, slay the serpent, revel in riches, command a band of heroes! Or perhaps have my toast and coffee at this computer, and amuse you again with my idiosyncratic blather and wistful repartee.

Most of you will never be slayers of dragons. You will battle with the IRS; rescue your cat from the road; stamp on the ant who wandered into your kitchen; shake your fist at the rain. We reap but merely a portion of what we sow; save but a tithe of what we might have shared; share but a morsel of what we know to be true.

And this I know to be true:

The spring that bubbles up from the earth amid a few moss grown stones, under the supervision of a single leopard frog, is only the libation of the spirits of the wood. Should you choose to drink with the Naiad, be careful not to trouble her tiny pool. Be careful not to cause her frog consternation. He is indeed a prince of this sacred realm. The trout lilies, stippled alike the trout, are most beautiful where not seen. The trout himself, downstream in that pool beneath the roots of the old red maple, is not only beauty but energy most regal.

Worlds exist of which you have no ken. The ocean is many times wider than the shore. The forest glade is a microcosm of wonder. The many kinds of moss; the delicate mayfly; the glint of quartz in the stream – all are unchanged since before you drew breath to wonder; or to ignore. The Green King rules here as Poseidon rules the sea. The Rat and the Mole's little boat can yet be seen on the River. Doff your disbelief and take off your shoes. Civilization is nowise as omnipotent as you fear.

Ratty and Mole were among the first of my friends. Summers, my parents would drive my sister and me to Rockport, Massachusetts to my father's family's summer house, now owned by his five-year-older sister. We loved Deborah. She was funny and smart and somewhat indulgent, somewhat strict. A school teacher from the days when women teachers were forbidden to marry, she made a virtue of living alone; made friends of all; gave her utmost energy to the teaching of high school English. She retired; substituted; returned to teaching full time; volunteered at the

Tales from the Sea

Old Folks' Home; ran a Great Books group; remained an active member of the Congregational Church. She never learned to drive, but walked and walked. It was only a mile to the village. Coming back laden with groceries, she would take the local bus that dropped her only quarter of a mile from her home. From the local paved road, one diverged into an unpaved lane that led between wild roses and emerged before a rambling, two and a half story, weathered shingled nine room house with a sturdy veranda overlooking two acres of hay.

The sprawling living room had an inglenook with opposed settles, a bay window with a window seat, glass fronted cases for books and more books. The dining room was full of light and faced the not too far off sea. Glass shelves spanning the windows supported little glass figurines and little glass cups and vases that caught and refracted the sun. The table and ladder back, spindle legged, caned chairs were painted bright orange; the tablecloth white with embroidery. The kitchen was old fashioned, with a slate sink and round- front refrigerator, and a hand cranked coffee mill mounted on the wall, and a drop leaf table.

On the second floor, to which you ascended by a broad staircase from the front hall, stood four bedrooms and a single bath with, of course, a claw footed tub. The third floor had sloping roofs, two small bedrooms, and attics. From Deborah's bedroom you could easily see the twin lighthouses on Thacher's Island, close to the rocky shore.

The basement was dim, with bulkhead doors. We helped Deborah stack firewood there, for she delighted in her fireplace and summer evenings could often prove wet and chilly. A large, silver candy box with a hinged, bas relief lid stood on a table by the inglenook, but we needed to ask permission to have a hard candy. The mantel piece supported candles and a six inch high old man and old woman hand carved, hand painted, and well content with their world. They now stand on our china cabinet, but I doubt they approve of their less than austere surroundings.

Long matches filled a small vase on the mantle and, wonder of wonders, a shaker held magic dust which, when sprinkled on the flames, turned them to myriad colors. What a treat! We had to take turns from evening to evening, adding color to the fire.

After supper we would walk the few hundred yards via sandy lanes to the sea. An acre-broad expanse of tawny granite ran from an old foundation down to the water. Here we could watch the sea in its many moods and play among the tidal pools. One of these pools was large enough for me to sail my very own, very first boat: a twenty inch sloop. This pool was near to the sea and received refreshment from each high tide. It supported a cast of snails, minnows and little crabs who hid amid the bladderwort and seaweeds. The pool was knee deep and several yards broad and exercised my navigational skills to their little utmost.

Some days we would walk into town to shop for groceries and visit the small library. It was here that I met the Water Rat and the Mole. At age seven, they were just my size, and I loved them at once and forever. The copy I read, and read, and read again had no pictures. It wasn't until decades later, on my third copy, that I encountered Ernest Shepard's delightful drawings.

Kenneth Grahame never talked down to his readers. He described, with love, the River, the fields, the byways. He explored the thoughts and emotions of his characters: their ecstasy, their depression; their lassitude; their delight. The emotional and egocentric Toad; the stolid Badger; the bold, ingenuous Otter – all came alive.

I purchased, a few years ago, a copy of Wind in the Willows for my grandson, replete with excellent illustrations in color – a vibrant and responsive interpretation of a lovely world still to be found if one knows how to look. But three of the dozen chapters had been omitted. Dulce Domum, The Piper at the Gates of Dawn, and Wayfarers All had been left out. This is a grave injustice to the children who read this classic. Some editor assumed that children have no need of wistfulness, nor religion, nor dissatisfaction with the mundane. I suppose that some good Christian took offense with the Pan-theism of the world of Kenneth Grahame's creatures. Or who couldn't abide the thought of Awe in a modern child's life. The cloven hoof reprehends the righteousness of the educators who think corruption goes hand in hoof with Panic.

We despise the thought of venery, of hunting. Bambi must not be harmed. But it's perfectly all right to encourage youngsters to play with video games in which they blow up cartoon enemies by the carload, and modern warfare is no longer a hand to hand battle to the death, but merely the video game of the high elevation bombers that murder thousands of women and children, level hospitals, schools, and churches with a single twitch of a trigger. Impersonal destruction can be such fun! Bam! There goes another village! My score's higher than your score! Bam! Kill some Commies for Christ!

But the frenzy of the ravening wolf for the rabbit must never be taught. Life and death and war must be neither a mystery, inspiration, nor a reality. I became a vegetarian forty years ago after having killed numerous animals. Did need demand, I would do it once again to feed myself.

The Wind in the Willows is an idyll, but an idyll inspiring thought. The gamut of emotion is probed, and only the harshest emotions, the throes of birth, of death, and mutilation, are omitted. An ideal world, perhaps, but necessary to show the plausible, peaceful interactions of simple souls.

The violence at the end of the book, "The Return of Ulysses", would not offend a novitiate at a nunnery. The beating of the weasels and stoats has not the blood and gore of a modern film, nor is it touted as being an ideal to which we should aspire. The Badger specifically admonishes the Rat for passing out a brace of pistols to each of the heroes. No shot is fired – a clubbing more than suffices. And, even so, no bones are broken. Various weasels come by the next day to apologize for their pillage. There are no grudges; no retribution or revenge.

The cudgels of the heroes are, metaphorically, soon cut up to feed the kitchen fire.

And I, more interested in kitchen fires than gore, destruction, and retribution, shall continue to rock by the fire and dream, or ply my local River with Ratty and Mole.

Our craze for violence, depicted daily in close ups of blood and mayhem, serves no end except to glorify, to promulgate violence. Shootings of schoolchildren, rape and murder, infest our televisions and computers every minute. As ever, Alas! Little boys stage mock battles to help become responsible adults. I, too, killed my enemies with a wooden sword and imaginary bombs, then graduated to hunting – but only animals. Generations of learning to hunt other men has left the mark of Cain on our brows, furrowed now by intolerance, love of violence and oppression.

Though domination is a virtue of the male of every species, it is limited, with the beasts, to the interests of propagation and food supply. Only man harbors desires to rule others for the sake of ego; to amass unwieldy wealth that must be defended; to design beliefs that demand the suppression, nay, the deaths, of millions.

Are we mad? And so I lounge on my river bank and dream of desultory days and starry nights, or else go off in my boat with Ratty and Mole, little caring if I return.

I still have hopes of running the Ditch with *MoonWind* – the ICW – the Intracoastal Waterway – that follows our entire eastern seaboard. If once I can attain financial stability, which the sale of our second house may impart, I may reward myself with a voyage to Florida. The ICW cuts across southern Florida, through Lake Okeechobee, connects to the Caloosahatchee River, and empties into the Gulf of Mexico at Fort Myers. Down the coast a short ways lie Naples, Marco Island, Everglades City, Chokoloskee, and the Ten Thousand Islands. These last inhabit shoal water, and *MoonWind* had best go tippy toes amongst them. But the lee of a sunny island might be the perfect spot to write a book. As I now write this book looking out at a drear and rainy October dawn,

Mole Sets the Spinnaker

I suppose I could do no worse in a pleasanter clime. I only wonder what success I should have in illustrating on a table that swayed a bit. I might have to set up my studio ashore. I picture myself rowing to and from work as once I paddled the Connecticut to earn my rice and beans.

This time of year the Connecticut would be shrouded in a chilly mist at daybreak, and at times I would wait for the rising sun to melt the moisture away. I remember the morning I ran down an oil tanker that waited by the day marker until the crossing had cleared. Her skipper leaned from her pilothouse window and contemplated the morning – what he could see of it – while his idling engines throbbed quietly below.

There wouldn't be any tankers nosing about the Ten Thousand Islands. The water there would scarcely come up to your nose. A centerboard boat would be ideal for messing about off the Glades. I doubt I'm going to trade in *MoonWind* at present. I haven't even finished re-coring her deck or painting her cabin. The reproachful glances I have to endure from my boat make me ashamed. Just you try to keep your mistress tied up without at least an attempt to refinish her drop boards.

Enough about boats – they'll take over your life when your will power's at its ebb. Not that you shouldn't be overwhelmed by something. Whether it be art or science or nature, let yourself be whelmed. Delve into the depths of learning; be passionate; be aware. Whatever demands your uttermost attention, be it your cat, your spouse, your art, your creed, dedicate that attention. You may have noticed I put the cat first. If you had twenty claws in your lap as you typed these lines you'd grant concessions, too.

Digression the Second

"Prowler"

Some cats demand more than their share of attention. It behooves you to teach your cat another pastime. Journaling, painting, and photography are all within the capabilities of the common, domestic pusslet. The results may well surprise you. Though not much better read than many cats, Squeedles improved her vocabulary every day by napping on a different page of my Webster's Unabridged. Try it yourself. The cuticular transpiration of vocabulary will surprise you. It always surprises me. I awoke from my nap on my Webster's just now with "cuticular transpiration" on the tip of my tongue. I only hope I get the chance to use it in my writing.

Perhaps I should return to talk about boats. Or butterflies. I always enjoy a visit from a butterfly when I'm sailing, especially several miles off shore. Nearly always, the butterfly is a monarch. This species is renowned for long distance migrations, so taking a bit of a flutter five miles from shore to visit a waterman is nowise a great journey. You might try it yourself some time when you've nothing better to do. Just perch on my weather lifeline and tell me the news from shore. I'm always amazed by what the world gets up to during the time that I'm away. And I'm blessed to know that I haven't been a part of it.

But butterflies are close mouthed for the most part. I needn't disrupt my idyll afloat by reports of elections for candidates whose primary concerns revolve around their own power. The only power concerning me is that of the wind and the water. What would this world be like without politicians? Would they were every one sailors, instead, each one alone in a little boat on the sea.

I fear to expound on politics, lest I forgo my calm demeanor and pummel my innocent keyboard. Let it suffice that my admiration for life, and love, and learning is a thing realms apart from the degradations of power.

*   *   *   *

When I listen intently I can hear *MoonWind*'s plaintive lament from her slip. I wanted to sail today, but I need to finish an illustration for a customer. It seems my fate to hunker down here at Griswold for the winter rather than indulge myself by sailing to warmer climes. The woodstove should be installed next week and suffice to heat this trailer.

Meanwhile, the world whirs by and I sit here admiring myself on the scrolling pages. Another author I know has just emailed me an excerpt from her soon-to-be-released journals of Mystic, Connecticut. As she herself said, "I can't imagine why anyone would want to read yet another book about Mystic, but I had to write it."

This is the way of most writers. We're a zany, compulsive lot who enjoy indulging our imaginations and talent for coherent prose. The result? More books to amuse, instruct, provoke, and inspire. Which is to say, we inspire ourselves and others to produce more books. Electronic books are a blessing, if only because they save the trees from being converted from producers of oxygen to repositories of blather. We love to blather, we writers. We smugly count the words we produce each day, and project when our next magnum opus will hit the market.

We mustn't forget that, courtesy of Berk Breathed, Opus is also a penguin.

My next "Great Penguin" should be complete by spring, if a ravenous polar bear doesn't eat it first.

I'm glad we weren't speaking of polar bears cause I don't know much about them, except for the big white bearskin rug with the head full of fangs on the living room floor before the fireplace in the home of friends of my parents. This was in New Milford, Connecticut, almost into New York State, and all I remember – being young beyond belief and almost recollection – was that rug.

*   *   *   *

I have but very few memories from before the age of three or so: picking up shingles on the lawn with my little red wagon; sleeping in a downstairs room in our home before I was allowed upstairs to have my own retreat.

By four I began attending a private kindergarten that met in the library basement. Most of those children would be a year ahead of me when we started elementary school. Perhaps someone thought I was precocious because I could read at four years old. It's difficult to remember not being able to read.

Perhaps I was born able to read. That would explain a lot. By the time I was six, I had written and illustrated a book about frogs. It was probably four pages long and undoubtedly the best thing I've ever done. I still have a short attention span and can only write stories a few hundred words in length. When I want a whole book, I have to string them together and pretend they've something in common.

Fortunately, I can read a long book all by myself, even if I do fall asleep once per chapter. I have made it through War and Peace, Anna Karenina, Don Quixote, Joyce's Ulysses – as well as Homer's – several historical novels by James Michener, Moby Dick – several times – and even The Wind in the Willows.

This last I've read so many times that the Mole's velvety coat has gotten rubbed threadbare, and Ratty's whiskers invariably get caught between the pages. To make it up to both of them, I always paint their boat in the spring before I commence my own. It's the least I can do.

I haven't even varnished the teak on my Whitehall pulling boat this year. She lies on her gunwales in front of the garage at our Stonington house, and her gunwales are all but bare of the eight coats of varnish that I lovingly applied two years ago.

MoonWind stayed on the hard last year at Shennecossett Yacht Club. I hadn't the money to launch her, or care for her, nor the time to take her sailing. I busied myself with two or three craft shows a week to supplement our ever dwindling income. But not many people bought books or cards or prints. The days of impulse buying have fled, and people would fondle my wares, and then move on to the next booth.

"Lovely work!" they would tell me.

And at four o'clock I would pack it all up in my truck and trundle home. Maybe tomorrow...

Half the readings I've had lately at libraries have been no-shows. No one at all shows up, and I sit with despondent librarians and discuss the future of books. Book shops are little better. People purchase Kindle readers and download bundled literature. When our local bookseller complained about the electronic competition, I suggested she advertise special downloads tailored to individual readers.

Book shops have knowledge of books that the average reader hasn't. They could offer you uploads of crafts, philosophy, local history, out of print works, Impressionistic painters, Restoration drama, Spanish poetry, herbal medicine. Books from any category imaginable could be assembled. You could go to your local bookseller and ask for a compendium of house plant care, and a week later, bring your Kindle into the shop and they would have found a hundred books and dozens of periodicals to upload into your reader.

Book shops of the future may not have many books at all. They may combine with libraries and be a place to read and write and study and upload books. As long as they serve good coffee, herbal tea, and ginger croissants, I'm sure they'll always keep busy.

It seems that more and more book shops lately have a bakery on the premises. Some even serve soup and sandwiches and encourage people to stay and study and read. A great idea, but I always wondered how much strawberry jam got closed into re-shelved books.

I've had an aversion to selling my books to bakeries and little ice cream shops. Especially as many small businesses want my books on consignment.

"Here – take this lot back – there's butter between the pages."

At least electronic books don't have that problem. Just wipe that crème of asparagus soup off your screen and continue scrolling.

In merely four thousand years, mankind's reading method has progressed from scrolling to scrolling. Perhaps some automobile manufacturer will soon produce an auto mounted on long, wooden rollers. It worked for the Egyptians.

An airplane that flapped its wings might also be innovative. And how about a boat powered only by wind? But who, in their saner moments, would ever want one?

When I suggest such frivolous ideas to *MoonWind* she turns her transom to me and distains to speak. My wife and my cat follow this procedure as well. "The reverse stare," we call it. "Scowl" might be closer. The pusslet thinks my sense of humor pathetic, but then her taste in literature is nearly the same as my wife's. I know this for a fact, for many of the books in our house reside on the couch where the cat sleeps, and the pages are invariably marked by fur.

I could have entitled this book, "A Predilection for Pusslets," but then you never would have purchased it. As it is, you probably haven't figured out yet what this book is about. If I myself knew I'd be sure to tell you, but mostly I just have two cups of French roast and then limber up my two index fingers on the keyboard. It's much like warming up at the piano – you never know what the outcome will be: Moonlight Sonata or Chopsticks.

I still harbor hopes that I'll learn to write someday. Still harbors not being conducive to getting under way by sail power, I generally stay in my cabin and scribble in a notebook. The results vary.

I rather enjoy composing in pencil compared with typing. I needn't sit up straight so my deportment goes all awry. I often knock over my coffee, and the stains suggest compositions to illustrate. Sometimes *MoonWind* lurches as a powerboat speeds by, and my calligraphy sports flourishes never before observed.

*   *   *   *

This morning we're having our first frost of the autumn. Not that this changes our plans for the day. I need to work at moving the last of our heaped possessions from the Stonington house, so the new tenants can paint some rooms tomorrow. Artwork and mirrors made the trip to Griswold yesterday. Soon, they will adorn the walls; boats and flowers and landscapes will strive to make this new house into a home. These, and the soapstone woodstove, which should be eating firewood by next week.

Once you have woodstove, a cat, and a painting, what more could you wish? Oh, yes – a sailboat. Personally – quite personally – I much prefer a home in my sailboat to a sailboat in my home. I have three pictures of sailboats in my study already. A small pencil drawing of a coasting schooner nearly becalmed; an amateurish little painting of a small open sloop underway, though no one can be seen at the hem; and Rosenfeld's most impressive photo of the schooner, *Nina*, coming straight at you, close hauled, rail down. This last stands thirty inches tall and, for composition, would be difficult to excel.

I haven't any compulsion to illustrate sailing boats – I'm not sure why. Perhaps because it's been done so often before. I'd rather draw mystical, metaphysical things: serpents and griffins. I'd rather experiment with light and shadow. I need to get more black onto this white, white, white, white paper. I need to experiment with broader strokes. Perhaps I'll try some Japanese brush painting one of these days, if only I can relinquish my propensity for precise, delicate lines.

Meanwhile, I have another commission to execute: the entryway to a hotel in Old Saybrook, Connecticut. A decent composition, but no ways exciting. But the hotel bought twenty of my books to sell in their spa's gift shop, and they may order hundreds of cards to be made of my drawing. And so I strive to build a business to sustain me that I may have the leisure to write, and draw, and sail.

If only I didn't need to drive my truck so far. I log thousands of miles each year and haven't much to show for it. I hoped I could build a clientele who would purchase from my website. I envisioned remaining in my study, here, responding to orders; stuffing envelopes with books and prints; then driving a handful of miles to the post office perhaps every second day. Would it were so.

Alas, I'll drive one hundred miles today to deliver an illustration and spend the evening at a soirée for local artisans at a high end gift shop. Hopefully, I'll sign a few books and prompt the shop to buy more.

Hopefully, the commission I'm to deliver will prompt my client to tout my competency to others. I need to remind myself that I've been in this business of illustrating and writing prose only a handful of years, and am just now reaping recognition on merely a local basis. Could I tap the market of even southern New England I'd be content.

$$*\qquad*\qquad*\qquad*$$

Another dull and drizzly morning. Yesterday evening I spent at the gift shop in Essex, Connecticut, talking to people about my work. I think I sold three books. That makes one book for every three crackers I ate. At that rate, I should sell two thousand forty one books for every two tons of crackers I ingest. By the time I attain four hundred pounds, I should be rich and famous. And then what?

The handful of local artisans attending the soiree wore name tags. The proprietress introduced us one to another in case we couldn't read.

"This is Matthew Goldman," she explained to a team of artists.

"I beg your pardon?" said the middle aged man behind me.

Turns out his first and last names are the same as mine, except he received his in Australia, and was just here on a visit. We had our picture taken together and he bought two of my books to read on the plane next day when he returns. His wife kept smiling at me and shaking her head at the coincidence. A lovely couple and I wish them joy.

An older woman bought one of Landmarks books to send to her daughter in Africa to remind her of what she's missing at home in Connecticut. She works for the American Wildlife Federation and tracks and records big game about the continent.

"I actually saw a pair of cheetahs devour a zebra when I visited her," the mother told me. "They aren't commonly observed."

People who stare at me while I'm eating don't generally get invited a second time, but then, I'm nowise as rare as a cheetah, but merely an underdone author.

Castor and Pollux

{A famous naturalist and illustrator who lived in Hadlyme where I grew up kept an ocelot for a while. When he let it into his house it would stalk without pause in a stiff legged stride, then suddenly bound to the farther end of the room. It was quite impressive, and I never came closer to it then the doorway. After all, I was ten years old and smaller than this cat, and couldn't be sure it had had enough for its breakfast.}

So, the soiree netted me enough for gas money plus four dollars and eleven cents I can spend how I see fit. Just now, it's going toward a half pound of French roast to prompt me to write about the books I sell.

If only I could write romantic fiction I might become famous.

"Make your sailing stories more erotic," one of my customers said to me. "Think of the potential – you're out on the ocean alone with some voluptuous maiden, when she proceeds to unbutton her…"

"Yes," I responded "but that isn't how it happens."

"Who cares?" he said. "You want to sell more books, don't you? I thought you wrote fiction."

Well, he may have a point. Perhaps if some maiden with ample buttons volunteers to show me the procedure, but it hasn't happened, yet. I suppose I could make it up out of my head, but then I'd probably be arrested for corrupting the morals of the reading public and have to languish on Letterman or Oprah.

The worst of fame is, I'd probably have to wear my best jeans and buy some new boating shoes. This pair is self-bailing and have served me admirably for years. I'm afraid that, as Huckleberry Finn, I grow more loathe, year by year, to return to civilization. It's hard for me to remember I went to a boarding school for four years where we wore ties and jackets the entire day, and had haircuts every two weeks.

Whatever could have gone wrong? You can take the boy out of the river, but you can never take the river out of the boy.

I'm still the same lad who used to row from the landing down to the cove to fish for perch in a leaky rowboat. That boat leaked so badly, I would keep my catch in three inches of water in the bottom of it until I returned. That little skiff was invariably full of river when not in use, and I kept a ten quart pail handy to bail it somewhat dry before I used her. I needed to tie the oars to the thwart so they wouldn't float off. At least I never had to worry that someone might steal my boat.

But, of course, in Hadlyme, fifty or sixty years ago, no one had the need to lock up anything. Or so we assumed. You could go away for the weekend and never lock your house. You could leave your car keys in the ignition all night. In a village of three hundred people, in a town of only three thousand, you knew nearly everyone, at least second hand, and never worried about the

But two houses over, up the hill, stood the old parsonage. A sturdy Colonial, built in 1747, it now served as the summer home to a well to do, elderly couple. One summer they ordered a new car from a dealer in New London, twenty miles away. They received a call informing them their purchase had arrived. On entering the dealership, they were met with vacant looks. The new car had not arrived and no one had called. Puzzled, the couple returned to Hadlyme – and found an empty house.

Furniture, silver, and paintings had disappeared.

Their house stood just within view of ours but had high hedges about it. We wouldn't have seen the moving van that conveniently removed all their possessions. There wasn't another house beyond for nearly half a mile. The old woman in the home between ours was so dim sighted she could just about see her house cat.

But that cat would have eviscerated anyone who presumed to mess with her mistress. I personally watched that cat kill and eat a ninety-pound German Sheppard who wandered onto the porch.

*   *   *   *

In Hadlyme, when I grew up, you either had been born there or you hadn't. I won't say you were invisible if you hadn't been – you merely appeared translucent. Fortunately, I'd been born there – but my parents hadn't. After twenty or thirty years, people could actually see them and would say hello, but I'd been born there. I was, "that Goldman boy."

The fact that my sister and I attended the Congregational Sunday school, the only denomination in our village, helped our assimilation. My sister was confirmed by Reverend Ficken. She joined the Pilgrim Fellowship that met in the one room North Schoolhouse. I made it through Sunday school without converting the teacher to paganism, but only because my powers of persuasion had not been activated. I actually sang, or squeaked, perhaps, in the church choir for a few months.

But the call of the wild overtook me at an early age, and I couldn't help but notice that the fishing was always best on a Sunday morning. I think it still is.

*   *   *   *

But I've digressed. Here it is Sunday morning and I'm sitting at my desk instead of walking out the door to be a part of the natural world. This has to do with both wanting security and wanting to possess things. Even possessing a boat has its drawbacks; especially a boat large enough to live in.

Ever since Grampy Noah "just had to have a boat," yachters everywhere have been under the curse of trying to maintain them. I doubt Grampy Noah took the trouble to varnish his drop boards and hatches. He had other distractions. Getting the lions and lambs to lie down together was not his problem. Retrieving entire lambs afterwards or convincing the ewes that their children were somewhere safe on board, might well have been.

At least I needn't shovel elephant dung out of my cockpit. Had Noah been alive today and tried to flush all that waste overboard, the DEP would have confiscated his ark. Even the dove, with all her persuasion, wouldn't have softened the obdurate heart of a DEP official.

But the harbors do seem to be cleaner than they appeared a decade ago. The things you find clinging to your hull during flood tide in your slip may be suggestive, but at least they're seldom odiferous.

Once you get offshore a ways the world is cleaner, fresher, more avid, and more salubrious. Life ashore seems noxious, futile, and filthy. Besides, none of the islands ashore have good harbors.

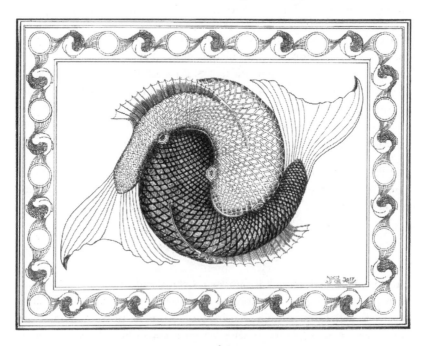

Yin and Yang

Ocean cruising makes you defer your anticipation of a snug harbor for days and days. I have a short attention span, and want to drop anchor after ten hours of sailing. Even if I never venture ashore it's reassuring to know there are rocks and trees and fresh water just a short swim away. I enjoy walking in villages. Even towns the size of New Bedford, which has more flounders than residents, don't daunt me till I attempt to cross the streets. If it weren't for the automobiles, New Bedford would be a pleasant town to wander.

The inconsiderate people who ran US Route 6 through the center of town certainly did not anticipate me and my proclivity for looking up at architraves and stumbling into the street.

I actually am a student of architecture and study buildings. I can be found out in the street with my camera on occasion. This is a harmless avocation as long as these modern, motorized vehicles drive up onto the sidewalks to avoid me. Having driven on three or four sidewalks myself, I can attest there isn't a knack required. It's amazing how quickly people get out of your way.

I still appreciate a stately building. That's why I've made so many illustrations of libraries and city halls and mansions. Below is a good example of Second Empire architecture.

I should remark that I wasn't run down by a single train while photographing this edifice.

I understand that really large cities put transportation underground to allow pedestrians the free use of the streets. This seems an eminently civilized solution. In some places, Montreal for instance, pedestrians have had control of the city streets for decades.

*　　　*　　　*　　　*

Art and architecture are what I most enjoy about cities. And second hand book shops always attract me, especially if I have my truck handy to bring all my purchases home. The past few years I've worked at illustrating and now keep my eyes alert for books with examples of pen and ink drawings or engraving. Fine lines get me excited. Gustave Dore is my present inspiration. His 241 engravings for an 1865 edition of the Bible are without equal.

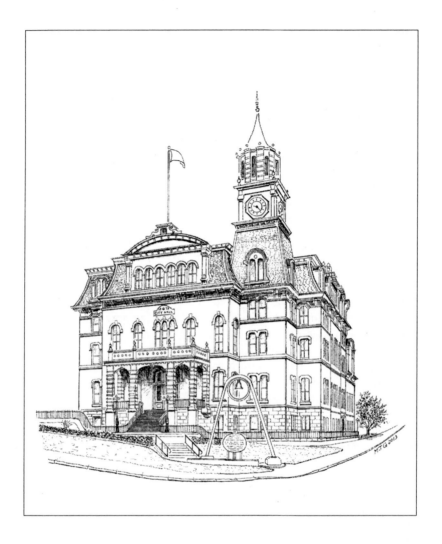

City Hall – Norwich, Connecticut

My pen with the finest point was a gift from a woman I met who studied illumination. I'm duly impressed by someone who spends the entire day to illustrate one word. William Morris's Kelmscott Press emphasized calligraphy and borders and embellishments. When you look at Morris's textile designs, you can see the correlation. I've tried to emulate some of his ideas but need to practice more originality.

This is what much of art comes down to. As with writing, most of us produce a great deal that is nearly good but not great, and then we have revelations and produce our very best work. So called geniuses have a high percentage of incredibly good work.

Genius denotes innate talent for exceptional creativity. Our current usage embraces mostly those who produce the best. This doesn't bother me, for those who produce the best are those who best represent our race. Leonardo and Rembrandt will be remembered centuries after I am gone. This is fitting. They worked at their art far longer and harder than I have done or can do, and had greater innate talent.

I'm satisfied by little things, unfortunately. Were I consumed by the need to excel, if only for my own satisfaction, my life would be outrageous, turbulent, fraught with the need, the drive, to be better and better. I have this at a modified level at best. Had I begun a serious career in illustrating as a young man, I should likely be a master of it by now.

I still get excited by sweeping curves, by intricacy, by chiaroscuro, by composition. I trust a few of the drawings in this book will represent what modicum of genius I have within me. Most of my illustrations, so far, are either architectural representations, sketches, or poster art. I need to obsess a bit more, crave expression a bit more, arouse my passion a bit more. This isn't always easy while I'm cleaning litter boxes…

I satisfy myself with very little of what I produce by writing or illustrating, but when I do, it abides within me irrevocably, and helps me to the next level. We need to gain confidence in our ability. When our abilities represent what we love rather than what is needful, it raises us spiritually. Being good at a job we don't care for doesn't enrich our souls.

I worked for years to become a better machinist because it provided my livelihood, but I never enjoyed it. I never felt so free as when I parted with my machine shop, and vowed never to take a job of similar work again.

I might have enjoyed woodworking if it didn't devolve into building mass produced cabinets. Even custom cabinet work using the same techniques would soon become boring. Building a wooden boat from scratch I would have found a challenge. But I looked at a little wooden boat at The Wooden Boat Show at Mystic Seaport and wondered who could afford the six hundred hours it took to make a fifteen foot, pristine work of art.

But it probably handled better in a choppy harbor than any illustration I'm likely to make.

Over and Under

Moonstruck

That's the trouble with pure art – art for art's sake – it is so impractical. At least a wooden boat has a function and is able to fulfill it. It takes a few hours to read my book. But a boat takes hours and hours, if not days, to take you to unknown shores.

It's difficult for me to think about books and boating at the same time. As winter approaches I'm more inclined to hunker down by my drafting board and computer. This is a good thing. In spring I have urgent cravings to be on the water, and who gives a damn about drawing. And this is a good thing.

Were I to move to a tropic clime, I could easily be converted to a boat bum. And were I to move to an igloo in the arctic, I'd probably spend all my time producing books with which to amuse the seals. Here in Connecticut, climate is problematic. There are days in January it climbs to fifty and I go sailing. There are summer days of rain and gloom and muskrats when I'm glad to remain indoors.

And who is to say what makes life worthwhile? A bit of self-indulgence, a bit of work, some love, some labor, some relaxation, perhaps a touch of anguish. Some of us have easy lives and good health; some of us struggle with misery, pain, and oppression. Tomorrow may find me confined to a wheelchair, my sailing done with; or blinded and unable to draw my pictures.

That "carpe diem" we banter about so blithely has its meaning. Most platitudes are merely truths with too many coats of varnish.

So here I sit on a Monday morning pecking at my computer. I need to start another commission: to draw a local hotel. Hopefully, one thing leads to another. When has it not? I'd rather illustrate eagles soaring than panes and panes of glass in countless windows. I'd rather sail on a rainy day than illustrate panes of glass in countless windows. But eating takes precedence over soaring and sailing.

Perhaps I should give up eating.

Perhaps all of us should give up eating. There'd certainly be less starvation in the world. There'd be more time for dancing and dreaming, for traveling and learning. Of course, when you went to a restaurant – just out of habit – the waiter would bring you the wine list. As you casually sipped the libation of your choice, he'd proffer you a catalogue of highly artistic placemats. You would order one, matted and framed, to hang on your living room wall. It would cost you no more than a decent dinner for two.

Art would flourish. Restaurants would flourish. Wine would flow freely. People would think with their eyes, not with their stomachs.

You could remove the door to your refrigerator and use it as your bookcase. Your cupboards could be used to store your clothes. Your dressing room would become obsolete. You could sleep on your kitchen counter. Your bedroom would become obsolete. Your kitchen range could serve to heat your house. Without ingestion, toilets would become obsolete. You wouldn't even need to brush your teeth. No more visits to the dentist!

If you installed a shower in your present kitchen you wouldn't need any other room, ever again. Swap your microwave for your television. We'd all have enormous kitchens and no other rooms. Building costs would be less, mortgages tiny; food bills nonexistent. You'd need to work but fifteen hours a week; retire at forty.

Without the need for farms, there'd be ample space for billions of more people, more state parks. No fuel would be needed to cultivate, process, package, transport, cook, or refrigerate food. The savings in fuel would decrease global warming. No ads for food would distract you from your program. No cow would mourn the slaughter of her offspring. No broccoli would ever be heard to curse a vegetarian.

I'm determined I'm going to try it. Just after I finish these waffles with maple syrup and sour cream...

On second thought, I couldn't give up my French roast. And what good is coffee if you can't have a muffin with it? Or a croissant? And how could I enjoy my wine without some Brie and crackers? And how could I read short stories without a toilet?

*   *   *   *

Writer's block is what they call it hereabouts. People not able to type or write the next page of their stories. These are the people who thrive on plots; on beginnings, middles, and endings; on conflict and character development; on protagonists and antagonists; on resolution. What a discipline. I'm glad I have such a short attention span and don't have to remember the name of my protagonist.

I enjoy reading fiction. I go to bed every night with mystery stories. Conflict and resolution are inherent in every one of them. But I don't have to write them. The speaker at our CAPA meeting last night lectured on all the facets of novel writing. Even memoirs, she said, have character development, conflict, and resolution.

I guess what I write doesn't qualify as memoirs. It must be journalism in its sense of ongoing-ness, but, otherwise, has little in common with the highly developed skills of the memoirist. I have to admit that my children's books and my plays followed those precepts. Plays, especially, demand you have mapped out a course of action, reaction, and resolution.

Maybe Waiting for Godot and a few other plays have fractured the rules, but mere exceptions don't console the normal, workaday writer.

Not ever having been normal, I haven't been burdened with strictures on plot or character. The first person singular serves me as it will. Our speaker said that we needed to describe our characters enough for our readers to empathize with them. Have I done that? Can you picture me sitting here at my computer in my union suit, my beard neatly braided, swilling French roast out of a flower pot? Or sailing *MoonWind*, my yew green sloop; hanging over the windward rail to converse with voluptuous mermaids? How can you not identify with that?

Excuse me while I make a fresh cup of coffee.

There. Now I can think more rationally. Notice I did not say, write more rationally. I've nearly given up any notion of doing that.

I'm too preoccupied, at this time of life, thinking about Eternity, and mermaids, and coffee to be rational. Rational is for youngsters of fifty who have jobs and children and parents and televisions.

Me, I have a cat, and a wife, and a sailboat – more than enough to occupy my time and keep me crazy. The cat shredded the carpet last night, my wife snored, and my sailboat whimpered that she needed another blanket. I managed maybe five hours sleep – about average – and arose late, at half past six, to find it light outside. And not knowing any better I sat down and continued this book.

*   *   *   *

When I look at my list of projects, I see I've accomplished a fair amount so far this week. Unfortunately, some scurrilous person has added to the farther end of my list. By next week I'll have as much, if not more to do, than I have now. Why is this? Why can't I catch up and have leisure to go sailing?

Perhaps I should ignore my chores and go sailing anyway. My wife accepts this as my modus operandi, and I make it a point not to disappoint her. Her expectations are not unduly elevated for either me or the cat. Unlike the cat, I know better than to jump on her at five o'clock in the morning. Unlike me, the cat knows better than to steal the covers.

The cat and I employ the identical mantra: "I didn't do it!" My wife staunchly refuses to believe either of us, ever. In this home, a quorum of one prevails, as she delights to remind us.

*   *   *   *

Tomorrow, my woodstove will be installed. As this entails cutting a hole in the roof of my trailer for a stovepipe, and cutting a hole through the tile surround as well as the wall for the intake vent, I've left it to a professional.

The following day, a woodcutter will bring me two cords of stove wood. As I've moved to a different town, I've had to find a more local source of stove wood. As I spoke to this fellow on the phone, he patiently explained to me the best way to build a fire. I had to interrupt to disclose that I'd not only built the first fire for Methuselah's great grandmother, but have learned the latest technology and now know which end of the match has the magic in it.

He told me it would surprise me how many weekend warriors, as he put it, couldn't build a fire in their stoves and smoked up their homes. It didn't surprise me all that much. I used to have a dragon who smoked up my home until I traded him for my cat. My cat has many bad habits but she doesn't smoke. The fumes from that catnip undoubtedly would overpower my senses, what few I have left.

It will be a comfort to have an efficient stove and a winter's supply of fuel. We still have propane forced hot air as a backup, so we can go away for a weekend without buying the cat wooly pajamas. She lounges about relentlessly as it is.

*   *   *   *

I've come to the foregone conclusion that I shall not end these journals until the final page. I think this rather perspicacious of me, for I have seldom attended to foregone conclusions in my past, trusting rather to my customary lethergy to curb my exposition.

Most writers who leave us journals have neglected to put them in book form with front and back covers and international serialized book numbers. They left that nonsense to editors in the future.

Henry David Thoreau and Virginia Woolf left us untitled volumes of introspective prose that later editors gathered, titled, and bound. As I have no expectations of journalistic fame, I've had to promote myself with neither shame nor anticipation.

Though not as fatuous as James Thurber nor as erudite as Sacheverell Sitwell, still, I may make a splash among my fellow sailors when I fall overboard. The journals I began back in the '70's lacked in humor. I was young then, scarcely thirty, and didn't know any better.

My attitude towards life has slowly progressed from sanguine to salubrious; my humor from comic to cosmic. I hope to end my stay on earth tickling other old people in our nursing home. For now I must process my words for the few people who profess to understand me. I have hopes that at least a few of them will be admitted to Heaven. The rest may be doomed to attend my nightly readings.

I have no Heavenly aspirations for myself. None of my friends will be there, and Saint Peter would undoubtedly demand I apply my drafting abilities to the tedious illumination of a billion Bibles. The pay would be poor; the retirement benefits much deferred; and the entertainment through the long evenings limited. Once you've seen a trillion gospel shows, you've seen them all.

But any bookie will cheerfully give you long odds on my chances of even showing in the umpty-ump furlong Heavenly Stakes. It don't matter to me. I'm here on Planet Earth for the duration and, afterwards, why, I may just take a long nap.

*   *   *   *

Meanwhile, the sun is shining and I ought to get outside and do some yard work. I've been exercising my right to mechanical drawing depicting, in utmost detail, every miserable pane of glass in this agonizing hotel. Thirty-something windows and glass doors with numerous light per sash. Not to mention all the spindles in all the railings around all of the balconies. Perhaps, in the future, I should charge by the window. At least I didn't have to build any of it.

Saybrook Point Inn
Old Saybrook, Connecticut

I need to mow the grass a final time, and place and block and shim half dozen pallets on which to stack my stove wood. I need to true and re-install about thirty feet of skirting around my trailer. I need to organize my tool shed. If I can organize my tool shed with half the success with which I've organized my life, I should be able to find half my tools per-haps half of the time.

This isn't the way I visualized the latter days of my life. Who would have thought I'd abandon so many projects: a sailboat, an island, a wife, a home, a business, a career.

Now I have a different boat, a different wife, a different career. Even my cat is different. I shouldn't complain – I have the cat to do that. It's only when she does it at three in the morning that I take exception.

*   *   *   *

I wonder if I should change my career, my profession, every ten years. I've considered being a sculptor, a photographer. With digital cameras and Photo Shop, the manipulation of apertures and stops seems nearly obsolete. The composition excites me most, although producing an impressionistic photograph appeals to me. I now seek unusual compositions for my pen and ink illustrations. Much of this seeking goes on inside my head. As my head is a virtual lumber room of discarded thoughts and images, it's a wonder I find anything there at all.

As the three princes of Serendip, I occasionally happen on something unique or useful. Sometimes it's even my coffee, and then I am energized to produce more books and art. Sometimes a fleeting image blips across the field of vision as radar, and I need to stare expeditiously into the dark to discover what I've glimpsed.

To become a sculptor, I should need to revert to using tools again. Clay is most forgiving, of course – one can add as well as remove material. Replacing chips of wood or stone never proves satisfactory as the joint invariably shows. Typing on a computer avoids such problems. I can remove a sentence quick as a wink with nobody, not even you, any the wiser. Ink, of course, has no forgiveness at all. But only scan the illus-tration and, Lo! A program exists by which you can add or remove lines.

I told an old woman this and she immediately stuck her head in my scanner, turned the resolution to 1200 dpi and clicked on 'scan.' After she opened herself in 'paint,' she managed to remove the lines from her face with no trouble, but she inadvertently removed part of her nose. She now has scarcely enough to insinuate it into anyone's business, and, consequently, has renewed numerous friendships.

Who says technology can't improve your life?

Had my intention been to produce a serious book, I should have needed help. I used to be quite serious, growing up. My parents were rather erudite and encouraged me in this pursuit. I was led to the trough and my head shoved under the water. I came up spluttering, ran my tongue round my chops, and decided it wasn't too bad, as long as I needn't imbibe it all at once. "It" being love of learning.

The trouble was, I had this streak of obstinacy, and insisted on reading Ogden Nash when I should have been reading Shakespeare. This corrupted me to the point that I regressed to James Thurber, Jack Benny, Newman Levy, Burns and Allen, Gene Sheppard, Garrison Keillor, and Horrors! Even Walt Kelly. But even Shakespeare had his brighter moments. Polonius skewered by Hamlet made me giggle. Desdemona smothered by Othello made me guffaw. Any hopes I had of becoming a serious playwright began with Uncle Willie.

I actually wrote several serious plays, and not that long ago, either. From age forty-five to fifty-five, I composed ten full length plays and twenty one act plays, about half of them tragic. I sent them to dozens of theaters about the country, and procured but a couple of staged readings for my efforts. I survived the first cut in several competitions, but never won a full production. The competition was too fierce, and my talent and technique not quite the best.

*   *   *   *

But I developed two comic characters who starred in several short plays: Acidophilus and Esmeralda. Acidophilus was, of course, a highly cultured dragon. He wore three piece scaly suits with outrageous neckties, had small wings, a long tongue and a longer tail, and a most salacious manner. His paramour, Esmeralda, was a plump, curvaceous, and all too human lady, ready for a romp in her dressing room between scenes. The two of them slurped coffee during performances, disparaged the management, drove their director crazy, and explored the possibilities of the triple entendre. They perverted Shakespeare, Greek myths, and Sherlock Holmes with equal merriment. Changing one's train of thought at every station may delay your reaching your destination, but allows you to meet many interesting characters on the way.

I had so much fun with these two zanies that, ten years later, I toned them down and wrote a series of children's books starring Vincus the griffin and his friend, Queen Portulaca. By the time I achieve total senile decay I shall probably write about dragonflies and worms.

Churchy la Femme, Howland Owl, Pogo, and Albert the Alligator remain my heroes. I take them to the toilet on any occasion. It's either them or Lord Tennyson, and Alfred never rolled his eyes as expressively as Albert. My education having devolved to the cult of silly animals, I sometimes need to take a break and read some serious journals or anthropology.

Annie Dillard, May Sarton, Henry David Thoreau, Barbara Kingsolver, Loren Eisley – all have impressed me. These writers spent much time alone, seeking answers to how to live one's life. And life alone; the life introspective; the life of thought; has resulted in most of the classics of all times. From the Confessions of Saint Augustine and the meditations of Marcus Aurelius to the wrenching commentary of Sylvia Plath and the scarcely concealed anguish of Dorothy Parker, we have struggled with our demons and our desires.

May Sarton and Henry Thoreau chose to dwell in the country; Loren Eisley, poet and anthropologist, spent much time roaming the wildest reaches in search of fossils. They hadn't demons so much as they had designs – designs for a life less encumbered by civilization.

Such is my life when I fare forth in my boat. I'm loathe to leave my mobile phone turned on; I never listen to music while under way; I seldom use my very high frequency radio except to get a weather report or contact a harbor master or a drawbridge tender. All my conversation is with myself, and, fortunately, I seldom pay attention. The cry of the gull, the sough of the wind, suffice me; the long susurrations of the heaving sea regale me.

I haven't the need to challenge all comers by rounding the racers' marks.

I haven't the need to frighten myself by sailing into the gale. Small measures of exuberance and a snug harbor delight me. It's wonderful to be as simple as I am. I get excited by a new, three dollar pen or a used paperback. A boiled lobster is my zenith of haute cuisine. The breeze in my sails fills me with awesome wonder.

Yet I'm aware that this world is no such luxury for millions. My self-indulgence pales at such suffering. Man and beast alike are led to the slaughter to indulge the vicious appetites of our race. Intolerance and greed have always been with us, but to what avail? The power crazed zealots who rule the world are just as sick as the cowering paranoiacs in sanitariums. Unfortunately, the power crazed zealots love to play with guns. Anyone who doesn't explicitly subscribe to their doctrines doesn't deserve to live. Kill or be killed; eat or be eaten. This is the law of the wild. But wild men used to be shut in cages and displayed for their depravity...

I try not to think such thoughts while I'm on the water.

Nor have I any answers to the questions posed by the wise.

Nor do I care to suffer in order to feel less guilty. My deprivations will not keep food in the mouths of starving children for very long. I could sell my boat and feed a couple of children for a year. Meanwhile, their parents would conceive a half dozen more children. Revolutionaries shoot down children, well fed or otherwise. They dump food into harbors that the children may not be fed. Crops from third world countries are sold abroad while the local children starve. Funds are allocated for arms rather than food and medicine.

I cannot take responsibility for the seven billion souls upon this planet. I did not bring them here. I have no wish to make them disappear. We have world leaders for that. I try to do good for the few dozen souls I know.

When I hear predictions that this world may end with either a bang or a whimper, I wonder if this would be a good thing or not. To balance our art and architecture and music against the greed and suffering presumes godlike omniscience.

I learned a new word this morning: theodicy:

Theodicy: the attempt to justify the existence of a benevolent God.

Considering the evil in this world, what could be more perplexing than attempting to rationalize the existence of God at all?

To quote the songwriter, Randy Newman:

And the Lord said,
"I burn down your cities;
How blind you must be.
I take from you your children
And you say,
'How blessed are we.'
You all must be crazy
To put your faith in me.
That's why I love mankind.
You really need me.
That's why I love mankind."

A not too encouraging set of lyrics for a rainy Christmas morning.

But by Sunday the sun will be shining, and God will smile down on all His people. Well, on some of them, anyway. The rain, today, will not dismay the scores of sodden corpses that rot in ditches about the world. These needn't worry, ever again, about dry clothes or a handful of rice to quiet their clamorous bellies. They needn't flee the assassin's bullets again. They needn't huddle in doorways and share their rags with vermin. They needn't resolve their theological doubts, ever, or research any erudition such as 'theodicy.'

Is it any wonder I attempt the study of humor?

It is easy for humor to emerge sardonic, caustic, sarcastic, or perverted. We who pen what's meant to amuse may also criticize. Dean Swift and Moliere had sharp points to their quills. Sheridan and Wilde a gentler touch.

No single recipe makes the pie that's palatable to all.

In His Hand

Bas Cuisine

Speaking of recipes, people think I can cook. Of course, I can scale and clean a fish, fillet him, slather him with olive oil, squeeze some fresh lemon on him as a benediction, sprinkle him with herbs de Provence, and put him on the grill. Any aborigine can do exactly the same. Of course I can peel and dice onions, garlic, pepper, and ginger as the basis for my stir fry. Making a pot of rice takes nearly the aptitude that it does to boil potatoes. Making muffins is akin to putting pancake batter – which I make from scratch – into a greasy pan. None of this is cooking but mere survival.

I've made yeasted bread, made yoghurt and cottage cheese, boiled down maple sap to make syrup, plucked and roasted a partridge; skinned and butchered and stewed some fat old woodchucks. But I can't be bothered to work so hard for my stomach's sake any more.

I've made preserves and pickles and mayonnaise – don't take a degree from the culinary institute to perform suchlike miracles. I enjoy making omelets – just don't let Julia Childs know that I make 'em in a cast iron skillet or sauté them in olive oil. Heaven forefend!

I've made a salad by walking about the yard with a colander and plucking half dozen herbs from amid the grass. Any herb wife can do as much. I make a mean pasta sauce when I'm so inclined, and various kinds of soup. The secret is cooking slowly and stirring often. Now that I've told you, I suppose you're going to let everyone know, and the world will soon be over-run with chefs.

Making soup is just an excuse for cleaning the refrigerator and throwing it all in a big pot to simmer for two or three days. If you have a wood range going all day you can heat your house, make soup and bread at the same time, heat water for a pot of tea, and dry your socks by hanging them from the door to the warming oven. Your cat will conserve her calories by sleeping behind the stove. Life ain't all that complicated.

Can I cook? Well, I can prepare most any ingredients and throw them into a pot with maybe some of the right herbs and spices and put them close enough to the fire to scare the daylights out of them. If you're speaking of haute cuisine, I'm not a subscriber. Alfredo and Hollandaise sauces and marinades don't appeal to me.

Avocado, lemon balm, and fennel cream sauce with citrons and crushed macadamia nuts to garnish a poached salmon is the gourmet's style. Holding his freshly speared salmon over the campfire on his spear until it finally ceases to wriggle, then tearing off great gobbets with his fangs and spitting out the scales is more the gourmand's style.

Mine is somewhere between.

A splash of white wine in my scampi is all very well and I always add a bit of white wine to my pea soup when it's almost done and thick enough that the wooden spoon that you stir with can't fall over. If that makes me a Frenchman, I'll need to curl and wax my mustaches.

I think I made an apple pie once and the dog enjoyed it immensely. We sawed the crust into sixteen inch lengths and fed them to the wood stove. I've never made pizza, I've never made ice cream. I did make a batch of wine once from elderberry flowers. It tasted quite strange but, after I'd left it to age for a year, went down rather smoothly. Good thing, too, as I'd made about forty bottles. Twiddling elder blossoms from their umbels disciplines your fingers and sends your mind onto astral levels, lest you go cross-eyed staring at tiny white blooms.

I had a neighbor who had his two children pick dandelions out of his lawn. Only the flowers, you understand; you leave the calyx behind. He'd had experience making wine and this tasted as though the yellow sunshine had been steeped out of the blossoms. Another time he brought over a gallon jug of pear wine. In case your thirst proved extreme, the jug had a finger loop at its neck to expedite your indulgence. Believe me, that wine would have made a believer of a fundamentalist.

"John," I said, when I saw him next. "That wine was delicious! What type of pears did you use?"

He looked at me rather sheepishly. "Bartlet pears in heavy syrup from the A & P," he said.

I kept hoping for another gallon to take to the lab for analysis as, obviously, he wouldn't tell me the truth. I never got it.

As far as indulging in gastronomic literature, you'll have to read "Under the Tuscan Sun," by Frances Mayes. The film was only so so, but the book was well written and amusing and informative, and lusciously descriptive. I highly recommend it. "A Year in Provence," by Peter Mayle, is another gastronomic imperative.

I don't always delight in my food and sometimes find meals a distraction. I'm often too busy to have any lunch until three or four o'clock. I scarcely take time for breakfast – my customary yoghurt and banana serves me well until I remember to eat again. The fact that I can cook is akin to stating that I am relatively competent at wood working but have no interest in repairing my furniture or building a closet or restoring all my old windows.

My loves are writing and illustrating and sailing, with paddling and rowing not too far behind. I enjoy the smell of sautéed onions and garlic nearly as much as the taste of them. A glass of red wine and some cooking fumes will keep me going for weeks. My French roast at daybreak I list as a necessity, not an indulgence. This book would scarcely get written were it not for some coffee roaster hard at work. My blessings on him and his craft. A cup of coffee equals four hundred words. This is an incontrovertible fact.

I put an ounce of coffee into a Pyrex measuring cup along with one teaspoon of raw sugar, and pour eight ounces of boiling water over it. I stir it and let it sit until it melts the bowl off the spoon. Then I pour it through an old, fine mesh, stainless steel strainer into my favorite, or second favorite, mug, and carry it to my computer. I pour it into the air vents at the top of my hard drive and, immediately, lights begin to flash and the keyboard produces sentences on the screen. Sometimes they're only sentence fragments, but these I deem more poetic. Not enough sentence fragments, ever, for my taste. And that's my secret.

When I'm aboard my boat, of course, I haven't a computer. Then I have to dip my pencil into the coffee every few words. It's a bit more laborious, much like dipping a quill pen into the ink, but it gets the job accomplished. I managed to write 15,000 words during a two week sail among the Elizabeth Islands a few years back. That's about a thousand words per day – about two and a half cups of French roast. Three cups of coffee is about my limit. After that, my stomach complains, my hand shakes, and I tend to utilize far too many adverbs.

Daybreak - at Anchor in Point Judith Pond
Whitehall tethered astern

Writing, Working, Thinking

I planned to go sailing tomorrow, as the weather promises fair, but my chimney man didn't finish installing my wood stove day before yesterday, and promised to return on Sunday to do it. As he'd never installed a woodstove in a mobile home, he wanted my help.

Although this mobile home has been up on blocks for years, its wheels removed, and its frame cabled to its concrete pad to secure it against a hurricane, it is still considered a mobile home by our astute authorities. Even though it consists of two separate modules, each on a separate trailer, that were spliced permanently together fourteen years ago, it is still considered a mobile home by our astute authorities. Even though it would take much work to separate the two modules before either could travel over the roads, it is still considered a mobile home by our astute authorities.

This means that the wood stove must be through bolted to the floor to prevent its sliding about when I tow each half of my double wide trailer down the road to my next stop. Regulations are regulations, after all, and the authorities take their responsibilities seriously hereabouts. Four holes need to be drilled through the tile hearth and the floor and strong backs contrived between the joists to secure my stove in place.

So, possibly, I may go sailing on Monday. Tuesday and Wednesday also bode fair. Could I possibly go off cruising for three whole days? I still have chores to do aboard, but *MoonWind* is all-a-tauto-o as concerns safety and performance. I need only pack a spare pair of socks, a bit of food, and some coffee, say goodbye to the cat, kiss my wife, and disappear into Ever Ever Land.

I've just remembered: I have a reading Tuesday evening with the Norwich Power Squadron. Ah, Lucre! Ah, Fame!

I need to dispose of all these books, and selling them to would-be readers seems preferable to heaving them overboard. A day sail on Monday seems indicated. Then I can have something to speak about on Tuesday evening. Otherwise, I might revert to my normal, reticent self.

And I need to complete my illustration of the grand hotel entryway I've begun. And I probably won't have finished stacking the firewood that's due to be delivered later today. And at five o'clock I need to feed the cat. The cat has promised that should I ever neglect this most important of duties she will lash me to the bed until I comply. This is why you should never, ever, teach your cat to tie knots.

Oroborus

Every winter I illustrate and write another book. Every spring I format and publish it. Every summer I'm on the road trying to sell said books. And you wonder why the serpent on my cover devours his tail? Did no one ever inform you what Eternity means? It means chasing your tail forever and ever. It means eating yourself alive to satisfy your craving for immortality.

And marinara sauce is not an option. And salad is extra. And the waitress is having a bad day: her husband just ran off with a younger woman, and she doesn't really care that you've dropped your fork.

Jean Paul Sartre's "No Exit" is a fair treat compared to the real world. 'Cause after you retrieve your fork from underneath your chair, the waitress still neglects to bring you more water.

And for most of us, the road is dry and the water holes far apart. At least, when I read at one of my groups, they supply me a bottle of water. They may or may not buy my books but at least they always – usually - supply me a bottle of water. It's these little things that make life nearly worth living.

I should have trained for a dull, prosaic job such as building submarines at our local facility. I'd be retired now with an ample pension, and could spend my days mowing the lawn, and spend my evenings in front of the television. What more could anyone want? Every summer I'd take my wife to a motel on Cape Cod to look at the sea and wander the little boutiques and gorge in restaurants. Then I'd come home and tell everyone what a wonderful time I'd had, and mow the lawn, and tune in the Red Sox game.

Just writing about it boggles my little mind. I think I much prefer to gnaw my tail.

*   *   *   *

So, this winter I mean to illustrate this book. I'll impress you, amuse myself, and possibly contrive a superlative illustration or two that make it all worthwhile. If I'm fortunate, I'll find a publisher or an agent to help me to sell a few copies.

I don't believe my present publisher will want a book that isn't sport oriented. My sailing books scarcely pretend to be sporting.

I don't think of sailing as a sport except for racing. Thousands of sailors race but I'm not one of them. I never especially care about getting somewhere first. The journey itself interests me, and having a marker buoy as a destination leaves much to be desired. Can you row ashore to a marker buoy, go for a walk along its shady lanes and talk to people? Can you buy more groceries on a marker buoy, mail a postcard home, or wander its sandy beach to collect shells? Not unless your marker buoys are larger and better populated than those we have in New England.

I enjoy a change of scenery myself. A cozy harbor surrounding a quiet village delights me. I don't need taverns and restaurants and discothèques to amuse me. I don't want amusement parks or dancing girls. One affectionate mermaid is more than enough, and even she can be dispensed with more often than not. I can perch by the wharf and scribble in my notebook and sip some coffee and be content.

Racing implies scheduling and deadlines. I deplore deadlines. I ran a business that required deadlines for every job I bid on. I stayed up nights to complete jobs for customers. To purposely declare my intent to do something I greatly enjoy as quickly as possible borders on the ludicrous.

"Gosh, this lobster is good! Let me see how quickly I can devour it!"

Imagine making love as rapidly as possible, and watching the clock in hopes that your duration is less than it was last Tuesday.

Languorous is a word I seldom use, but it best describes how I wish to live my life: slowly and calmly and getting every last bit of enjoyment from it. If you care for a thrill, take your boat out to sea when it's blowing a gale. I'm much too phlegmatic to care who comes in first.

So I don't consider what I do in my boat as sport, but merely travel and relaxation. And yet I can't write for travel magazines, for they are supported by ads for hotels and restaurants. Therefore, they solicit writing about hotels and restaurants. They want you to go ashore and go to a fancy restaurant and review the cuisine and service and décor. They seek writing that will bring more boaters and tourists to that town. They want the marinas, hotels, and restaurants to purchase advertising in their publication. It's very simple and very self-serving and the poor little serpent chases his tail from restaurant to restaurant to restaurant, searching for the best marinade to paint on his scaly tail.

My tastes being rather plebian and my pocketbook rather empty, I couldn't envision myself as a travel writer. I couldn't envision myself waxing ecstatic over standing rib roasts and St. Emillon Bordeaux at eighty dollars the bottle and four poster beds with satin sheets and gold-plated faucets and spouts on the Jacuzzi.

I prefer a shower to a bath, I prefer flannel sheets to satin, the wine sounds heavenly, but I haven't eaten red meat in forty years.

I decided I wouldn't become a travel writer. My sort of travel doesn't appeal to many. My sort of sailing doesn't arouse the competitiveness of the average American male.

Below is a picture of someone in a hurry. There doesn't seem to be a sailboat in sight.

My sort of travel involves not worrying who sees you where or with whom. I can wear my ratty sneakers. I can leave bits of sautéed garlic in my whiskers, though I'm scrupulous about keeping my galley and dishes clean and my food properly cooled. I check my aids to navigation and don't take many risks. I admonish *MoonWind* not to drag her anchor while I go ashore for groceries. She generally smirks and pretends to agree that this would be sensible. *MoonWind* has a fondness for forty-foot ketches with glistening winches and indulges her fantasies about rafting with them when she's left to herself for more than a few hours. A headstrong lass, but I dote on her nevertheless.

Once on board for the evening, I get to listen to my kind of music while I chop my broccoli, ginger, onion, and garlic. Sometimes it's classical, sometimes it's jazz, sometimes it's rock and roll. I was born in '47 and grew up with the Stones, the Beatles, the Doors, Led Zeppelin, the Allman Brothers, Jimi Hendrix, Bob Dylan, the Eagles, and Joni Mitchell. I've also grooved with Ray Charles, Johnny Cash, Aretha Franklin, and the Everly Brothers. Vivaldi, Beethoven, Mendelsohn, and J. S. Bach delight me. So does Dave Grisman. So does Stephane Grapelli; so do those Gershwin boys, Scott Joplin, and Fats Waller. The list goes on. When Billie Holiday croons to me, my stir fry takes on a flavor out of this world, and I wouldn't trade it for anything a five star restaurant might concoct to tempt me.

My little cabin is my special lair and I find it secure and comforting and relaxing. I don't relax in prestigious surroundings. My mother enjoyed serving dinner on her best, gilt edged porcelain. I'm content if my dish has faded violets painted on it. Every chip in its rim recalls a story. My mother's crystal rang if you touched two glasses together. I drink green tea out of a stoneware mug that's been glued together. What must be wrong with me? My parents sent me to prep school to become a little gentleman. I wanted nothing better than to boat with Ratty and Mole on the river.

It must be that my dear aunt Deborah corrupted me when she encouraged me to read The Wind in the Willows. Deborah never cared much for porcelain dinner ware and crystal goblets. She preferred to walk by the sea on the shelving granite from which the town of Rockport, Massachusetts took its name, and never basked on a blanket on a public beach. She preferred to walk, to talk of books, to teach, to help the less fortunate, to feed the birds, to play with her little dog, to sit by her fire. She hadn't a television, she hadn't a car. She lived a rich and rewarding life and the whole town grieved at her death. I loved her more than I loved my mother. I wished I could live with Aunt Deborah forever and ever.

*　　　*　　　*　　　*

Yesterday I stacked two cords of stove wood. A slow but not laborious undertaking. Perhaps three hours of stooping and straightening up and reaching, never lifting more than ten or fifteen pounds. Yet I could feel the complaint of dormant muscles, and even though I stretched a bit, endured a slight ache in my back. I need to exercise more and remember my body.

I may be in better shape than some my age, but I need to improve. I need more exercise; I need to stretch more. If I mean to sail for many years more, I must, must stay agile, coordinated, and strong. Aboard a boat, sore muscles and lack of agility may lead to disaster.

I imagine that when I grow old and feeble, I'll revert to little boats on stiller waters. A paddle on the pond, perhaps with a fishing rod or camera, will suit me just as well. I'll still be able to write about it and make up glorious lies to amuse my readers. This is significant as it gives me a purpose in life. Not everyone can claim to have frivoled away scores of years lying about their lives. It takes a certain integrity to persevere at something so intrinsically unimportant.

Today I mean to go sailing. Though October twenty-second, it threatens sixty degrees and a ten knot breeze and I haven't taken a day for myself in two weeks. Here is a journal entry from October fifth a few years back when my second book of sailing stories had just been released:

I can't imagine how October arrived without my awareness. I should have smelled the leaves as they slowly changed from green to gold. I should have remarked the coolth when I opened the French window for the pusslets after their breakfast. It should have occurred to me that it wasn't always this dark at six AM.

This is what happens when you become infatuated with sailboats. Just now *MoonWind* languishes on her mooring. I didn't even sail her last weekend, though I went aboard her one day to effect repairs.

The features editor at a local paper tentatively offered to pay me to write about boating events. If nothing else, it will flaunt my nom de plume before the public. The flurry of publicity that surrounds any new book is apt to fade, and mine will become just another book among many on book shop shelves.

A year from now I should be repairing boats at Shennecossett Yacht Club, which I've just joined, and making double what I presently earn. Hopefully, I can write for more and more publications that either pay me outright or allow me publicity that helps to sell my books.

I'm off to Jamestown tomorrow with a surveyor to look at a boat: an old Caribbean 35 I discovered during my recent trip through Narragansett Bay. This is a rugged, blue water sloop with a small center cockpit, lazarette stateroom, large water and fuel tanks, and a fifty horse diesel. A commodious boat designed to go anywhere. But she needs much work. I'm looking forward to cruising and living aboard such a roomy and rugged vessel. I suppose I should purchase her first.

Meanwhile, here in the world of reality, I need to reinstall the forward hatch on a thirty-four foot trawler this afternoon; I need to strip and renew the varnish on a Dyer 29; I need to finish painting a venerable wooden rowboat for a lady on Groton Long Point. My own varnish will have to wait a while.

The remaining days of another year trickle slowly away. The pusslets chase brown and yellow leaves that swirl about the deck. My heap of uncut, unsplit wood in my yard demands strenuous attention. There's something reassuring about a few cords of seasoned stove wood neatly stacked by the door. If it never gets cold they can oxidize and provide warm homes for the mice and their close companion, the garter snake.

The morning mist has dissipated. The temperature soars to seventy. Some of the sailboats here at Noank have doffed their covers and now cavort, half naked, about the Sound.

If our climate in New England grows much warmer, the cormorants may migrate north for the summer. The seas may rise till we all have mummichogs living in our basements. A boat may become the only viable means of transportation. This might necessitate tacking out to Watch Hill to catch enough breeze to sail back to Noank to go to work. I'd much prefer sailing fifteen miles to driving a mere seven. The benefits of global warming to avid sailors cannot be exaggerated.

*   *   *   *

Little I wrote of five years ago came to pass. I completed all of the work on customers' boats. I never got the job to write for the local paper. I haven't earned much more money since I joined Shennecossett Yacht Club. I never purchased that larger boat – she needed many more repairs than I had ever imagined. I cut and split and stacked five cord of wood, which duly impressed the pusslets. And my house remains about twenty feet above sea level, so I seldom find more than two or three mummichogs in my basement following a nor'easter.

*   *   *   *

Went out for an afternoon's sail yesterday. Tuned my VHF to the marine weather forecast while I rigged *MoonWind* and confirmed what my senses told me: 10 to 15 knot breezes, with gusts to 20. Well, I've been out on days like this with a full suit of sails – even with a 150 genoa, but it wasn't relaxing. So I left the reef in my main and bent on my storm jib. The wind blew from the northwest. I motored out past Avery Point and hoisted my rags. Even with the motor engaged and the helm secured, *MoonWind* didn't want to head upwind, and the battens caught in the lazy jacks because I was too lazy to bring them all forward of the boom vang but, eventually, the main went up. Hoisting that tiny jib proved a minute's work – until I returned to the cockpit and noticed that the jib halyard was snagged on the port spreader.

I wore my safety harness but, of course, didn't secure it when I went forward. The chop was only a foot or so and I kept my footing without any difficulty. Finally all-a-taut-o and sailed out to the center of the Thames and headed out the channel. With only half my sail plan I still made four to five knots with little heel. I set a course for Little Gull Light, give or take an island, and settled in to enjoy the wind and the water.

Little Gull Light stands on a tiny island amid the Race — that turbulent deep reef where the Atlantic pours into Long Island Sound at its east end. An eighty foot deep reef divides two hundred feet of water, and the surge of the tide throws up a nasty chop. The current, in places, exceeds four knots. What a fun place to play in a twenty-six foot sloop.

Half way out, about three miles off shore, I encountered three footers and the twenty knot gusts the forecaster had mentioned. Whitecaps began to form, as the wind backed up the brunt of the incoming tide. I began to get spray in my whiskers. Salty dog that I am, I'd forgotten to ship my foul weather jacket. After a rousing slosh in my face, I determined enough was enough. The chop increased as the Race drew nigh, and *MoonWind* began to cavort. Although the air was sixty degrees, and the ocean not much cooler, I prefer my bath water hotter.

The ten knot portions of the wind proved reticent. I actually had to brace myself for the puffs and work the tiller. Something told me summer might be over. I decided to come about between this puff and the next one. *MoonWind* has always been skeptical of heading into the wind. Not that she has a lee helm. If you let go her tiller, she'll head up until she luffs. To get her about often requires backing the main or the jib. After two tries by just putting the helm hard down, I decided to jibe her. *MoonWind* enjoys jibing – with or without my consent. This afternoon she swung her little stern to the breeze, pirouetted, and headed for home.

I headed for the weather bank of the Thames and kept my sails near flat. I took the traveler most of the way to windward, and settled in for a lovely ride. The seas abated almost immediately, though the wind remained gusty. I managed to beat to windward without any trouble, having the tide to abet me.

Four ferries - converted landing craft - maintain an hourly schedule from New London to Orient Point, nearly twenty miles distant. I entered the Thames accompanied by one of these Behemoths. A second ferry emerged from the river simultaneously. I kindly avoided running either one down by keeping out of the channel. There are gallons of water from bank to bank of the Thames about its mouth. *MoonWind* would be hard pressed to find a rock smaller than a house on which to lavish her affections.

As soon as I entered the river mouth I was in the lee of the shore. The water flattened, the breeze abated, summer returned to Connecticut. I took off my clothes, slathered myself with oil, and worked on my tan.

About July, I looked up to see the draw bridge. As the architects of this contrivance failed to leave enough clearance for *MoonWind*'s mast, I had to decide whether to rouse the bridge tender from his nap or to come about. As it had, unaccountably, succeeded to four o'clock, I determined to drop my main and whisper home to Pine Island Sound under just my headsail.

Against the end of the incoming tide I made about one knot. Having but a mile to go, this suited my mood exactly. The ferries came and went to Orient Point. The smaller ferry to Fisher's Island shoved off from New London and passed me close aboard. The little oceanographic research vessel from the state university branch at Avery Point messed about the river mouth.

I wafted by Eastern Point, then by Black Rock; rounded Avery Point with its stately mansion, and entered the channel to Pine Island Sound.

But the breeze frustrated my intention to sail into my slip. Inside Avery point it blew due north – right on my nose. I dropped my jib and motored toward my slip. The breeze grew puffy and I played with my throttle as I tried to sneak into my slip. At the last minute, a puff flung my bow around. I slammed my motor into reverse and just escaped swiping my neighbor's transom. As it was, I banged the piling at the end of the finger pier with my rub rail. My neighbors roused from their lassitude below and came on deck to see what disaster impended.

Branford House – 1904
Avery Point, Groton, Connecticut

Meanwhile, the breeze had slewed *MoonWind* right about. I tried to back and fill in the fairway but that breeze proved uncooperative. I had to motor out past the end of the pier to execute a half circle. This time I allowed myself more room to turn at the end of my finger pier. The couple I had aroused stood by to catch me, and all went well.

After we secured *MoonWind*, we chatted for a bit and introduced ourselves. I told them they had saved the infamous Constant Waterman from totally disgracing himself. If they were impressed, they did their best not to show it. This raised them considerably in my estimation and we had a most pleasant ten minute's conversation.

By the time I unrigged and squared *MoonWind* away, it was half past lunch, about five thirty, and I trundled on home to fall on my face into a heaping trough of cheese and pasta.

Tomorrow night I get to blather to a new audience – the Norwich Power Squadron. As a concession to these salty dogs, I've determined not to rinse the spray from my whiskers.

I gloried in the wind and water and sunshine. No phones rang; no emails required my response; nothing got in my way except a few waves. Whenever I'm on the water, I wonder how I've survived life ashore. As everything moveable needs to be stowed before I get under way, there must be a secure place for everything aboard. I can't leave a notebook and pencil and coffee cup on my table. The dish soap and sponge and kettle hide in the sink. If I don't put away my pajamas, they'll suffer the disgrace of adorning the bilge. The tissue box lives on the shelf behind the pin rail. Magazines and brochures go in the chart rack. One good roll of the boat disposes with anything not securely stowed. Except for loose sails in the vee berth, and my bedding and some tote sacks tucked into the quarter berth, my microcosmic life exemplifies the advantages of having few possessions. I can carry nothing superfluous save a few books. I never need wonder where to find almost anything.

Actually, when I day sail, I'm a bit more lax. I had two buckets closed in my head: one full of cleaning gear, the other with caulking and scrapers and putty knives and blue tape. I left two extra life jackets and an extra safety harness on the settee. My mother was right: I'm slovenly.

Would that my office here at home were as organized and uncluttered as my boat. Perhaps I should rent a slip for our trailer and step a mast on her roof. With a waterline of sixty-five feet, her hull speed would equal almost eleven knots. We could make it to Block Island in less than three hours on a broad reach; make it to Cape Cod in less than a day. With a beam of twenty-six feet and a flat bottom, she'd scarcely roll.

And commodious? You bet! We could carry a cord of wood aboard for the stove; carry enough provisions for a six month's cruise. With central air, plush carpets, washer and dryer, lots of closets, a queen sized bed for the cat - what more could anyone want? What a great idea! I'll have to tell my wife...

She only rolled her eyes. The cat winked once and continued to hold the new blue carpet in place. Such is the response I invariably receive at home.

Fortunately, the members of the Norwich Power Squadron last night proved receptive. They paid close attention and laughed a lot, bought my books and told me how much they enjoyed my presentation. I came home with my pockets crammed with cash and shared a bowl of ice cream with the cat. Life is sweet.

I have been looking over a booklet I just obtained from the free books shelf at the Mystic & Noank Library on the oracle at Delphi and the cult of Apollo. Interestingly, the earliest worship at Delphi, perhaps fourteen hundred BC, was that of Mother Earth, personified by a goddess. Later, when Apollo became the object of devotion, his oracles were pronounced by the Pythia – a venerated priestess. Always the male and female elements balance how we see, and learn; interpret and resolve. The Pythian Games, unlike the Olympic, were those of music and poetry, rather than athletics. Apollo received at his birth both a bow and a guitar. Would all youth might be as balanced in their ventures.

Meanwhile, here in the real world, I needs must complete an illustration, retrieve some of my work from a nearby shop, make a run to the recycling center tomorrow, and prepare to set up for a craft show early Saturday morning. The weather bodes fair, though the show will be held indoors. At last year's show, this same weekend, we had rain mixed with snow to regale our customers. This weekend promises temperatures in the sixties. Polar bears should check their coats at the door.

Paula worked her final day teaching yesterday. Now we shall see if we can survive on our own wits and initiative for the next year or two until out tenants, hopefully, purchase our house in Mystic. In addition to working on this book, I must take every repair job or illustrating commission or opportunity to sell books and cards that comes my way. And I must create some of those opportunities by being more assertive.

If I'm willing to work for less, I shall undoubtedly get more work, both repairing boats or writing and illustrating. How much should I compromise? When I make an illustration and earn six dollars an hour, that seems like more than enough compromise. When I bid jobs at ten dollars an hour, I usually don't get them. Illustrating is considered a minimum wage occupation in this economy. Or perhaps I should not be so fastidious in my drawing – not so attentive to detail. Working more quickly would be most beneficial, but mistakes are too easy to come by as it is, especially while inking. Perhaps I should just look for some mindless job at minimum wage, such as writing for newspapers.

Or I could be perfectly stupid and start a literary magazine. I certainly know plenty of writers who would contribute. Some of them might be persuaded to buy a copy. Distribution and sales prove the problem. I can scarcely sell my own books. I'd make more, perhaps, submitting my work to magazines, though often my work has been promised publication without results.

It sometimes seems I was born a century too late. Black and white illustration no longer enjoys popularity. Color films and television cured us of that ailment. And journaling has now devolved into memoirs telling all, or into travelogues, or into diaries that disclose what Susie wore to her Junior Prom. I grew up reading sketches by E. B. White, who wrote for the New Yorker for years and years. He wrote of New York City, of his homestead in Maine, about little excursions he made hither and yon. His writing had humor, wit, and perspicacity; impeccable grammar, syntax, and punctuation.

Charlotte's Web and Stuart Little, with pen and ink illustrations by Garth Williams, set a high standard for children's literature. I miss White's gentle humor; his insights; his positive energy.

Henry David Thoreau wrote of his travels. He spent a summer with a friend and an Algonquin guide messing about the uninhabited reaches of Maine by canoe. He traipsed the dunes and villages of Cape Cod. He rowed on the Merrimac River with his brother one memorable week. He never stayed at a hotel. He never ate in a restaurant. He seldom had to wipe his boots on the mat. His travel was of the most rudimentary kind. The thoughts he penned and the language in which he couched them make it memorable.

But who, in this rapidly paced computer age wants to listen to someone who paddles a handful of miles per day? Who wants to listen to a scruffy poet who loves the wilderness? We have become the mere cogs, the computer bits, of civilization. We are not a part of this world as much as a part of what flashes by on a screen. We are whelmed by sports and politics and glamour; caught up in the lives of individuals only because they're paid fabulous sums by consumer products of dubious value to entertain us with vicarious thrills. Our modern heroes and heroines dazzle us by their looks; their sex appeal; their common repartee; their abilities to run and jump and throw.

Those famous for their thoughts and artistic merits molder in little used libraries and museums.

Euripides, Voltaire, Copernicus, and Darwin would never make it on prime time TV. The clever hosts of late night talk shows wouldn't begin to know what to say to them.

Those of us intelligent enough to want to know about philosophy, drama, and science are considered elitist. College professors are not considered as important as baseball players or movie stars. After all, you don't need to go to school to earn millions of dollars. And money is power, and money and power drive industry and advertising and politics and consumerism, all of which provide ongoing entertainment for the world.

The basic choices are entertainment and/or war. Both involve massive expenditures of time and money. And even war provides entertainment. From films to books to video games to televised bombing raids, man is obsessed with destroying his fellow man. As long as his house and town and children avoid destruction, he's happy to open another beer, dote on the gore and misery, and cheer for the winning team.

It's so much simpler to take your canoe for a paddle in the marshes. The stately heron strikes a pose that unabashedly flaunts her naked body. The osprey shrieks as she murders another fish. What better drama? Sex and death at their finest.

And the wild iris reach to kiss the glorious sun; and the cattail reeds rustle sensuously, caressed by lush breezes; and a hundred red wing blackbirds praise the season with uplifted voices.

And the worst of all this? It doesn't cost any money. Admission is free. You can even enjoy it without a canoe. You don't need a politician or an actress to endorse it. You don't need an education in drama to appreciate the scene changes. Big business needn't deplete the earth of resources to help you enjoy it. Worst of all, you can satisfy your craving for immortality with only a notebook and a pencil and a grade school education.

Here is your world: see to it when you can.

All you need is awareness and introspection. And these you can learn about at any library for free. Yes, the library, Molly. That funny old building that needs a coat of paint. Perhaps if each of you children grabbed a paint brush...

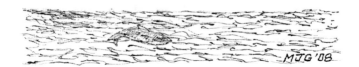

Hurricane Sandy

Today we're battened down in expectation of a hurricane or maybe tropical storm with the name of Sandy. Perhaps a nickname for Cassandra, that wise woman of Troy who prophesized doom and disaster, and aptly so.

Yesterday we spent removing *MoonWind*'s mainsail and boom, fuel tanks, bell, and other paraphernalia that might go adrift, and rigging her with numerous extra mooring lines and fenders. Many of the boats at SYC opted, after conferring with their owners, to be hauled. As participation by owners in this process is required, and as many hands make, if not light work, at least massive conversation, a crowd gathered at the lift slip to aid, abet, comment, and drink coffee. As everyone knows, conversing with one's hands carries more emphasis, and leaves the mouth free to rinse with hot, sweet coffee.

By midafternoon, with the wind without the harbor at twenty knots, gusting to thirty, the club advanced into hurricane mode, and desisted from unrigging sailboats that they hauled. To have *MoonWind* on jack stands with her stepped mast providing leverage for the seventy knot gusts expected seemed ludicrous. I rather she roll in her slip than on her jack stands. It's only the surge that needed to be considered. A ten-foot surge on a high tide would carry the piers above the pilings provided and leave *MoonWind* stranded in downtown Milwaukee.

I trusted we should not get a ten-foot surge. The latest prediction to my knowledge showed Sandy's landfall close to Atlantic City. And we all know what a gamble forecasting is.

This morning shows Sandy's track about the same. Here in Connecticut, naught but winds of forty knots with occasional gusts to seventy need concern us. A gust of seventy suffices to turn a seagull inside out. For those of you who don't think this an improvement, we suggest you keep your seagull in your bedroom where she belongs.

After we had secured *MoonWind* and told her we loved her, we trundled over to nearby Noank to secure a customer's boat. This is a Bristol 24 – a sweet sailing, ruggedly built little sloop with a proud heritage, lovely lines, and a fondness for her white-haired owner.

We removed her mainsail, secured her halyards, and rigged some extra dock lines. No one at the boatyard seemed worried about the eventuality of hurricanes, squalls, tidal surge, or even barnacles. On a Sunday afternoon, one expected flocks of boaters to be caring for their craft. Many boats had no extra spring lines and loose gear was in evidence.

We ran across friends just done securing their boat, and stopped for a chat. Willie, the dog, poked his head from the back window so Paula could scratch his ears.

"Wish we hadn't so much windage on our forty-foot cabin cruiser," remarked her skipper, "but what can you do?"

"Have you ever considered taking a reef?" I suggested.

He chuckled and gave me a wink.

"Any time these past twenty years," he replied.

We then assaulted the grocery store and purchased lots of food that required neither cooking nor refrigeration: apples and crackers and cheese and canned tuna and juice and nuts. We bought potatoes to wrap in foil and set inside the wood stove. If we manage to start a fire first, the potatoes may bake a lot quicker. Laden with plunder we scuttled for home.

We weighted down the tarp that covers our wood pile with numerous concrete blocks, gathered anything light and loose that might take wing in the storm, and proceeded to rig an anchor for the cat.

We filled the bathtub with water for flushing the toilet, and stowed two dozen liters of bottled water. All this accomplished, we contrived some supper, and secured the dock lines and fenders on our queen-sized bed.

This morning the wind intends to blow. This afternoon, I may not have electricity to continue this narrative via computer. I've been told that a pencil, a notebook, and a candle my serve the same purpose. If the power fails, I mean to find out.

Now, at 0949, wind at New London Airport registers 25, gusting to 40. Nothing untoward or alarming. Seas running ten to fifteen feet. A bit too much breeze and sea to sail in *MoonWind*, but a heavily built forty-footer would have no problems if she took a reef. Storm supposed to peak this evening and hope not to see any stormy petrels in the wake of my trailer.

Not too much rain or wind here in Griswold. Need to dry off the cat when she comes in, and she follows me to the kitchen, explaining vociferously what I'm meant to do. Then she looks in her empty dinner bowl, then looks at me, then looks in her empty dinner bowl, then looks at me once again.

"How could they have assigned me such a dull witted human keeper," she wonders aloud.

Yes, Gertrude, all of us ain't been blessed with your mental acuity. Remember that the next time your bowl is empty.

Now, at 1457, wind at New London Airport has increased to 40, gusting to 55. Seas off Montauk Point are 20 feet. Hopefully, they're just a tad bit less in *MoonWind*'s slip. Montauk is the absolute, easternmost end of Long Island. Beyond, especially due south, lies open ocean. Seas here can build to the height of houses, and sometimes do. Tonight, they predict 26 to 31 foot waves 20 miles off Montauk Point, itself a mere twenty miles off the Connecticut shore.

MoonWind is blessed to be behind Avery Point and Pine Island, in turn protected by Fishers Island and Long Island. I imagine ten-foot white horses with frothy manes gallop the length of Long Island Sound just now. I'm glad not to be riding them, for some undoubtedly smell the sea oats, and gallop up the beach in search of supper.

I can only hope my old green sloop weathers this violent weather. She has a six-foot seawall a hundred feet to the west behind her, and a four story granite building just back from that. To the northeast, where most of this wind originates, nothing interferes save a field of boats on jack stands. That should help some. Ahead of her, due east, three piers intervene twixt her and weather, and Bushy Point, a mile beyond, limits the fetch within Pine Island Sound.

Our power failed about 1500 and came back about two hours later.

Now it is 1858 and Sandy due to make landfall in New Jersey as a category 1 hurricane, soon to diminish to a violent tropical storm. God save sailors and others on such a night.

Cap'n Salty Whiskahs called my cell phone from across the Pond just after we lost our power. He was concerned I might have floated away. Actually, he was bored reading my two books over and over and wanted to preview what I've been writing here. I promised him he could have a free book when he sells my first million copies to the Common Market. What could be more fair?

I'm more than ready to have a best seller. I'm more than ready to have a sizeable royalty check every month. I'm more than ready to sign more than five books at a reading. I'm more than ready to afford the leisure to write another book without worrying how to feed my boat.

Word has just come from the boat yard: *MoonWind* is safe!

My boat is unharmed, my power is on, I have a house full of food, and my roof doesn't leak. Life is grand. I think I should celebrate by continuing to breathe for another day. There's them what can't.

Now, the morning after the storm, nothing save gentle rain. Oh, yes, and it's dark. With any luck, that will soon be rectified. Seems as though it's never light when I rise from my little bed. Must have to do with retiring too early in the evening. With Sandy gone ashore to distribute her charms, there is nothing for me to do but return to work.

Digression the Third

Another hour should see me done my latest commission. Then I can deliver it to Old Saybrook, and pick up prints I consigned to a shop in Essex. I also have prints to retrieve from a shop in Sterling. I may have as many as eighty prints all together, which make an impressive display at arts and craft shows.

As soon as my drafting board is cleared of this latest illustration, I mean to give it a coat or two of primer and sand it smooth as smooth. Then, back to work on this burgeoning work before me. Perhaps something rare and wonderful may come of it – a few illustrations worthy of my ripe imagination.

And I need to re-rig *MoonWind* and sail her over to Noank for the winter. With Paula away in Peru, I hope to find time to sail off into the sunrise – at least to Cuttyhunk and Point Judith Pond. I haven't wetted my roding at all this season, and I fear it may dry out and prove unmanageable. There should be a few more days of temperate weather ere Boreas descends with his snowy whiskers to obviate my plans to pursue some whitecaps.

And a customer threatens to bring his twenty-nine-foot sloop into the shop for total refinishing. This probably involves two hundred hours work. But first my partner's shop needs to be organized and cleaned – a full day's work for the two of us.

This Autumn I mean to confer with printers or galleries or art suppliers as to what paper best exhibits my drawings. Then find a printer to quote making this book. I need to compare digital versus offset printing; smooth versus glossy paper; hard cover versus soft. I need a professional presentation to send off to agents and publishers. I don't mind driving all over the world as long as I sell more books. To spend fifteen dollars in fuel to sell a dozen books that net me thirty dollars verges on ludicrous. A publicist may be a better expedient than a publisher.

I'm at an age where I need to budget my days, my months, my years. Though I may enjoy another twenty years of productivity, I won't want to be on the road to market my wares at eighty. At this particular midpoint of Eternity, I have as much energy as I need to accomplish nearly all I wish to accomplish. Tomorrow may bring a greater storm than Sandy; one that will wreck my every plan on that grim reef of mortality. For now, I should sail as far off shore as allows me to set a true course to my next destination. The rocks and shoals have always been there, and my job, as mariner, is to avoid them – to bring my mortal craft to her ultimate harbor in ship shape fettle.

Through most of the surrounding area is still without electricity, I must put my energy into this book; re-rig my boat; finish securing my woodstove; replace the skirting around the trailer; mow my lawn a final time if it ever stops raining.

I have a reading at Stonington Harbor Yacht Club a week from Saturday – my second reading at a yacht club. The first was at Hamburg Cove YC a couple of years ago, and I'm trying for a reprise. I read at four power squadron events this year with moderate success. Perhaps a series of readings at yacht clubs over the winter will help to pay *MoonWind*'s fees. Perhaps *MoonWind* herself should read from my books in her breezy whisper. I would need to rig her new boom cover and polish her mast a bit better and paint her cockpit before she debuted, but I have no doubt she could do it.

What can we not do if we only set goals and discipline our lax wills? I can be happy on the sofa, reading light fiction, eating pretzels, and drinking a glass of wine. But that ain't how books get written or illustrated, or, most deadly of virtues, even how the lawn gets mowed. A hay field is best suited to one of my temperament.

I still have this yearning, this affinity, for the Old Haying Grounds - that island where, a century ago, the locals used to pasture their stock and harvest salt marsh hay. That overgrown, that salubrious, that fondly idyllic island and its many memories.

I built a cabin there, and canoed the mile and a half from the ferry landing to get to it, just so I could have some peace of mind. At twenty-five, having lived a couple of years in the fast lane, I had an urgent need for some peace of mind.

I sank some cedar posts and, not knowing any better, attempted to float some hickory poles there to make my sills. Well, they were green, and weighed more than water, and it's fortunate they didn't drag me and my canoe to the river bottom when they sank. I settled for some old, chestnut three by eights about twelve feet long, which I stood on edge atop three cedar posts each.

My cabin would be only eight by twelve, and four of that I determined would be a porch. With a fold up bunk, an eight by eight living space sufficed. As a ship's cabin, everything fit and everything was provided. I had a big mop sink in one corner, provided water by hanging tanks which in turn were provided by runoff from my aluminum-clad roof. I had a two-burner wood stove, a wicker rocker, a tiny table, a built in chest, an old metal locker to keep the mice from my food. A broom, an ax, a Coleman lantern, a skillet, and a teapot completed my repertoire. I even had a shelf with a score of books.

There wasn't much I wanted. A book and a drink and a smoke and a load of quiet after a day's work in the machine shop. And when it proved too quiet, I would drag my canoe through the whispering ferns the hundred yards to the river, slide her in, and wend across the water.

A couple of miles brought me to Chester Creek. A mile up the creek stood a restaurant where friends would gather. A mile walk would bring me to the village of Chester with its friendly tavern. A two-mile walk would take me to Deep River. I could settle into the local inn, and spend the evening with friends and music and undemanding conversation.

And then would arrive that hour in the early-on when the inn would close, and I had to trudge the well-known road that returned to Chester Creek. Then I would drag my little canoe from its hidey hole in the marshes, and begin the three-mile paddle back to my island. Against the breeze, like as not.

Would I live those evenings again? Hell, yes. And I'm over sixty. This present living on a lousy two acres between two other houses gets me down. I'd sooner live aboard my boat and anchor in the river. Things aren't all that inspirited living ashore. It's having all this space beneath a roof that spoils the passage. I can't get on enough sail to make any headway. All I do is lay aloft and lay below and count and discount my belongings.

I'd sure like to make the passage inside on down to Florida one of these years before I trip on my beard. Bring the old Whitehall traipsing astern behind *MoonWind*. Pack my forepeak with sails and gear; my quarter berth with clothes and bedding and books. Don't want anything fancy; don't want anything doesn't serve my needs. Maybe some tools in case I need to work. Maybe a pencil in case I decide to draw. Maybe a laptop.

Then again, probably not. If I did, I'd need a cell phone for the connection. Then I might be tempted to call one of you very early some morning to describe the sun coming up over some marsh, and turn on speaker phone so you could hear the red-wing blackbirds amid the cattails. That might take so long that your coffee would get cold. I'd hate to antagonize a potential reader at five thirty in the morning.

Comstock Comstock Bridge
Salmon River State Forest

Question is, if I go, will I ever come back? May not know till I'm halfway home again. May find a harbor that suits me. May find a reedy refuge from all this carking responsibility. May settle down for a spell and write some more books. Might just sail as much as settle down.

Home is where the boat is, don't you know?

Meanwhile, here I abide in my study on an even keel.

For those of you unable or disinclined to sail off into the future, here is an alternative: just stroll across this little bridge. When you get to the farther side, it will be the Future.

I just re-read "The Elephant's Child" by Rudyard Kipling. Besides the magnificent illustration, the story is plausible, whimsical, and downright hilarious. It provokes me to complete my last Vincus story about the ozone layer.

This features good Queen Portulaca and the Queen of the North Atlantic – no name mentioned. It shows the greedy, self-centered rulers of many far lands, who all drive enormous limousines – huge enough to house tennis courts and airstrips – that pollute the atmosphere. These rulers constantly compete for prestige without a thought for their people – why should this be? Vincus cannot even reason with them until he plies them with several quarts each of maple pistachio birch beer raspberry ripple – that magical ice cream capable of resolving the world's problems. Were it only so!

Imagine the rulers of every nation eating ice cream for breakfast. Greed and hostility vanish from their agendas; jealousy and suspicion fade to naught; anger and self-righteousness deflate and wither. Ice cream forever! Who says I can't be rational? Who says I'm not realistic? Vote for Vincus the griffin this November! Vote for change!

This is my take on politics: that until the leaders of the world set examples of peace, humility, conservation, and economy, all their rhetoric and all their promises are but the wind that wails in the woods and tears the limbs from the trees. Mother Theresa for president! Lao Tzu for emperor!

I cannot conceive –
Other than children, words, and deeds;
I cannot deal with droves of days.
This world is – and I,
I am blessed to be.

I cannot imagine –
Other than all I shall.
I cannot linger – life's away!
Foolhardy as life
I am blessed to be.

I cannot forgo –
Other than pride, wealth, hate;
I cannot part with power –
Power to raise this self
I am blessed to be.

I cannot accept
All of the differences but
Not all of the differences
Among all of the men
I am blessed to be.

I cannot annul
All I have done, will do.
I cannot beg this world's pardon;
A part of that pardon
I am blessed to be.

Meanwhile, in my miniscule portion of this world, I delve, and dream, and deliberate as ever. The storm has passed; the calm spreads onward forever.

Tomorrow will be the first day of November, 2012. Where has this month, this decade, disappeared? This month began so summer-ish, this year so sane. Sanity and summer have both departed, and I sit here, amazed, who only wanted a day to wind up loose ends. A day indeed!

The years now flit with the inhumane haste of Eternity. I've already reached its midpoint. What can remain save a smattering of seasons; a zillion years? Now I must step out bravely, not only to a different drum, but perhaps to a different vision. I fear to be circumscribed by too small a world; too tame a life. My youth approaches its end, and what may middle age bring? Hopefully, longer cruises on my boat; more time to reflect; less scrabbling after money.

Tomorrow is nearly now, and yesterday this sentence I've just completed. These etceteras extend nearly forever. These exclamations exhaust my enthusiasm. Off I should go, to wrest a dream from the stars. I began this book barely a year ago – how it has grown! "The Care and Feeding of Journals", by Constant Waterman, might serve as alternate title.

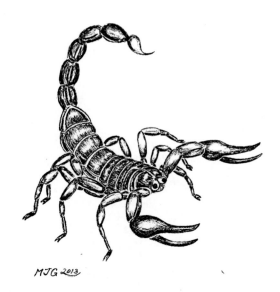

MJG 2013

Messing About in Boats

At a practical level, I need to ready *MoonWind* to sail away. I presently suffer ennui and lassitude; debility, lack of direction, and decaffeination. This weekend bodes fair; I should sail *MoonWind* to Noank for the winter. I'm more at home in Noank than Pine Island Sound. Apart from the boatyard, Noank remains a village with direction and organization and community. Pine Island Sound is boatyard, yacht club, and University, and all embrace but a wide place in the road. There seems no settlement there.

Noank has a church, a garage and filling station, a cafe, some restaurants, a market, an art gallery, a second hand shop, a package store, a post office, an historical society with museum and meeting house, several full service marinas, a shellfish hatchery, a blacksmith shop with art and sculpture studios, a firehouse, two yacht clubs, two lobster pounds, two tiny parks, a playground, the Park & Rec' department for the town of Groton, a veterinary clinic, and a lighthouse. All these are spread about a square mile surrounding West Cove and fronting Mystic Harbor. Residents, tourists, and boaters come and go.

If you can't find something to do, you can perch on a stool in Carson's Store and wait for someone you know to come by for a gossip. Meanwhile, have one of their fresh baked morning glory muffins.

MYSTIC & NOANK LIBRARY 1893

So, sailing *MoonWind* the four miles to Noank is nowise arduous. I've friends, acquaintances, customers there. I can sit at the counter in Carson's and pen my journals. I can walk to the market and feast on delicious options. I can walk to the Noank Foundry and hobnob with other artists. The drive to Noank is five miles less than to Shennecossett. And Noank lies only two miles from downtown Mystic. Mystic has nearly everything a civilized person could want. On days I choose incivility, I can find some curmudgeonly boater to growl with. Half dozen local venues sell my books and cards. I can hide in the library; lounge by the breezy river; gorge on ice cream; visit the art museum. Mystic Seaport has world fame; so has the Mystic Aquarium. The Marine Consignment of Mystic has been a favored haunt of mine these many years. I've rowed and paddled and sailed the Mystic River.

But Noank nearly qualifies as my home. Another few hundred years and I may fit in.

Here is a journal from November 2009:

It's been brought to my attention by the powers that be, meaning my own inadvertent prowess, that most of what I compose is consummate drivel. Therefore, I've decided that this episode of my journals will be among the best I've ever written. Now listen and attend, Oh Best Beloved.

Tomorrow I shall either sail *MoonWind* to her winter slip in Noank, four miles to the east, or else row my Whitehall pulling boat the identical distance to the identical location. Now, this is explicit and estimable prose at its finest.

I could, of course, sail *MoonWind* and tow the Whitehall behind her. I've done this dozens of times with no ill effects – not counting the time that the Whitehall surfed over a wave top and surged downhill right at me. In the snick of time, I put the helm over and just avoided the demolition of my outboard.

But that isn't what this is all about. I want to row the four miles in order to row them. [Again, succinct and un-extravagant prose] I actually enjoy rowing my Whitehall. At eleven feet, six inches and one hundred thirty pounds, but with little wetted surface, she speeds as a hungry albacore pursuing a frantic mullet; rides three footers as effortlessly as a seal; surfs down waves as a greater shearwater, barely brushing the heaving sea with her wingtips.

Hopefully, tomorrow will bring no three footers. The forecast calls for a six knot following breeze with the tide in the same direction from breakfast time till two in the afternoon. If I can't row my little boat in those conditions, I should relinquish my title of Constant Waterman.

I've been reading Breakaway Books' compilation of the late Robb White's marvelous stories, "Flotsam and Jetsam." I keep this massive paper-back aboard *MoonWind*, and nibble at it while swinging on my hook in far off harbors – some of them as distant as Rhode Island. What with a rainy summer, and my spending September and part of October rebuilding *MoonWind's* deck house, I haven't been abroad that much and, consequently, have read only half the stories.

This is good. I wouldn't want to get through them too quickly – I'd rather save them up.

MoonWind has come to Noank. Now that she's in a slip for the winter, and the weather is not conducive to faring abroad, I'm forced to drive the seven miles to the boatyard, crawl beneath the tarpaulin over the cockpit, remove the drop boards, descend the companionway into the galley and main salon, brew myself some French roast, and curl up on the settee with Robb White's book, and read some more of his stories.

Maybe by April I'll have savored every page. Then I can start again.

Without a doubt, Robb was a better sailor, boat builder, and curmudgeon then I'll ever presume to be. He also excelled at hunting, fishing, and stomping on alligators. I only wish I'd had about forty years to make his acquaintance. We could have swapped yarns and practiced our lies on each other. If we'd sailed together, I could have inflicted my sense of humor on him – at least until he held my head under water.

His frequent columns in Messing About in Boats delighted me. Fair winds and calm seas console you, you old waterman!

And so may someone write of me in the not so distant future.

The people who enjoy my writing seem to enjoy it immensely, but it is not everyone's cup of quahog chowder. The sailors who race; the sailors who polish their wheels; those with large, powerful motor boats; those whose idea of boating revolves about fishing – these find little save the writing itself to recommend my journals, and not so many take interest in the joys of well-wrought words.

I look forward to my reading next week at the Stonington Harbor Yacht Club. I may just find a following of local sailors there.

Digression the Fourth

Meanwhile, I should write for a more diverse audience. Many of you don't know the difference twixt a batten and a bar mitzvah. I know I don't. Battens are the strips of wood or plastic that stiffen the edge of the sail. Their favorite pastime is working free of their fabric pockets and testing their wings on windy days. And a bar mitzvah — well, I had a couple of cousins who endured them as I watched with great concentration from the congregation, but my time spent in a synagogue is not much greater than that I've spent in the hallowed sanctuaries of Greek Orthodox churches or Buddhist temples.

I grew up a Congregationalist. These are the people who worship coffee in the basements of old white clapboard buildings in quaint villages all about New England. As a child, I didn't like coffee. I also didn't appreciate fine wines, good sex, or theater. How our tastes change!

So I grew up proud to call myself a heathen, and shocked any number of avid church goers of various sects and religions with my revelation. This was the first time I appreciated the benefits of shocking more than one person at a time. I've since incorporated this procedure into my normal conversation. However, I have still that cloak of diplomacy left me by my iconoclastic father. I don it on state occasions such as my readings. It happens to be a good fit and not quite so scratchy as you might imagine. Sometimes I forget to take it off for months at a time, and people forget what a curmudgeon I am. Or perhaps I tend to mellow with advancing age, as does a pear. Hopefully, unlike a pear, I won't become totally mushy and sentimental as I age.

The good news is, I'm only at the midpoint of Eternity, so many more years and decades stretch before me. What can I not accomplish in such a span of time; what can I not endure forever and ever?

*   *   *   *

From the Journals of Constant Waterman

Monday we had eight inches of snow. Wednesday it was zero degrees at daybreak. By Friday it surpassed forty and the snow melted slowly, dripped from the eaves, receded from my overturned yellow kayak by the garage.

Saturday dawned overcast, but quickly ascended to fifty degrees in the forenoon. The weather channel threatened fifty-five. I secured *Goldfinch* into my pickup truck, discovered my life vest in the garage, and stowed my two piece paddle inside the boat. I struggled into my wetsuit and boots, found a hat, forgot my gloves, remembered my camera and water bottle, and drove down the river road to the public landing.

The Mystic River is mostly an estuary perhaps four miles in length. It commences as Whitford Brook, a knee deep, fast moving stream that has its source a few miles back in the brush behind my house. It joins the estuary by the old brick mill, whence it spreads to a quarter mile in width to the loud delight of the ducks. It constricts as it nears the village. There's perhaps two feet of tide – just enough to float off some of those intrepid mariners wont to go aground.

A mile downstream lies the public landing on the west bank – nothing more than a gravelly parking lot for twenty cars and a slot to the river worn smooth by many feet. Most of the people who park here are cyclists who parade the river road. I've found that a bicycle makes but wretched headway against the tide and, besides, the handlebars invariably interfere with my paddles.

I carried *Goldfinch* down the bank and set her into the stream. In moments I was away. A mile downstream on the eastern bank stands famous Mystic Seaport with her vintage fleet of tall ships, schooners, and sloops, her antiquated village, her wharves, and her boat shop.

Below the Seaport juts the Schooner Wharf, where berth the charter schooner, *Argia*, {damsel fly} and the tall ship, *Mystic*. Below this lies the quaint, historic settlement of Mystic that straddles the river. A bascule bridge with an eighty-five foot span connects the two shores. Once an hour during boating season, the bascule bridge rears up to allow tall ships and little boats to ply the channel.

Below the village on the west bank stands Mystic Arts Center; the old, brick trolley barn and power house – now condominiums; and Fort Rachael Marina. On the east bank spreads a narrow public park and dinghy dock, then Seaport Marine. Wharves and slips filled with lovely craft adorn both banks of the river for a quarter mile.

Next comes the pivoting railroad trestle, part of our Northeast Corridor. The hooting of the Acela locomotive contributes to the mild din of the village. Below the trestle the river again spreads wide for its last two miles, becoming Mystic Harbor. Marinas proliferate. Shipbuilding, fishing, and lobstering were major industries here. Lobstering and boat repair remain.

I paddled these placid waters in search of nothing. The breeze from the sea caressed me, but scarcely rippled the river. By the Seaport I took some photographs. A lovely old gaff rigged schooner, *Star Bound*, from Brooklin, Maine, nestled against the quay. The larger schooners, *Dutton*, *Conrad*, and *Amistad*, slumbered their winter away. The sticks were out of the *Conrad's* steel hull. I rounded the tiny lighthouse – a replica of Nantucket's Brant Point Light – and passed the huge red boat shop where wooden boat restoration goes on daily. *Charles W. Morgan*, last of the wooden whalers, stood, propped, ashore, undergoing a total refit.

The fishing smack, *Emma C. Berry*, built in nearby Noank in 1866, is pictured below. She was donated to Mystic Seaport in 1969, and designated a National Historic Landmark in 1994.

I paddled to the Schooner Wharf, just downstream from the Seaport, tucked astern of *Argia*, and made fast to a floating section of pier. I walked up the ramp and across the lot to the Marine Consignment of Mystic – that second-hand shop that delights the boating community. I greeted the owner, then crossed the shop to the street door in time to meet my wife and her friend returning from their lunch. Not everyone paddles downtown to meet his spouse.

After she left, I climbed into my kayak and cast off my painter. I passed beneath the rugged wharf, patted *Mystic's* broad transom, and made my way the last two hundred yards to the bascule bridge. Clearance beneath this bridge is about four pigeons. I proceeded another quarter mile, took a picture of the Mystic Arts Association, turned and ascended towards home.

The gentle breeze blew at my back. I could feel a bit of sweet fatigue in my arms. The grey sky stooped to kiss the river upstream. The scores of

Emma C. Berry - 1866

usual waterfowl had flown. Aside from a couple of very young mermaids teasing an old striped bass, I saw no one enjoying the Mystic River.

Paula is off for Peru. My first night as a bachelor for a goodly time, and all I can think about is sailing from this coming Sunday until perhaps Wednesday. Temperatures bode in the fifties with furtive glimpses of sixty likely. What more could one expect the second week of November in Connecticut. Best of all, the nightly chill will not decline to less than forty-five. My yoghurt won't freeze. I needn't chop the ice from my toilet. Penguins won't be inclined to skate in my bilge.

I may just cling to the coast. Two nights out; one night returning; home by evening of the fourth day. Not a momentous undertaking, but further and longer than I have sailed in the past three seasons. It doesn't seem possible that all my extravagating with my girl, *MoonWind*, has been so long in the past.

Tomorrow I must take gear aboard: a second anchor and roding; a second six-gallon fuel tank and fuel; bedding; propane; food; clothing. I don't imagine I'll change clothes much or cook elaborate meals. Perhaps one or two to remind myself of humanity. Crackers and cheese and fruit are all very well for a while, but a good hot meal reminds me that I still am nearly civilized, though numerous people have evinced skepticism on that point.

And I need to stow my nine-foot yellow kayak on edge between the shrouds and the deck house, just in case I aspire to go ashore and accost the natives. As I plan to make it at least as far as the outreaches of the Commonwealth of Massachusetts, it's possible I may want to explore a town and hone my predilection for a foreign tongue. As I was somewhat educated at the headwaters of Buzzards Bay, I can generally make my needs known to the natives. Even though watah is what may go into my jugs, I'm sure the result will be nearly wet enough to dilute my French roast.

Otherwise, I plan to "make myself scarce." Perhaps I'll stop in Padenarum, where Concordia Yachts used to make some pretty, wooden boats. Be nice to smell a few oak or mahogany shavings instead of polyester resin and epoxy. If they offered me a job, I might just sail home and fetch my tools.

Mostly, I'd like to sail by Allen's Pond between Horse Neck Beach and South Dartmouth. Here I spent many pleasant and leisurely hours with my wife and sons, paddling and sailing and chasing the wily blue crabs. It's been over twenty years since we all vacationed there in an Airstream trailer.

After driving two hours, we'd come to the head of a private road. Unlock and open the upper gate; close and lock it behind you. Drive a half mile of rutted road between high stone walls. Open the Cow Gate at the bottom. Be sure to latch it again. Don't need Flossie and Evangeline strolling, naked, down to the beach with their blankets and oil. Hard enough keeping them Holsteins in the pasture. After the Cow Gate, another half mile of sandy, rutted road, then twenty cabins and trailers all in a clump for another quarter mile. Then another mile and a half of dunes – a posted sanctuary for the terns and plovers.

Plovers ain't no way aggressive, but the terns have read the notice boards and take it upon themselves to enforce regulations. You haven't known rigorous discipline until you've been disciplined by the local terns during nesting season.

North of the dunes, a long and shallow salt marsh pond connects to the sea by a little breach way. Swimming in this breach way proved a challenge when the tide was running. Was all you could do to stay in one place no matter how strong a swimmer you thought you were.

The trailer had running water, thanks to a point we drove. It had a generator, and a toilet that led to a sump. You could cook blue crabs, take a hot shower, and keep your ice cream cold, thanks to a tank of propane. Little Beach was idyllic. Of course, during Hurricane Carol, in '54, all the cottages took a cruise cross the pond. It made most sense to replace them with trailers and take them away during the winter. Or when a hurricane threatened to redistribute the dunes and shingle.

My wife's father kept a small sailboat there and we took her out. My wife and I taught out sons to sail. One of my boys now keeps a Cal 25 on Lake Champlain. My other son lives near San Francisco and admires the Golden Gate Bridge. It makes no difference. I love them for what they are. My sister's boating has consisted in messing about for an hour once every five or ten years in a canoe. Not all of us can claim to have a weather eye, webbed feet, and tell-tale whiskers.

Off to Noank today to provision *MoonWind* for a little cruise – perhaps sixty miles each way, which I shall punctuate with stops at lovely Point Judith Pond, about midway, both going and coming.

Coffee, sugar, GPS, oatmeal, raisins, sleeping bag, and pillow. What more could a waterman want? Maybe remember my sunglasses and gloves. Maybe remember a spoon. Maybe take a book to read and a notebook to record my thoughts. Maybe remember a pencil. Pens tend to freeze, though NOAA predicts balmy weather. Maybe take copies of my books to astound the natives. I know there's a library in Padenarum, but I've never ventured inside.

I began to make piles last night when I couldn't sleep. Food, clothing, accessories. I also leveled my drafting board once and for always. One illustration per week? Twenty by April? I would need to drive myself and not have too many other commitments. Like repairing boats. Or sailing.

*   *   *   *

Hopefully, I can cease to write this book sometime soon. The joy of blather is, I can always begin another book at any point whatsoever. No need to wait to see "who dunnit;" no need for resolution of conflict; no climax; no dénouement. Just plain old, everyday journaling, on its way to nowhere in no great hurry. By the time I record my journey to Padenarum, I may have a book.

I tend to be lax on the water in the morning. I want to savor my notebook, my French roast, and utilize my head without interruption. Sailing the boat begins bright and early – perhaps by eight o'clock. By which time I've been up for two or three hours.

We are back on standard time again, so sundown comes about five o'clock. I like to anchor by then in case of problems. I've had my anchor drag at night and had to start up my motor and change my berth, but there's always the chance of running down a mermaid in the dark. Not good karma.

Besides, if I anchor before sundown, I get to brew a cup of Lapsang Souchong, sit in my cockpit, and watch the sun sink slowly into the sea.

Even on a drizzly eve, it's worth it to rinse my whiskers for the view. Aren't but so many sunsets left for an old waterman to savor.

POINT JUDITH LIGHT
POINT JUDITH
RHODE ISLAND

You need a goodly horizon for a proper sunrise or sunset. The prairies, the ocean, or a hilltop all suffice. *MoonWind* isn't much enamored of prairies. And sailing on hilltops means tacking among the trees. Sea level suits the both of us and, fortunately, there's a goodly supply of it just a bit south of here. It's sometimes lumpy; then we find a snug harbor. It's sometimes so calm that, Horrors! we need to motor. Inevitably, the earth rotates, and the sun slips away to lighten another's morrow.

And, with any luck, Apollo returns for breakfast. Fortunately, he prefers my kind of coffee fixed my way, so I expect him to grace my mornings a few years more. And though the far isles of Eternity may know but endless night or endless day, I'm glad to thrive at this midpoint where days and nights display such variation. The isles here have hospitable harbors where *MoonWind* can swing on her hook; and if, perchance, she chooses to drag discretely to nuzzle the shore why, who can blame her? I, too, need to go ashore on occasion to shake the wet from my whiskers and stroll the strand.

*　　*　　*　　*

Getting back to illustrating, I determined I would do a series of black and white drawings depicting white, or black and white, birds and beasts:

Pas de Deux by Moonlight

White bison, snow leopards, ermines, white owls [barn owls] white ferrets, white foxes. I did a white peacock which was criticized by an art teacher I know. A friend of mine, however, paid eight hundred dollars for the privilege of having my white peacock hang in his kitchen, and asked if I were sure I had charged enough.

And then I look at Salvador Dali and Marcel DuChamps and wish I could charge ten times as much as I do. They may have talent; they may be crazy; but who is to say what intrinsic value should be ascribed to so called works of art. At least Salvador Dali was a master artist. If Andy Warhol's cans of soup and Claus Oldenberg's clothespins are works of art, then I should have stayed repairing boats at forty dollars per hour, and listened to the studied complaints of my customers.

The White Peacock

It's late Saturday night and my tenants informed me first thing this morning that they tried to burn down my house - and what am I going to do about it? And quickly.

After almost seven years in that house and hundreds of fires in the fireplace with no mishap whatsoever; I hear that the wooden panels surrounding my fireplace have smoldered and charred and filled the house with smoke. Now I must take down one wall abutting my central chimney and rebuild it from the masonry out to the nearby doorway and round the corner into the adjoining room. But first I need professional cleaners to deal with soot and ash.

And I doubt my insurance company will be interested in being involved as I never informed them I planned to rent my house.

And I hoped to take *MoonWind* out to taste the sea spray tomorrow morning. I had plans to sail away for four entire days. Tomorrow, Sunday, I promised to meet with my renters. Monday I shall have to begin the work. Tuesday I should have been worlds away on the water.

Instead I shall probably begin to dismantle – literally – my house. I knew I should need to work at something this winter to support myself. Be careful what you wish for. I wanted work. I never mentioned the pay. I always knew that the gods had a sense of humor, and also how gratified they are when we suffer. I shouldn't complain; my house could have burned to the ground.

Meanwhile, the pusslet went out; she came back in; she had her cookies and some fresh water; and now she naps on a chair. Some days – today – I'd gladly change places with her. But the pusslet has no aspirations to make her life either a hell or a heaven. Her gods make sure her bowl is filled every day. She needn't put on her trousers and go to work. She does enjoy fresh doughnuts and French roast coffee, but she needn't work especially hard to get them. She hasn't the satisfaction of creating the book or work of art that makes life such a pleasure.

And now I need to put on my trousers and go talk with my tenants.

*　　*　　*　　*

At least I got out sailing, if only for the afternoon. *MoonWind* decided to ride the ebb to Watch Hill. With one reef and my smaller genoa still made seven knots over the ground. Breeze perhaps ten knots and steady, but seldom healed more than ten degrees. Not having canvas high aloft makes the difference. All the way to Watch Hill Point – seven miles - in a little over an hour. Point Judith Pond beckoned from not too afar, but I shut my ears. *MoonWind*'s ears stood right up. She wanted to keep on east-ing.

We had a bit of an argument till I put the helm hard down and headed her home to Noank. But she got even. After I dropped her sails within West Cove and put the motor in gear, she found a likely rock and climbed atop it. We came off after a minute, and I reined her in, cantered into the marina, and put her back in her stable. Glad the tide was coming in. No leaks, but probably a nasty gash in her keel. Perhaps I can sail to Shenny for a short haul and inspection. But not this week.

Helped a fellow sailor warp his boat about the end of his pier to get her into a berth as his motor proved unresponsive. Then helped him haul his outboard out of its well and trundle it up to the shop. He retaliated by handing me a moderate, unmarked bill to line my pocket. Every little bit helps just now.

Today's agenda includes contacting the insurance company and getting my house in Stonington cleaned up. That and mowing the back lawn and maybe moving my jack stands to the yacht club in case I'm short hauled. I still need to replace some skirting around my trailer and install the intake vent for my wood stove. Tomorrow the cleaners come. The next day I take down panels.

If ever I wake up with nothing to do, I may just take the time to write a book.

Would everything I undertake, or aspire to undertake, be as simple and rewarding as writing a book. I can shove a thousand words a day into this file for days and days at a time. There is always and ever something to write about, if nothing else but the whim and execution of writing, itself.

Writer's block is something I've seldom experienced. When I've something to say, the keyboard blathers for me. When I've nothing to say, or have other projects that take priority, then nothing is here to happen; the keys are silent. But I'm not dismayed.

*　　　*　　　*　　　*

Yesterday morning a professional photographer met me at the boat-yard and spent an hour admiring my face via an enormous lens. The sky proved drab – a uniform grey in all directions. Then we went to Carson's and had morning glory muffins and hot drinks. She wants to shoot me again when the light is better – when the sun hangs low in the sky. "About three in the afternoon or seven in the morning," she said.

She's an interesting woman; she has a degree in sculpture and studied sculpting marble in Florence She grew up in Calabria and came here as a girl. Though she still sculpts, she has made her living as a photographer these past twelve years.

* * * *

Yesterday afternoon I motored *MoonWind* over to SYC to be hauled to repair her keel. Hopefully a quick process, as I need my jack stands to support a customer's boat in the shop soon. And the season for hauling boats in this part of New England is at its end.

Good news. The damage to *MoonWind's* keel is minimal, and I had it repaired in an hour. Amazing that hitting a rock at three knots feels as though the keel has been wrenched from the hull and must be hanging by one barnacle, while, in reality, only a divot that requires a cup of resin has been displaced.

* * * *

Monday I helped my partner haul his eighteen foot skiff and that of his late brother in law. As neither engine cared to cooperate, this necessitated ferrying both skiffs a mile to a public ramp. This we accomplished using an eight-foot inflatable dinghy having a five horse outboard. It proved a sultry day in the high forties, but not too breezy. Quite pleasant for mid-November.

First, we needed to pump up the dinghy, then mix some gas and oil for the two cycle motor. Then we gave the dinghy a little ride in the truck to Palmer's Cove. We carried her to the water, walked her out the pier, and lashed the dinghy alongside one skiff. I puttered out of Palmer's Cove beneath the causeway. My partner met me at the ramp with the trailer behind his truck. Of course, nothing is simple.

First, we needed to offload a little sailboat from the trailer. We drove it from one house to another, removed the boat, and flushed the cockpit of sand left behind by Hurricane Sandy. The inflatable and its outboard needed to be fetched from the boat shop, driven to Palmer's Cove, and carried down to the water.

I found that to direct the course of the skiff by steering the dinghy no problem at all, especially at a judicious rate of two knots – until I needed to make a sharp turn at the piers before the launch ramp. Then the skiff headed off on some divine errantry of her own, dragging the reluctant dinghy in her wake. I put my motor into reverse and steered for the open sea. I'm proud to say that the skiff hit the piling head on at only one knot. A bit of judicious backing and filling, and I brought the skiff to the ramp and made a perfect landing onto the half-submerged trailer. Really quite simple.

My partner drove the skiff back to Palmer's Cove. I returned there via the dinghy. Without the headstrong skiff alongside, I had no problem roaring back at ten knots. We then drove the skiff to its new home and unhitched the trailer. Then we removed a thirteen-foot Blue Jay sailboat from the second trailer after draining the rainwater from it. We hitched up this trailer and returned to Palmer's Cove to repeat the procedure.

By this time, the tide was at its flood, reducing the clearance beneath the causeway to perhaps four feet. My partner removed the awning support from the center console for additional clearance while I attached the dinghy and checked my fuel.

"The wheel bearing on this trailer sounded noisy," my partner remarked. "Fortunately, we've only to drive this skiff a couple of miles."

This trip I merely grazed a piling with the rub rail of the skiff. But I made a poor landing and the skiff lay thwartways to the second trailer. We finally straightened her out and got her secured. We decided to carry the dinghy in the truck. First we should haul the trailer and skiff a bit farther up the ramp.

Then the starboard axle of the trailer bent and jammed the wheel against the frame. It would not be possible to trail the skiff the two miles to its winter home.

Should the skiff return to Palmer's Cove?

After debate, and a couple of cell phone calls in search of another trailer, without success, we backed the trailer into the cove, removed the skiff, and tied her off to the pier. Then we dragged the complaining trailer a quarter mile to a relative's yard and unhitched it. And there stood another trailer.

My partner called its owner, the landlord, who promptly appeared, unlocked the trailer, swapped his ball hitch, and attached the trailer to his truck. We returned to the ramp and hauled the skiff. We removed the outboard motor from the dinghy and put both it and the dinghy into my partner's truck. The skiff returned to the landlord's yard where he graciously allowed it to remain for the time being. We returned to the shop and stowed the dinghy and motor.

Total elapsed time: about five hours for each of us.

And who says messing about in boats is anything but rewarding?

*   *   *   *

Saturday a craft show at Stoneridge, a local independent facility for seniors. This includes children of fifty-five who tire of maintaining their own homes. One purchases a condo and a meal contract and settles in to any lifestyle compatible with life in a four-acre building complex. There are woods and shores nearby; state parks; good restaurants [and plenty not-so-good]; art galleries; theater; dance; and music. When driving one's own auto becomes impractical, Stoneridge provides a van to get you at least beyond the parking lot. After that, you crawl to your favorite venue. And of course, there's a social life. Four hundred souls of a similar generation herd together for companionship, cocktails, love, and Scrabble.

Every November, they host a holiday bazaar of local crafters. Today is it. I normally do quite well. In this economy, clearing one hundred dollars beyond the setup fee is satisfactory in the four hours allotted.

And it proved slow, indeed. The first hour I sold nothing – not even a postcard. By the fourth hour I'd grossed about seventy-five dollars. In the last ten minutes I sold two prints and a box of cards – another fifty dollars. So I just cleared one hundred dollars beyond the twenty-five dollar setup fee – still not a great return. It pays the setup fee and the fuel to attend the three day show in Hadlyme next week. Hopefully, my client brings his sloop into the shop for the winter to have refinishing done, otherwise our personal economy will tread a narrow edge.

This life seems naught but tradeoff between security and freedom. To have freedom one must have independent means, a vocation that pays well, or the ability to live with a minimum of possessions. To enjoy absolute freedom, one would aspire toward an ascetic end, else live in a wilderness and be able to provide everything necessary. Going into the woods with an ax and a knife is not an option for many civilized persons. To join a monastic order, or the equivalent, takes strength of will.

To live without a television I find no burden at all. My computer keeps me in touch with the publishing world. As it is, half the emails I send never get answered. I imagine few would respond if I were to correspond by letter. Without a telephone, I should not be able to run a business, and have to work for someone else. Without an automobile, I should have to work within a few miles of home. Having capital, I could manage some sort of house, however lowly, though building codes in this part of the civilized world demand electricity and running water as adjuncts to every dwelling.

Places can still be found, not too far from here, where one could live in a shack without amenities. One could return to the glamorous life of a sixteenth century peasant, stitching one's rags together, and huddling with the mice on a bed of straw. Good for the soul perhaps, but tough on the bones. At sixty-five, I enjoy a few creature comforts, even though I don't demand a wide screen television and roasted cows. Even a cabin with hand pumped water and a bright Aladdin lamp would be acceptable, and my rattlely truck to take me grocery shopping. This would be deplorable enough by modern standards. And not having modern communication would preclude publishing ventures. Perhaps I should bide a while yet and tell you another tale.

15 December 2012

I brought *MoonWind* to Noank from Pine Island Sound the day before Thanksgiving. I hate to tell you that I motored the four-mile trip, but that's what I did. It was midafternoon by the time I was under way, and I was impatient. If this becomes a habit I may think to trade in *MoonWind* for a trawler.

One of these days in the not too far off future I hope to be caught up with all these carking projects that distract me from the ocean. If and when I sell my rental property in Mystic I'll have a bit of capital and far fewer responsibilities. What a novel situation. Income enough to feed *MoonWind*, and leisure enough to go sailing for weeks at a time.

Now that it verges on winter, the days to sail are limited by my reluctance to freeze my fingers. What with the wind chill factor, I seldom experience joie de vivre at half my body temperature. My elderly bones take longer to thaw; my frosty whiskers dismay my wife; my frozen fingers send the cat under the sofa. I have to sit on the wood stove half the evening before I'm allowed into bed.

Unlike Tristan Jones, who doted on icebergs, I prefer to bask in the sun rather than have to sweep the snow from my keel. I'd rather laze on a sunny day and actually see my naked toes than scrabble for a tissue with my gloves on.

This is why I went sailing last week – just to prove to the world I wasn't a wimp. After all, it was forty-eight degrees with an eight-knot breeze – Indian summer. I have to admit, I sailed for only three hours. Long enough to make a round trip to the lighthouse at Latimer Reef, four miles off.

Of course, I had to steer around all those ice floes, but I saw only two polar bears, one of whom was eating a lobster boat. A flock of penguins passed overhead on my return, but I hadn't time to watch them, as I needed to point as high as I could to clear a monstrous iceberg. It was nearly noon and the sun had just set and I wanted to make it back to West Cove before the grease in my relative bearing froze.

In the interests of a good story, I ought to tell you my sails blew out, my motor wouldn't start, and that killer whales boarded my boat and ate my best pair of sea boots.

Alas! None of these happened. I enjoyed my sail at a leisurely three knots, refrained from climbing on any rocks – to the disappointment of *MoonWind* – and puttered into my slip a little earlier than I'd planned. I could nearly feel most of my fingers and so could tie my shoes all by myself.

Oh, I forgot to mention – I needed to strip off my wetsuit and booties and don some lubberly duds. The Annual Jack Stand Party at The Mystic Boom Vang Association began at five o'clock. Here was my chance to brag about the ice floes and the polar bears to all those sailors who hauled their boats in October.

But nobody paid me the slightest attention.

"That's just Constant Waterman," I heard one sailor confide. "He never goes anywhere unless he can write a story about it, but I doubt he gets anything published."

"Poor old guy," the second one said. "Imagine someone from Mystic writing stories about sailing."

"Yes," said a third. "That's all he ever seems to do is put varnish on his drop boards. And do you know what? He doesn't even have a lock on his cabin. I slid back his hatch one afternoon to see what was down below."

The other two leaned forward in anticipation.

"And?" said the first. "What did he have below?"

"You wouldn't believe it," the third one said. "There wasn't an air conditioner or even a television. There was nothing but sails and coils of line and charts."

"Poor old guy," the second one said. "Maybe we should take him sailing some time."

"I'll have Sea Puss launched by June," the first one said. "Some sunny day we'll invite him for a sail. We can bring some pizza and beer and watch a Red Sox game. I have my TV mounted in the cockpit. We'll anchor somewhere calm so we don't slop our beer."

"Like behind the breakwater," said the third.

"It'll be a real adventure," said the second.

And it will be. The Red Sox are going to beat the Indians, five to four, in the bottom of the tenth on a walk-off double. I just know it.

Virgin Gorda

A few years back, I went to the British Virgin Islands, Virgin Gorda to be explicit, and met an old classmate who'd asked me to help him and his friend sail his Jeanneau 37 back to Portland, Maine. Paula and I spent two weeks on Virgin Gorda. Then she flew home, while I spent the next two weeks out sailing. She and I spent the first week camped on the boat, the second week ashore.

Most of my writing concerns our stay ashore. The sailing proved rather boring: Aside from being seasick most of the trip, I found it uneventful. We saw perhaps ten vessels the whole two weeks. We saw two whales lazing on the surface. No violent winds accompanied the rain squalls we encountered. One stood at the helm for three hours and maintained the same course one had maintained the day before and the day before that. There was nothing to see but wind and sky and water – vast portions of each, punctuated by stars at night and sunbeams during the day. There were few seabirds until we came near Bermuda and Casco Bay, Maine. The Gulf Stream disappointed: no barefoot boys sat on its banks and fished; no canoes rode its ample length to the sea. What sort of stream was that?

I should probably begin at the beginning – what a novel idea! Even though this isn't a novel, I think I'll give it a try.

It's five AM. The muffin and coffee in my stomach get acquainted as the shuttle finds its way to United Airlines at Bradley Field outside of Hartford. We check our luggage then lug our carry-on bags aboard the aircraft. We have just settled in for a comforting nap when we touch down at Dulles Airport in DC.

It's seven thirty and a bit of breakfast is called for. Instead of checking in at our gate, we settle into the little restaurant next door and order omelets. By the time the waitress has discovered where the hen has hidden her eggs, it is nearly flight time. We inhale our meal and dash to the airline counter.

"The plane has departed," the clerk informs us. "We paged you and paged you."

"Was your microphone plugged in?" I inquire.

She is not amused.

I explain to her about the uncooperativeness of the chickens. She fixes me with one of her official airline scowls. She can do nothing for me, she says, as we have been proven negligent. They have another flight to San Juan tomorrow at this same time. Would I care to purchase another pair of tickets?

Tomorrow?!

Purchase?!

Now it is Paula's turn. She approaches the man making reservations at the farther end of the counter. She explains to him that she's diabetic; that her medicine is in our forwarded luggage. She describes – though not from personal experience – the progressive symptoms of diabetic convulsions. She waxes descriptive. She greatly regrets that she might die in his terminal.

Beads of sweat develop on this honest fellow's brow. He quickly books us – free of charge – onto a competitor's flight that departs in forty minutes. We'll have to touch down once in Charlotte, but only for an hour.

"Time enough for a second breakfast," I wickedly suggest, and get punched for my impertinence.

We arrive in lovely San Juan, Puerto Rico. We go to the baggage office to collect our errant luggage. It's nearly four o'clock. The luggage office has closed. We go to the ticket counter for United. As their last flight of the day has departed, this has also closed.

We go to the information counter at the other end of the terminal. It's a three day hike, and our carry-on luggage is cumbered with lead ingots.

The attendant calls United and finds that one of their baggage men is still there. We drag ourselves and our ingots back to United and find our man.

"I would have gone home at four o'clock, but something told me I needed to stay awhile," he informs us.

Paula doesn't tell him that she's conversant on astral levels.

We trudge to the baggage office and discover our luggage snuggled in for a nap. The baggage man finds a porter to trundle our things upstairs. As we've missed the three thirty flight to Virgin Gorda, we have to pay Air Sunshine extra to take their final, five thirty flight. Fortunately, they have space. When we walk out on the tarmac to our plane, it is easy to see how a single goat or a crate of chickens could have spoiled our final chance of seats.

This aircraft to Virgin Gorda holds eight people, one of whom is the pilot. This lanky young man, who wears his captain's bars pinned to his short sleeved white shirt, and who sports neither tie nor jacket, tips back a seat, crawls into the fuselage, and stows the luggage handed up by the clerk. The skipper then appraises us carefully, with avoir du pois in mind.

"You will please sit here, my lady, and you will sit there, sir. You will please sit by me in the co-pilot's seat."

Having arranged us with an eye for the trim of his aircraft, he gives the motor's rubber bands a final winding. He hops on the wing and swings himself through the door and into his seat. Being tall, his seat is shoved back within two inches of mine. I'll spend the fifty minutes riding side saddle, my legs in the aisle. At least my seatbelt's secure.

They release the rubber bands and our little airplane zooms into the sky. We level off at sixty-eight hundred feet. We fly at one hundred sixty-five miles per hour. The young man steers with his knees as he fills out all the paperwork for this international flight. Virgin Gorda will be our point of entry to Great Britain.

We land in St. Thomas and swap four breathless passengers for four others. In twenty minutes we'll land on Virgin Gorda. As we approach I see that the tiny runway is only gravel. It crosses a small peninsula and appears quite short: perhaps about a yard long. The Caribbean Sea extends most wetly and generously beyond. There's a jutting promontory that we need to pivot about before we descend. I watch this point of rock approach but manfully refrain from clutching at it as our port wingtip scrapes by.

With a rush we descend and hurtle onto the runway. Our young pilot executes a perfect landing. While we remind ourselves to breathe, he taxies up to an old, two car garage that bears a signboard reading, "Virgin Gorda International Airport." This sign is slightly wider than the building. The pilot unstacks and hands me down everyone's luggage.

Behind a glass counter, the official reads our papers, then approves them. He's not impressed that I plan to depart and sail home via small boat. Other mad men have passed this way before.

We stand by deferentially, waiting for our baggage to be inspected. No one seems interested. What could anyone care to smuggle into Virgin Gorda? Piña coladas?

An affable clerk comes out from beyond and kindly shoos us away. In San Juan, we asked that Air Sunshine leave a message for my friend to expect us on this later flight. We ask the clerk if anybody here relayed this message.

"Doan know, mon," he shrugs. "Go out back, see if your friend be there."

We go out back. In the dusty parking lot beneath the two palm trees stand a pickup truck with a dented fender, a hatchback, and a Jeep. My friend gets out of the Jeep and extends his hand.

"You haven't changed in forty years," he lies.

*   *   *   *

Virgin Gorda Yacht Harbor – slip D-87

Having coffee in *Wanderer's* cockpit. Secure in her slip, *Wanderer* dances gently to and fro, exercising her spring lines. Beyond the surrounding arm of land that forms this perfect harbor the surf builds up, and roars an invitation to the sheltering boats to come outside and play. Paula sleeps soundly below despite the attempts of the ship's clock, just inches from her ear, which strikes its tale of bells every half hour. It has just told seven bells and the sun is high and bright in a perfect sky. Beneath the foregathering cumulus a number of muted, low mountain peaks dominate the skyline to the west: Great Camanoe, Beef Island, Ginger Island, and, in the misty distance, twelve miles off, Tortola.

This yacht basin is a nearly symmetrical rectangle of a half dozen acres surrounded by a low, concrete retaining wall. Along the shore runs a broad, concrete walkway, which, at its southern end, turns and fronts the boatyard. It runs alongside the fuel pier and terminates at the lift slip.

Behind the lift slip spread several acres of beautiful boats on the hard; waiting their owners' seasonal indulgence. A stroll among these stranded vessels is a lesson in geography. Their transoms proclaim their homeports to be both exotic and local. A few of these former are Rotterdam, Netherlands; Sarnia, Ontario; Rockport, Texas; Honolulu, Hawaii; Wayzata, Minnesota; and Maryport, on Solway Firth in Cumbria, England, just a few miles south of the Scottish border.

A dive shop and the harbormaster's office stand by the fuel pier. The chandlery is set back from the water. Now, during off season, the yard remains mostly quiet. Yet, a seventy-foot wooden schooner, *Southern Cross*, having a distinguished bowsprit and filigree work, hangs in the slings this morning. I take some photos of her when she lies alongside the pier an hour later.

*   *   *   *

Back a dozen yards from the inboard edge of the harbor spreads a parking lot with shops at either extreme. The Valley's main road, two lanes wide, parallels the walkway along the harbor. This little commercial complex serves us the two weeks of our stay.

The shops at the north end of the parking lot, and closest to *Wanderer*'s slip, are dominated by Buck's grocery market. Buck's has everything you could possibly need at only twice the price. These are the islands, and everything is imported save coconuts and concrete, and needs to come hundreds, if not many thousands of watery miles. The orange juice comes from Florida, nearly a thousand miles to the west. The butter comes from New Zealand; produce from Puerto Rico; the bottled water from Maine.

The only good deals are on the liquor shelves. Rum, from any of the islands, cost half what it does in the States. The cheapest white rum, concocted by an old woman back of the Dumpster, cost only four dollars the bottle. This and ice and Goya piña colada mix supplied us with an antidote to sultry tropic evenings.

The walkway surrounding Buck's has a broad veranda covered by the overhang of its roof. Several café tables invite the languid to sit outside with their coffee and deli fare and comment on the fact that today may prove warm. Numerous scrawny feral hens come by in hope of a hand-out, while the colorful roosters, having waked us all at four AM, strut their turf and glare at one another.

The many taxi drivers who serve the tourists congregate at Buck's for the very good reason that cell phone reception is better here than elsewhere. They sit outside Buck's and talk among themselves in that patois of the islands that seems akin to Creole: a mix of French and African with a sprinkling of Spanish and English. To us it is totally incomprehensible: this free-flowing, languorous language of the islands.

Taxis here are generally pick-up trucks with bench seats down the back, and canopies to keep off the sun. Tour "buses" are larger, gaily painted trucks with seating for a dozen. Though many of the smaller boutiques and services operate on "island time" – which has about eighty minutes to the hour – taxi drivers are extremely prompt and courteous.

The first thing you notice on Virgin Gorda is courteousness. Everyone bids you "good day," or "hello," or, occasionally, on a Sunday morning, "God bless you." Small talk is expected in restaurants and shops before any mention is made of anything so crass as a table for four or another pair of new sandals.

Now that tourist season is mostly over island time obtains more so than ever. Buck's share their large building with a perfumery [seldom open], a store having pirate regalia [occasionally open], and the office of the tourist bureau [will return at three o'clock – but doesn't mention what day].

Around the corner are the locked heads and showers reserved for boat owners who rent a slip. No matter who might be lounging nearby, however late at night, you had nothing to fear. You could stroll up to take a shower at midnight and always expect a "good evening" from anyone you encountered. The numerous, buttery blossoms of the squat, wide spreading Golden Shower Tree [Cassia fistula] outside the heads are dutifully swept up three times per day by the cheerful woman who keeps our heads and showers so clean.

Across the parking lot are a grouping of shops that surround a partially canopied phalanx of tables. A couple of palm trees help to support this roof. The parking lot end of this little mall is dominated by the restaurant sporting the unlikely name of the "Bath and Turtle." Across the corner of the parking lot, it has its own open air bar where live music is offered on Wednesday nights. Each of the local restaurants about Spanish Town features live music one night out of the week. And this is off season. The music generally stops at midnight, though the jukebox from the pool hall across the road often blares till early in the morning.

Air conditioning isn't prevalent here, except in the smaller boutiques. The Bath and Turtle has overhead fans and a fan outside to cool its share of tables. The doors stand open and people casually wander in and out. We always dined outside. A television hung from the corner of the building – permanently attuned to news, sports, and weather – and kept at a rather subdued, considerate level. We always enjoyed good meals at the "Turtle," which served all day. If you have a chance to try their crab and shrimp fritters, don't pass it up.

The other amenities offered at this mall are a full-service bank [on island time], with an outdoor ATM that talks to you in French, Spanish, English, or Dutch and, on select occasions, condescends to dispense US dollars – the local currency. Also present are a self-service laundry, an ice cream shop that serves a half dozen flavors, public washrooms, a computer store, a camera and video store, a high end jeweler [island time only – come back after four o'clock], a tiny grocery market with a bake shop, the dive shop – busily selling beachwear and scheduling trips – and a half dozen small boutiques filled with cordiality and surprises.

*   *   *   *

Now evening flows over Virgin Gorda. The marina is quiet save for some night bird I've yet to identify. We sit in the cockpit and watch the near-full moon ascend to her pavilion of pale cloud that surmounts the tallest palms. Without the basin the surf mutters disconsolately, but the wind has died away. The tropic night is still and filled with stars. Tall night beckons, and who are we to refuse?

No matter how steeply this moon filled night may spire, one thing is certain: at seven AM, Buck's will serve hot coffee.

16 May 2008

Yesterday we rested and exercised our ability to do as little as possible for protracted lengths of time. Most people refer to this as vacation. To vacate: to empty. Can't imagine a duller existence than ongoing emptiness. A day or two is more than sufficient for me. True, we strolled a bit about the harbor village. We swam in the sea, stumbled a mile of stony beach, indulged in food and drink, and read our books.

It is said one needs to empty oneself in order to be filled, but I don't believe to become entirely empty would prove beneficial. We need to empty ourselves of preconceptions to acquire knowledge, but surely all our conceptions can't be false? I hope I've learned a few worthwhile things in sixty years.

However, there are things I wish to do, and sitting idle for days accomplishes nothing.

This day is a mix of sun and clouds, and already early this morning we've had a shower. The little, black headed laughing gulls are noisy creatures but more amusing than our herring gulls at home. A pair of them alights nearby and carry on an animated conversation, and nag each other up and down the pier. I could invest these creatures with personalities and build a sitcom about them. I haven't observed the smashed remains of crabs or mollusks about the piers, so assume these birds subsist upon nothing save Oolong and buttered toast.

We saw a pair of brown pelicans yesterday, and, while we lunched at The Bath and Turtle, observed a bird like an oversized thrush who comported himself as a catbird – perhaps a brown thrasher. Spotted what appeared to be a frigate bird high above the harbor, his tail closed tight, but hadn't the initiative to break out my binoculars.. As I write this, he returns. His wingspan appears to be about four feet, though my bird book suggests they attain as much as seven. We startled an unusually marked duck along the beach and have seen mourning doves, plovers, and a few sparrows. Aside from a dragonfly patrolling the harbor and the usual geckos there hasn't been much evidence of wildlife.

Moon Maidens Spangle Heaven with Flowers

Some low peaks on the farther islands are bathed in light; some shade one another. As the sun ascends, some will be in the shade, or partial shade, of the cumulus clouds that tower above the islands. Many clouds are smoky below but luminous and cottony above where they catch the light. The British flag flogs heavily from its pole out at the point; the BVI flag below it wraps and unwraps itself with the lethargy of the tropics.

A large ketch under power backs and fills to align herself with a slip. The massy clouds have moved aside and the sun streams hotly down. The ship's clock, below, strikes eight bells: time for breakfast. We tune the VHF to the weather channel and I try to interpret the Spanish. I comprehend but half the words but finally get the gist of it, confirmed in English several minutes later. Seas will run five to six feet; wind will be out of the southeast, eight to twelve knots, and bring occasional showers. Once I master this forecast, it serves our entire vacation.

I'm out at the mouth of the harbor, opposite the breakwater that shelters the entering channel. Nearly beneath the flagpole stand a pair of commemorative benches of unresilliant concrete that provide an excellent view of the shore in either direction and prompt me by their hardness to write more quickly.

To my left is beach with occasional resorts of vivid colors: yellows and pinks and aqua marines. Inland, the boulder and cottage strewn hills rise gently. Some of the boulders are smaller than the cottages. Betwixt and between stand pipe organ cactus, their clumsy arms uplifted in amazement.

To my right, half a mile away, the customs pier juts into deeper water. Here the small freighters, container vessels, tankers, and ferries moor and declare their contents. Beyond the customs and immigration office, a couple of acres within a chain link fence contain offloaded freight.

Ferry passengers visiting or returning with taxable goods from another country must check in here. As it's possible to visit France, the Netherlands, and the USA all in one long day, customs needs to oversee just what comes into Great Britain.

Infected plants are high on the list of items refused entry, yet every day a thirty-foot skiff brings landscaping plants into the Yacht Harbor. I trust she's gets scrutinized by the eagle-eyed customs official. Then again, she needs no clearance if the plants come from the other British Virgin Islands. Does anyone check? Does anyone care? What if that agave wasn't really grown by the local boatman's grandmother? Do you know how sharp agave spines can be? You could conduct an uprising with no more than a dozen large agaves.

And what of these raucous laughing gulls? Does anyone check to see where they catch their fish? Are any of them denizens of a foreign, hostile nation? Think of a French colonial wielding escargot. Think of a Dutchman hurling large ripe Goudas. If a gull from Saint Martin, subject to both these empires, can fly right into Virgin Gorda without even showing his papers, are the rest of us secure in our bunks at night? Who knows what subversive interests these gulls may foster; what disregard for democracy they may share; what manifestoes of gross egalitarianism they may distribute – every gull equal by birthright to every other; every gull entitled to his share.

In front of my bench a small, green frenzy rises from beneath the low bank that confines the channel and hovers on whirring wings – a hummingbird: a tiny whirlwind bent on ravishing flower after flower. Where's an environmentalist when you need one? She dips, she swerves, she makes a low beeline back toward Spanish Town. May we see your passport, madam?

17 May 2008

Late afternoon of a hot but drier day. The heavy shower we had during the night decreased the humidity. Our forward hatch was wide open with a wind scoop rigged to give us a breeze. When the rain began about three AM, the skipper was on deck in a flash to loosen the scoop from the head stay, drop it into the forepeak, and close the hatch. I, meanwhile, stupidly made my way forward, below, and stood looking up at the wind scoop, unable to unrig it from down below. We lay in our bunks and were lulled back to sleep by the downpour's luscious drumming upon the deck.

This afternoon I study photography – the old-fashioned sort with stops and apertures, light meters and film. When I later switch to a digital camera, I can spend more time on composition and light without the nuisance of changing film while the shadows are perfect and the lion leaps at the moon.

I learn about immigration procedure from the skipper. In the BVI, as in other islands, mariners are expected to report their comings and goings to the authorities, unless they mean merely to anchor in territorial waters for fewer than twenty-four hours and not come ashore. Then they must fly a yellow flag from the spreaders to indicate that they haven't yet passed through immigration.

Drugs, fresh food, and firearms must all be declared though customs. Smuggling illegal individuals to and from the islands is frowned upon. Heaven forefend that Uncle Fidel finally get to play for the Brooklyn Dodgers.

*   *   *   *

I'm seated at a table outside of Buck's, sipping cold ginseng tea, listening to the patois of the locals, and telling the persistent chickens I haven't anything for them. It's grown quite hot; understandable at eighteen degrees above the Equator, though the sea breeze assures it seldom exceeds eighty-five: a perfect day to be hung out to dry.

The skipper has expressed a need to lace new leather boots on both pairs of spreaders. Trouble is, both our arms together won't reach that high. We add Paula's arms and we still fall short. One of us must be hauled aloft in the bosun's chair – the lightest of us, obviously. I eat as much breakfast as I dare and put lead weights in my pockets to no avail. Later today I'll get to direct just how far the sun is over the yardarm.

We'd had a late and leisurely Sunday brunch at the Bath and Turtle. We sat on the shady patio and stuffed ourselves with eggs and fruit and muffins. The graying couple at the next table talked to us about sailing. They spend a fortnight every year to charter a boat, returning to Virgin Gorda year after year. They asked us if the corned beef were good.

"You can scarcely tell it's made from iguana," I said.

"Speaking of iguanas," the man replied, "I came across one recently lying beneath the overhang of a rock."

"Yes?" I responded politely.

"Well," he continued, "I was walking by, but I paused to have a smoke."

"Yes?" I responded politely.

"Well," he continued, "I finished my smoke and tossed my lighted cigarette to the ground."

"Yes?" I responded politely.

"Well," he continued, "that iguana leapt on that cigarette, took it up in his mouth, dashed back beneath his rock, and smoked the rest of it."

"You know," I said, "it's extremely wicked to lie on a Sunday morning."

"How about all the other days?" he grinned.

"Those are my days to lie," I said as I handed him my card. "You're talking with a professional."

Returning along the harbor front to *Wanderer*, we spot two four-foot barracuda cruising the perimeter of the basin. They kindly consent to wait until I dash to the boat for my camera, but then the female thinks she really ought to go home and fix her hair. The male follows in her wake, visibly remonstrating. It's not every day you get to be featured in a column by Constant Waterman.

19 May 2008

Full moon last night and a lovely, cool breeze. Music, mostly Reggae, but some Cubano, reached us from ashore. Slept well enough and up at half past five; the blue lights lining the pier soft in the twilight.

Another perfect day; how can one stand it? The sun grows nearly too hot to enjoy the early afternoon; the boat too hot to nap. Swimming in the sea is delightful, but an hour in the water suffices. Mostly, it is just too hot. Oh, for some freezing rain or a bit of snow to brace up these islands. Oh, for a frosty morning with crocuses taking shelter beside the wall and a pusslet, tail well fluffed, scratching at the door in hope of breakfast.

Today we choose to replace the spreader boots. I'm elected to swing in the bosun's chair. The skipper does the winching, Paula tails the halyard. The pre-cut, pre-punched pieces of leather need only be stitched together. How long can it take?

I take a round turn through the first pair of holes with the whipping twine, then tuck an ample tail alongside the row of perforations to be captured by subsequent stitches. When I get to the spreader I take another round turn through the last pair of holes, then knot the two tails together. I snip the twine and begin again below the spreader.

It takes me twenty minutes to complete a spreader boot. Then I sway myself to the other side of the boat, twine my legs around a sunbeam to keep from swinging, and begin again. Including the time to ascend the mast and discover the perfect height from which to work, most of an hour has elapsed before I've completed the higher pair of spreaders. It's eleven o'clock and my legs are beginning to sun burn and I've developed an uncommon thirst, and the bosun's chair has lined my legs with creases and welts and similar distractions.

We leave the lower pair till five o'clock. These go more quickly now that I have the knack. With a little judicious hauling by the crew on deck I manage to shift the glowing sun from beneath the yardarm to over it. Just in time, as I need to apply some native rum to the wheals on both my legs. This bosun's chair hasn't a hard bottom and, consequently, drives its heavy edges into one's flesh. I wear its colorful welts for half a day.

*   *   *   *

Today Marya and Clare arrive, and we find there's a vacancy in their hotel. We take it. Hotel is not the right word. The Bayview consists of three attached, split level apartments having porches or balconies at each level. The center apartment has a thousand square feet; the outer two, fourteen hundred.

There's a full-sized kitchen, small dining room, and down a few steps, a twenty by twenty living room with a lavette. Above this is a bedroom just as expansive with a private bath. Half a level up, above the kitchen and dining room, is another spacious bedroom with a private bath. The entire Virgin Gorda army could easily be housed in this apartment. Each bedroom has a roofed-over balcony. There is air conditioning only in the bedrooms, but a huge efficient fan cools downstairs.

Being the end of May and mostly off-season, we rent this huge apartment for just under six hundred dollars per week, tax included. Our landlady locks our upper bedroom to keep it clean No telling what these mad Americans might do if they chose: they might want to play in each bed just for the fun of it.

The building stands back from the road a hundred yards, surrounded by gardens and shady palms. The flagged paths are crowded by bougainvillea, ixora, crown-of-thorns, and red hibiscus. Geckos dance down the path underfoot and run up and down our screens. There are birds and shade and quiet – delicious quiet. Because of the shade the nightly showers don't evaporate till late in the morning, and the hungry mosquitoes defy us to step outside. We're appreciative of the screens. The second story balcony has less shade, more breeze, and fewer insects. By afternoon, all is dry; the mosquitoes have all gone home to have their naps; and we drape ourselves on the porches.

Our landlady offers to pick up my sister and cousin from the airport, three miles away. She calls up taxies for us; offers brochures and advice; sends in a woman every other day to clean our rooms, change the sheets and towels, wash the dishes. There is a little laundry room at the end of one of the paths we are welcome to use, and loads of hot water for showers or baths. Compared to living aboard a thirty-seven-foot sloop, this equates to owning your very own village: we can't use all the space.

There are ample shelves and closets and drawers; utensils enough in the kitchen to start a restaurant. Clare and Marya and the skipper come by for dinner. There are pots and bowls and dishes enough to feed and serve twenty people. We don't know twenty people.

We stuff the refrigerator full of produce and shrimp and juices and ice from Buck's, a five minutes' walk away. There's a blender, a coffee maker, a microwave, a toaster. There's a huge arched pass-through between the kitchen and dining room. It has a broad counter with several stools. We stack it with cracker boxes, cameras, books, coffee mugs, and brochures.

I spend the early morning drinking strong Latino coffee and keeping my journal. I take a hot shower. At nine o'clock we scramble eggs and pan fry the delicious, local corn bread. Late in the morning we stroll the quarter mile to the all but deserted beach and splash in the sea. On our way back we stop at the little restaurant for ice cream.

We hang out wet bathing suits and towels from the clothes line on the balcony. They are dry in an hour. We take another shower, this one cool.

During the heat of the day we read and doze with the air conditioning on.

We arise when the sun is half way down the palm tree and dump ice and rum and coconut milk and pineapple juice into the blender. We push the "play" button, then dump this delightful mixture over our heads. As it evaporates it cools us off. Then we dress down and stroll the quarter mile to our choice of two restaurants, both with excellent food. This time of year there are, perhaps, three couples having dinner. The waiter has time to talk with us about the cuisine, the island, his aunt, and the weather. We always have hors d'oevres and leave room for dessert. The restaurant keeps a wheelbarrow just outside the door to deliver us home.

By the time we turn in, the tree frogs have tuned their instruments and serenade us till dawn. We seldom hear anything past the overture.

All this decadence produces alarming effects: we come to enjoy it.

Next time I need some peace and quiet to write another book, I'm going to stay at the Bayview.

20 May 2008

Talked with the skipper this morning of dinghies and knots; of shipboard cooking and recipes and coffee. People who aren't sailors – and I've heard there are such creatures – think that we talk of nothing save taverns and women. Now, taverns and women are all very well in their way, but what can compare with a really outstanding recipe for pesto?

The flat-bottomed cumulus clouds that rise above each island seem stationary, albeit a ten-knot breeze tickles the ocean. The pale blue sky arches beyond comprehension. The crisp horizon and striated sea must have been laid out with parallel rules.

We're moving from on board to our apartment at the Bayview this afternoon. The skipper will motor *Wanderer* the mile out to her mooring north of the harbor and save the fifty dollars per day dockage fee he's been paying.

I wander out to the harbor mouth with my camera and my note-book. I try the second concrete bench in hope that it may be softer.

The hummingbird busily assaults the sea grape tree, though most of its pale blossoms are blown and fallen.

The proud wooden schooner, *Southern Cross*, departed this morning without my awareness. Now she stands three miles out, her sails swelled and lifting. It isn't likely I'll see her again in this lifetime.

*   *   *   *

We drag our belongings from *Wanderer* over to Bayview; all but my duffel filled with sailing gear. Books and camera and everyday wear; then back to Buck's to provision our ample kitchen. Not liking the taste of the tap water from the catchment, we buy bottled water and ice from Buck's, as well as libation and fruit and crackers and cornbread and eggs and garlic and onions and lemons and sugar and coffee and paper towels. We begin to make shopping lists and wax domestic. We try to shop early before the heat makes a chore of dragging our groceries home. Were I to spend much time here I'd invest in a shopping cart.

Out first night here we dine with Clare and Marya at the Bath and Turtle. Afterwards we walk along the harbor, and watch the little land crabs emerge from their burrows. Any one of these crabs would fit in your pocket. They sit at the mouths of their lairs with one claw hooked about the edge of their hole. When startled they yank themselves out of sight with amazing rapidity. When it grows truly dark and no one large is around they scuttle about the shops to buy what they need.

We sit out on our balcony with a nightcap. The full moon ascends majestically above the royal palms. Numerous footloose clouds attempt to seduce her. She disappears momentarily in their indigo embraces, imparts a luminescence to their margins, then emerges undiminished, unravished, from their billows. The show proves easily worth the price of admission.

*   *   *   *

Next day the skipper takes *Wanderer* from the local anchorage round Spanish town, the lower portion of Gorda, to an anchorage in North Sound, a large protected area in the hilly northern section of the island. North Sound consists of a deep set, two-mile bight of land sheltered on the north side by Mosquito, Prickly Pear, and Eustatia Islands.

There are several harbors and villages on the mainland: Leverick Bay, Gun Creek, and Biras Creek are the most sheltered. The Bitter End Yacht Club and its surrounding development form a village of their own. Between Bitter End and Prickly Pear Island lies tiny Saba Rock, all of which is covered by an eight-room resort, a restaurant, and a gift shop. A water taxi scuttles from village to village.

Friday, the five of us shall sail to Tortola, twelve miles off. Virgin Gorda has just over three thousand residents; Tortola nineteen thousand: eighty percent of the whole population of the British Virgin Islands. The capital, Road Town, nestles at the mouth of an excellent harbor deep enough for transatlantic freighters. Its government buildings and port and commercial interests mark this as a proper town – nearly a little city.

It will take us two to three hours to sail each way. It may take the better part of an hour to drop people off at the fuel pier; take *Wanderer* back to the outer harbor; anchor; dinghy back in; then reverse the process. This time of year there won't be any dockage for the begging.

If we set out early we'll have three hours to traipse about Road Town, then meet for lunch at the harbor. The skipper plans to sail from North Sound early Friday morning to pick us up, drop us back at Spanish Town by nightfall, then sail the eight miles back to North Sound. Or perhaps he'll simply drop his hook a mile outside the Yacht Harbor.

I have a couple of bookstores and chandleries lined up for assault by Constant Waterman. When I write of the British Virgin Islands, perhaps I'll have the chance to impress the locals. For now they'll have to study their atlas to find out where the village of Mystic lies. They'll have to learn how to pronounce "Connecticut." They'll get to wonder how short a Hunk is a Cutty.

22 May 2008

A little gecko on the screen door at daybreak – on the outside, fortunately, where he's far more likely to catch a bug to enjoy with his morning coffee. I have Demerara sugar in mine – espresso grind Latino that's strong enough to keep my beard well curled.

Off to the Baths this morning via Andy's Tours. Though Andy has a couple of large red trucks that seat a dozen or more, he picks us up himself in a shiny, new pickup that has an extended cab, a six-foot bed with opposing benches, and a canopy. We sit outside for the view and the breeze. He slides open his rear window in order to talk with us. Andy is a swarthy, affable man in his sixties. He wears a grizzled mustache above his smile. He's willing to take us anywhere whatsoever.

You probably wonder: how dirty these folks must be after a week, and how unfamiliar with bathing. Look! They have to hire a tour guide to take them to the Baths to wash themselves.

Let me explain.

The Baths are a phenomenon of nature on Virgin Gorda, at the southern end of The Valley – the lower portion of the island. The upper portion of the island, connected to The Valley by a narrow, low neck of land, consists of spine of low but steep hills and precipitous roads and gorgeous, heady views of the surf and sea.

Andy agrees to drive us about both portions of Virgin Gorda and show us the sights. As Gorda is only ten miles long and covers but eight square miles, it shouldn't take him more than half the day. He agrees to drop us at The Baths for an hour and a half.

Before we stop at The Baths, Andy takes us through different parts of Spanish Town. He points out the old Methodist Church and the modern Catholic Church alone on its height, its single pitched roof receding from its massive, cruciform steeple. We stop at old hotels; we stop high up for a frigate bird's view of the airport. He drives us up and down the steep, steep road that sinuously winds itself about the island. You shouldn't fear heights if you plan to drive this road. Andy's truck curvets; it caracoles; it slides down slopes on its little haunches.

*   *   *   *

Andy stops at various places – some designated lookouts – and encourages us to take pictures. He talks to us over his shoulder from the wheel. He gets out with us when we stop and points out the sights. The highest point on Gorda is thirteen hundred feet. The road ascends to at least a thousand. The view correlates to having a private cloud: Lilliputian villages; rocky heights; beautiful harbors; pristine beaches; remote mansions hanging above the ocean; distant, grey-green islands; sailboats drawn with a needle-sharp H-8 pencil; the azure sea abruptly turning to aqua marine where it shoals along the shore.

We return to The Valley and visit the Copper Mine: cobblestone ruins of the only copper mine in all the Caribbean. Long ago, two hundred men and women and children slaved to bring ore up narrow shafts that groped well below sea level. Now there is only the ruin of a cobblestone building and the bottom half of the cobblestone chimney that rose above the smelter. These ruins perch above the shore, but there are only dirt trails with occasional frail railings to assure you don't fall the hundred feet to the sea. There are old shafts covered over, inaccessible. An informative plaque stands by the small paved parking lot that might accommodate half dozen vehicles.

Twenty minutes suffice us to clamber about and study the fallen stones; admire the view. Now to visit The Baths.

The Baths have been commercialized, of course. You need to pay three dollars for admittance. A restaurant and gift shop adjoin the large parking lot. From the parking lot there's a quarter mile of sandy, rock strewn path amid palms and flowers descending to the water. A little shop will rent you masks and flippers. Changing rooms and lockers and showers, and a booth selling towels and hats can be found by the beach, just beside the grottoes. Here you swim, or lie on your towel and bake, and wait for the sizeable hermit crabs to drag you home for their supper.

The Baths are a jumble of large, volcanic boulders by the sea. Though just a few acres in extent they form a series of grottoes and caverns and are even more picturesque then depicted in our glossy travel brochure. These boulders have hemispherical divots in them from the erosion of softer bits over the eons. Some of these boulders jut out of the foreshore; some lean over the water from dry land. There's a balanced rock that everyone since Adam has tried to topple; there are narrow, contorted paths from grotto to grotto.

Most of these caverns open to the sky and are not oppressive. A few of the paths require you to squat like a duck to pass between the rocks. In a number of places wooden steps aid you up or down the boulders. Some of the grottoes must be waded across. A few lead out to the sea, and a couple require that you swim through narrow openings before you surface in waist deep water just a few yards away. Beyond the grottoes, scuba divers float face down to appreciate the delicate flora and fauna that thrive in this ecosystem. Small angelfish and parrotfish scoot from beneath the rocks and play amid the coral.

It's advisable to have some sort of footwear as the rocks and coral can shred your naked toes. You are cautioned not to tread on the coral as these colonized little animals tend not to find us amusing. There are numerous large brain coral attached to the rocks and colonies of red coral. I discover a large, cadaverous black crab ascending a perfectly smooth and vertical rock above the water. Though it had no footholds, up he went – no pitons, no top rope, no carabineers, no nothing.

We wash the sand from between our toes at the changing room and shed our bathing suits. Andy meets us promptly at one fifteen. Can he take us to Fischer's Cove for lunch? Indeed he can. This is a resort and restaurant in Spanish Town that overlooks a pretty, sandy beach. At this time of year there is no one on it. The accommodations consist of a couple of brightly colored small buildings set amid paths and lawns and flowers and trees.

We dine al fresco on a broad veranda with an unobstructed view of South America. The restaurant is immaculate and airy and inviting; the food superb. The waitress tells us that Andy owns Fischer's Cove.

No wonder he encourages us to take a leisurely lunch. The food is sublime. I have red snapper with roasted potatoes and vegetables. I then indulge myself with a chocolate gateau that could fuel a cigarette boat to Tortola and back. The waitress has the temerity to try to remove my plate before I lick it. The divine coffee restores me to equanimity.

They roll us out to the parking lot where Andy waits by his truck. He hoists us inside and gently props us up. Scarcely a mile will see us safely back to cloistered Bayview. My sister wonders aloud through the sliding window – can she possibly buy some stamps? May she impose?

"Of course, m'lady," smiles Andy.

He makes a short detour to the spruce Municipal Building. He escorts her inside. There she needs to log in, as do local people, to gain access to the post office. She mails her single postcard. Andy escorts her outside and helps her up the steep step into the truck. Aspiring gentlemen would do well to spend a day with Andy.

He drops us at our door and hands us down. He waits politely for us to broach the terms of remuneration. He tells us he would like twenty dollars apiece. We give him a hundred dollars and thank him profusely. We compliment him on his driving, his patience, his cheerfulness, the food at his lovely restaurant.

I won't forget his smile any time soon.

24 May 2008

Yesterday went to Bitter End Yacht Club with Clare, who'd reserved a spot on a charter boat to snorkel about North Sound. Bitter End has its home at the foot of Biras Hill at the eastern end of North Sound. Once through the passage between the main and Prickly Pear Island, you leave the shelter of North Sound. Were you headed for Europe, Bitter End would be your last resort

The yacht club and its attendant shops and restaurants and beaches and marina; its sailing school, boat rental, pool and piers extend for most of a mile, connected by a sinuous tiled walkway bordered by shops and trees and flowers and flowers and flowers. I call it a walkway, yet golf carts commonly use it. One cart can normally pass another if one of them keeps their off wheels in the sea and pedestrians fling themselves into the cactus. This complex, though not a village, is at least the tropic equivalent of a mall. Hipped roofed cottages straggle up Biras Hill behind the shore.

Christmas palms and coconut palms and organ pipe cactus, cordia, and hibiscus constitute most of the trees. Agave, large aloe vera, crown of thorns, ixora, and smaller hibiscus; spider lily, lantana, poinsettia, periwinkle, prickly pear, and turk's cap overwhelm the eye with luscious color. Bougainvillea, in startling shades of magenta, pink, vermillion, and purple, is prevalent as a weed. Various ornamental grasses act as foils to the flowers. Low palmettos diffuse the rippling light. Flower and foliage spill about the buildings; overhang walls; drape from huge hanging planters. The sky, the sea, the shore are alive with light and shadow and breeze all the time.

There is no forest primeval. No towering shade trees offer the traveler refuge from the sun. The only shade is beneath the palm fronds strummed by the wind, and beneath the thunderheads that grow and darken above each island every afternoon. And that faint shade hangs only directly overhead and won't interfere with your tan. The merciless light streams in from every direction.

You can tell I'm from New England. So much light is unnatural. The hillside behind my home is covered in hardwoods. My yard abounds in century-old maples. Across the road stretch several acres of woods. We enjoy direct light from ten until two, and that at the height of summer. Before and after ten and two it filters through the trees and we tan like leopards. In the winter we need a flashlight to find the sun.

Direct and intemperate sun for hours and hours and hours is overwhelming. Perhaps this is why I much prefer coastal cruising in my sloop. I can always take refuge behind a shady island.

Clare and I left the Valley by walking up to Buck's and snagging a taxi. Then we hung on as it reared and plunged and galloped over the steep sided hills and slid on its rump the last, nearly vertical, thousand yards to

Gun creek. There the driver pried our fingers open and dragged us out on the pavement.

We found ourselves at the tiny tourist center with its porticoed rotunda – fronting the road and backing on the harbor. The rotunda was twenty feet across and boasted a pair of benches. Here we sat and waited for the free water taxi to take us to Bitter End.

"But the boat has just left," the young woman seated next to us exclaimed. "There won't be another for an hour."

She dialed a number on her cell phone and spoke with someone from the yacht club, two blue miles away.

"They're sending a boat to pick you up," she told us. "There won't be any charge."

In just a few minutes a center console skiff throttled down and pulled alongside the single pier that services Gun Creek Harbor. We literally hung on to our hats as we roared across the water. In just a few minutes we tied up at Bitter End. I tipped the driver and we headed for the charter boat office nearby.

Once we checked in, we had an hour to have our belated lunch. A hundred yards down the pristine walk we came to a bar and grill. The bar and pool table were within; the restaurant was on the patio, six steps up from the walkway. We sat beneath a striped umbrella and had ice tea and shared a flying fish sandwich. It took a firm grip on both slices of bread to keep our lunch from soaring back to the harbor.

Clare went off to explore the reefs and fishes. I took my camera and walked about, trying to do some justice to all the beauty. I took so many pictures that I needed to visit a local shop and buy new AA batteries. I stooped to fondle a bushel size century plant, also known as agave, and ran a terminal spine into my wrist. I am now blood brother to the flora of Virgin Gorda.

On the sea side of the walkway stretched piers and beaches. At one long pier lay a ninety-foot crimson sloop whose deck stood as high as my head, even though the pier on which I stood was four feet above her waterline. This lovely belonged to Sir Robin Knox-Johnson, early single-handed circumnavigator, who made his remarkable passage without once going ashore.

Smaller yachts and dinghies, kayaks, and sailboards abounded.

The roadway forked at a little brick roundabout edged with shops and more flowers. I followed the shore – what else would a waterman do? A small beach had a row of chaise lounges, striped with white and blue. The palm trees waved above them. The sparkle of the sea defined the sands. In the near distance lay islands with shaggy slopes. I felt myself trapped within a travel brochure: every image clear cut; every color unclouded; every person tanned and athletic and smiling.

Beyond the beach, beside the shore, was a swimming pool surrounded by a terrace with wrought iron café tables and filigree chairs. A little service bar stood a few yards off. People here took vacation with a vengeance. They reclined by the pool, by the sea, surrounded by flowers. They sipped piña coladas from glasses that never emptied. Cubano music wafted from speakers hidden beneath the palms. All that lacked were beauteous maidens to peel shrimp for them and to wipe their mouths. I suppose, for a price, that, too, could be arranged.

Beyond the pool the road devolved to a boardwalk that shortly led to the sea. I made my way the half mile back to the yacht club.

The clubhouse is a three-story structure whose lobby lies wide open to the weather. This lowest story is supported by wrought iron posts and surrounded by a wrought iron filigree valance and filigree railing. It is set about by wrought iron filigree benches. The effect is tasteful.

The lobby has several life sized wooden statues of women and warriors. Up the imposing central staircase is a landing having more statues. Along the balcony on the second story more statues face the sea. On the steep, paneled walls above the landing hang life sized leaping marlin carved of wood. There should have been a sea serpent, but perhaps the sea is too warm for them in the Caribbean.

Beyond the clubhouse runs a beach; above sprout cottages for guests. This complex has half dozen restaurants, from formal to English pub. It has a spa. You can spend a pleasant month just wandering this mile of lovely resort. You can bask by a pool or sail in a regatta There is boating of every variety. There is fishing and swimming and snorkeling; shopping and dining and dancing. You can bake on the beach until it

grows dark or drink dark rum until the iguanas come home. For true romantics, your wedding can be arranged. The sun always shines, flowers are always in season. What more could you want?

As an avid New Englander, may I suggest a month of cross country skiing?

24 May 2008

The following day the five of us sailed *Wanderer* to Tortola. Road Town, the major municipality, takes its name from the harbor: a "road" is another word for a safe place to anchor. The outer harbor has depth enough for freighters and a huge pier to accommodate them. The inner harbor has piers and slips and moorings for hundreds of pleasure craft.

I can't really claim to be an authority on Road Town, though I did spend four hours there. As the sailing and anchoring took about twice that long, I thought I'd tell you about the entire day.

Wanderer had been riding on her thirty-five-pound plow anchor in North Sound the previous couple of days. Soon after daybreak the skipper weighed anchor and single handed her down to Spanish Town – about eight miles. He hailed me via VHF and we met him at the fuel pier at 0850. Within a few minutes we were under way. We motored out beyond the last of the markers, then hoisted sail. We left the single reef in the main to make for a calmer passage, unfurled most of the genoa, and killed the motor.

Paula took the helm the entire passage of a dozen miles. We enjoyed a breeze of ten knots and made about five through the water. The day was superb, the views splendid, the company amiable. No one complained; no one contracted mal de mer; no one fell overboard – at least, not that I noticed.

We entered Road Town harbor and the skipper took back the helm. We doused our sails and motored in as a freighter motored out. We passed the huge piers built for both freighters and cruise ships and entered the inner harbor. There were no vacant slips to rent, and the fuel pier was busy, but we found a temporarily vacant tee headed pier and dropped off the ladies. We headed back to the outer harbor to anchor.

Another marina does a brisk trade in chartering catamarans, and a number of these forty-footers played about the harbor. Some of their skippers seemed amply qualified to count their spokes. They somehow avoided running *Wanderer* down - for which we were grateful - and we complimented them on their speed in spinning their wheels.

We dropped our hook; backed down *Wanderer* to set it; waited to be sure she held; then puttered to the dinghy dock in our seven-foot inflatable.

The skipper went off to purchase provisions he couldn't purchase on Gorda. I went round to galleries and shops to sell my books. At a bookshop named Serendipity a beautiful young black woman took my flier, showed me books filled with photos of sailing vessels, and told me what she'd been reading. The owner, an older, red haired English woman, returned and put the young woman back to work unpacking cartons of books. We then proceeded to talk of the publishing business. I found her both informative and receptive: she agreed to buy my book through her distributor.

It was time to convene for lunch. We ordered some simple fare that was served in island time. That is to say, they dispatched someone to catch the fish and grow the salad greens. After a couple of last minute errands, we reversed the boarding process. I took the helm as we backed away from the pier. Then I proceeded out of the harbor at half a knot as catamarans steamed by at two thirds throttle. Some skippers have no clue how to behave in crowded harbors. "Would-be yachties" know but two rules of the road: "I wanna get there first," and "my boat is bigger."

Once outside the harbor I set a course for Spanish Town, pointing as high as possible. I quickly learned how responsive *Wanderer* is. The skipper pointed out an old mansion on a headland, and gave us a bit of history about its Danish owners. As I peered beneath the boom at this now abandoned building I felt *Wanderer* swerve.

"Up with the helm!" roared the skipper.

I spun the wheel. Too late. *Wanderer* came up and crossed the wind as rapidly as a raptor stoops on a rabbit. She backwinded her jib and was on a course for Tahiti in a flash. The boom hung up on what a moment before had been the weather backstay. Fortunately, there was no one within a mile of us. We need only swap the backstay. After we sheeted in the jib we determined to make as much to windward as practicable before tacking for home. A couple of miles brought us close to Salt Island where we came about – this time on purpose.

Lesson One: steer small and pay attention.

I guess I'm spoiled. *MoonWind* would never resort to such a trick. She tends to be inquisitive when it comes to crossing the wind, and pauses to sniff the breeze. She always looks over her shoulder at me before she comes about to be sure this was really what I had in mind.

But *Wanderer* is more a racing boat, and, although she can sail herself when she's on the wind and her sails are nearly flat, she often takes the bit in her teeth and tries to leap the curb.

The rest of the way to Spanish Town I kept her close to the wind; one eye on the luff of the main, the other on Virgin Gorda. By six o'clock we lay three miles from the Yacht harbor as the breeze began to fail. The knot meter dipped to 2.8, then to 2.5.

Paula, in the stern sheets beside me, had felt a bit queasy coming back. As our speed diminished she started to feel better.

"Perhaps we should shake out our reef," I said to the skipper.

Wham! Paula's formidable right cross connected to my shoulder. The skipper's eyebrows disappeared under his cap.

"Mosquito," I told him, "but she nailed the little whatsis."

"I was just beginning to feel human again," Paula explained.

It's difficult to resist a lead like that, but my shoulder began to stiffen. Sometimes I need to save my clever remarks to try on the Pusslet, first. There's nothing worse than a mutinous crew when the hot sun's snagged on the yardarm.

Behind us the sky turned twenty shades of mauve, hot pink, and magenta. Ahead of us, along the shore, a big red cigarette boat practiced maneuvers.

She crossed our bow at half a mile doing maybe eighty. Then she shook out her final reef. She was quite impressive. She headed for Great Dog Island, three miles off, and went so fast that her transom nearly arrived before her bow. The sound waves she created filled our sails. *Wanderer* kicked up her heels and made six knots. I knew those cigarette boats were good for something.

At the entrance to the harbor we started the motor, headed up, dropped our main, and furled the jib. I motored into the harbor, and, as light began to fail, throttled down, spun the wheel hard to starboard, and laid her neatly alongside a tee head pier. All of us save the skipper stepped ashore. He motored out and anchored beyond the channel, then stayed aboard.

*   *   *   *

The four of us walked the half mile back to the Bayview where we taught some ice cubes to swim in a glass of fermented sugar cane. We added some pineapple juice and coconut milk until those ice cubes purred. We like our ice cubes contented.

The dark came down and the little frogs and night birds sang of summer. We made a huge salad and fell asleep in the bowl.

26 May 2008

This afternoon we stopped at our local hangout, The New Dixie Restaurant, and, after exchanging generous salutations – the practice here – enquired concerning ice cream. The choices seemed to be strawberry or more strawberry. We ordered two of each.

As we spooned pink ice cream into ourselves two local fellows escaped the heat and draped themselves over the counter. One of them wore a tee shirt proclaiming a fondness for poker runs.

"Was that your boat outside the harbor last night?" my sister asked. "The big red one?"

Yes, it was. Turns out he had to pass on the current race. He'd been losing too much oil around a main seal. Our seals in Connecticut that come from Maine each winter know better than to leak any oil – but that's another story. We concurred that running his cigarette boat at over a hundred knots without enough oil might prove a disaster.

"Have to pull my engine, mon. First time in two years."

The race he will miss is from Virgin Gorda to Peter Island and back again, outside: perhaps forty miles. His boat has two engines of a thousand horsepower each. When he opens the throttle all the way he burns about a hundred gallons per hour, and fuel down here cost more than it does at home. But cruising at a quarter throttle, once he's up on a plane, takes little fuel. What you might pour on your cereal could take him to Tortola.

*   *   *   *

This is our last full day on Virgin Gorda. We packed and did laundry this morning. This afternoon the skipper will bring *Wanderer* back to her slip so we can provision. We need to deflate the dinghy and stow her aboard; top off the fuel and water; purchase and stow last minute provisions; pick up our second crew member at the airport; and, hopefully, clear customs and immigration before they close.

Off to the customs house at four o'clock, only to find that immigration is closed until the morning. Back to the harbor where skipper and crew are hauling the latter's half ton duffel bag out the pier to *Wanderer*.

Later we all convene at our apartment for a drink. Clare has just returned from snorkeling up at Little Dix Bay where she saw a barracuda about "this long." About the size, I observe, to fit in the kitchen sink, though why you should want a barracuda – no, she agreed – why would you?

Conversation digressed to seasickness. Clare confessed to queasiness while crossing the Roaring Forties to Antarctica, while Marya recalled a Channel crossing when the wind blew Force 9 and the bar – Alas! – was closed.

Guess I've got some catching up to do. All the puddles I've ever jumped were relatively placid. By tomorrow, this time, I'll be a blue water sailor. Our first leg, 357 magnetic, will bring us to Bermuda in about eight days. Hopefully, I won't have been lost at sea any more than usual, nor eaten by whales, nor violated by mermaids.

*   *   *   *

We call a taxi to take us a mile to a restaurant we haven't tried. The food is decent, not memorable. The conversation halts and flags; begins again; then dies away. I only half pay attention. Am I really departing tomorrow to sail fifteen hundred miles in a little boat? Perhaps I should have chartered a sloop and just messed about the islands for the month. But this should be an adventure. I only hope we don't encounter gales and twenty-foot seas, although, if we do, I'll never again think twice about the thirty knot winds that currently keep *MoonWind* embayed in Connecticut.

Tonight, my bunk will neither pitch nor roll. Tomorrow I'll have a canvas baffle to keep me in my bunk. Tonight I can sleep the sleep of repose and wake whenever I please. Tomorrow someone will shake me from sleep to take the helm in the dark. Three hours on and six hours off until we reach Bermuda: a cloistered world in the midst of the broad Atlantic, six hundred miles from the mainland.

And *Wanderer* will be but another of those wandering islands we call a boat: a little vessel within an empty bottle of sea and sky; and perhaps not so much a vessel as a message.

27 May 2008

0500 and sleep eludes me. Think it may be the rum. As of today, no liquor at all until we reach Bermuda. I bet by then that when I turn into my narrow bunk sleep will whelm me utterly and absolutely senseless.

The first part of this month's vacation has come to an end. Now the adventure begins. Early this morning we had a rain squall for half an hour. I hope that once away from the land we leave such afflictions behind, but I hardly count on it. Don't know how quickly I'll learn to reef in the dark. *Wanderer* has no deck or spreader lights and everything will have to be done by feel. I won't be too proud to call below for some help. Only hope I can sense a squall coming in the darkness.

Coastal cruising is such a placid animal for the most part, with sheltering harbors and lees in which to anchor. Not to mention the option of not leaving harbor at all in wretched weather. The skipper admires my coasting abilities. Avoiding rocks and shoals is a greater challenge than ocean cruising, he admits.

En Route to Bermuda

30 May 2008

Third day out from Virgin Gorda. Steering 015. Today quite calm, but *Wanderer* sliding along at four to five knots, which ought to bring us near Bermuda in plenty of time for Christmas.

First couple of days were lumpy and, despite wrist bands, was seasick much of the time. Finally put on a patch and ate some Dramamine, and by yesterday evening could hold down some chow. My appetite returned. Bathed this morning till the skipper scarcely recognized me. Now soaking my laundry.

Skipper, at the wheel, requests I report that we have yet to see evidence of any urban sprawl. Not surprising as we currently lie three hundred nautical miles from Virgin Gorda, about five hundred from Bermuda, and at least six hundred from any American shore.

Since our first day we have seen no other vessel and little animal life. One frigate bird yesterday; a greater shearwater and two Bermuda longtails – white tailed tropic birds – today. These latter behave as terns at home: squeaking and diving and endlessly circling, eyes on the sea for fish. As to these, we've seen but a handful of tiny flying fish.

Mostly just clouds and more clouds and the sea. Every known genus and species of cloud known to the taxonomist can be seen, and we often encounter showers late in the day. If I die of boredom, I hope they keep me on ice till we reach New England.

Yesterday, at daybreak, the skipper had the wheel. I was below in my bunk, wrestling with another bout of nausea. We encountered a handy thunderhead and charged right through it, rail down. With full press of sail, *Wanderer* re-attained hull speed for the first time in two days. When I looked aloft, the skipper was wearing an expression of utter bliss. It nearly cured me to see him.

Despite feeling ill I took my tricks at the wheel, but kept a bucket handy. Being on deck and having something to do always improve my mal de mere.

Eagle View

Our first twenty-four hours we logged exactly one hundred fifty miles. The five-foot seas were either abeam or astern. Having my stomach five feet above my head makes me question propriety. Going below was agony with a bucket. Staying on deck kept me on an even keel.

As *Wanderer* is a racing boat she tends to be rather tender. "One hand for yourself," was always the rule. The skipper eschews life preservers, but insists on safety harnesses. A jack line runs the length of the deck by either rail with six-foot tethers in abundance. Our rule was never to leave the companionway without being tethered. I generally slept in my harness in case of alarms. Finding and donning one's harness in the dark during a squall might prove disastrous.

I neglected to mention that our departure from Virgin Gorda was anything but auspicious. The man at Immigration at Spanish Town flirted with incivility. He had the disposition of a snapping turtle. "Yes, sir," and "Thank you, sir," did nothing to appease him. After an hour with Customs and Immigration we raided Buck's for produce and ice and stowed everything for sea.

We finally shoved off about noon. We cleared the last channel marker, and went into stays to raise our main. We left in our single reef until we knew what awaited us beyond the islands. As we winched in the main halyard the boom vang tackle parted. We fell off quickly and picked up a nearby mooring. In half an hour we had a new line reeved and were under way. We left the Dog Isles to starboard, Great Camanoe to port. We found a delicious breeze beyond and helped ourselves to a serving.

Three hours sail brought us to Anegada, a coral atoll several miles in length, and the northernmost and easternmost of all the Virgin Islands. Not caring to add *Wanderer*'s bones to the tale of wrecks found here, we passed downwind at a salutary two miles, then set a course for Bermuda, a mere eight hundred forty nautical miles nearly due north.

We presently pass through clumps of brown Sargasso, and one has clogged the wheel of our knot meter. We thought to draw straws to see who would have the privilege of going over the side to clear this mess, but we couldn't remember where we had stowed the straws. The rest of this trip we go below and check our GPS to log our speed. As this shows speed over the ground while the knot meter shows our progress through the water, the GPS has more validity calculating position.

31 May 2008

Met with a rainsquall during my afternoon trick. We furled the genny and single reefed the main, but received no more than a deluge and twenty knots. And this was our last good breeze.

When I resumed the helm at midnight, what breeze there wasn't came from abaft the beam. With scarcely steerageway *Wanderer* traipsed and lollygagged and extravagated, both her sails wrinkling in a most unseemly manner. The skipper awoke and laid aloft and asked me what I was doing. After catching my breath from blowing on the sails I explained our predicament. After half an hour fiddling with the sails he agreed to start the engine.

Although we're more than halfway to Bermuda it seems the least love-able of our crew, the diesel engine, may begin to stand some watches.

When I awoke this morning, a magnificent rainbow covered the western sky. And look! Another sailboat under power paralleling our course beneath the rainbow. I tried to capture this beauty with my camera, but I all I heard when I clicked the shutter was a tiny voice imploring some coffee: my batteries were dead. The other boat, a catamaran, passed us to port at a couple of miles. It's good to dispel the rumor that we are the only vessel afloat upon this broad, broad sea.

Our ice is now consumed. Next will be our diesel, then our water. As we left Virgin Gorda with sixty gallons of bottled water we ought to be within a short swim of Bermuda by the time this commodity's gone.

A Greater Shearwater has overtaken us. She comes and goes, skims the waves with downturned wings, flaps a few times, then skim some more, her wings nearly touching the water. She's a brown and white gull-like bird, rather quiet. Occasionally she settles amid the gentle swells to rest. I haven't seen her catch or eat anything. Perhaps she is only a spiritual vision: the soul of some bygone sailor lost at sea, here to encourage us upon our journey.

Eventually we receive a portion of breeze. It being my trick I swap the running backstay, trim the sails, and attempt to head due north. The breeze veers round to aid me; then veers a bit more. Motor sailing, we race towards Bermuda with expedition. When the skipper lays aloft at noon, he shuts the engine off.

Soon we are on our course and making four knots. Off to the east a couple of miles a rainsquall shares its libation with the sea.. We fall off a couple of points to avoid it – the race is under way! We furl part of the genoa and flatten out the main. We get about twenty knots of breeze and just avoid the rain. We have a glorious ride at hull speed before the squall passes astern.

Then we resume our plodding course to Bermuda. We pass what appears to be a huge ray basking abeam a couple of boat lengths away. A second sailboat under power overtakes us a couple of miles to port, crosses our bow, and heads for Europe.

It's nearly time to log our fourth day's run. Of 826 nautical miles we've covered about five hundred, but the wind south of Bermuda can be fluky. I realize that our trip so far, and for days to come, takes us along the eastern edge of the infamous and arcane Bermuda Triangle. Will something extraordinary happen to us soon? If not, it will be my job, as chronicler of our journey, to come up with a plausible tale. Nothing unforeseen should be left to chance.

The sea is naught but blue and silver ripples; the long swells but a couple of feet in height. What lurks beneath this placid surface? What depraved monsters monitor our voyage?

1 June 2008

Nothing and nothing and nothing for leagues and leagues. Oh, for some rocks! We set the blue and white spinnaker to harness the little breeze. And still there is nothing to see save only clouds in every direction. These you can ponder until you see faces and forms and fictions, but after an hour the mind has wandered away. When at the wheel you must watch this mischievous spinnaker every moment; straying off the wind a few degrees causes the edge of this sail to sag, and then collapse. In seconds this rag can wrap itself round the head stay; lash itself into a tangle. I glare at it and fondle the knife in my pocket.

"Just you try it, lass," I warn it.

The spinnaker smirks and wriggles and flaps. I spin the wheel half a turn, then spin it the opposite way but not as far. The spinnaker fills proudly. It waits until I spot a cloud that looks like the Loch Ness Monster; like the Loch Ness Monster after a hard day's night in some Scottish pub. I can picture this pub. The barmaid comes to the table to take my order.

She's young and pretty and lush. She leans across me to wipe the table. She has the most ripe and voluptuous...

Snap! The spinnaker half collapses, fills, and shudders; again collapses. I hurriedly spin the wheel then spin it back, then spin it in shorter and shorter arcs till the spinnaker stabilizes. *Wanderer*, of course, caracoles through the sea during this interval. The skipper's stern frown dismays the companionway.

"What the devil you doin' up there?" he growls.

Nereid and Porpoise

2 June 2008

Wind has veered around to our quarter. We fly both spinnaker and a small forestaysail whose tack is secured to the weather toe rail. This stay-sail supposedly helps our mainsail draw. My theory is it interferes with the draw of the spinnaker.

Last night as I stood my six to nine watch I espied an empty oil tanker headed across our wake; leaving the States and headed for some eastern oil field.. She passed a couple of miles astern and vanished into the dusk. Our only other company has been a few birds and some Portuguese men - of – war, no doubt headed to Portugal for provisions.

We're closing on the thirtieth parallel. With luck, or breeze, or internal combustion, we should be ashore in two days. No rain or squall for hours and hours and breeze enough to keep us making five knots.

My writer's world has been stripped to its bare necessities: a notebook and a pencil. Without my phone and email and computer I'm no more a member of this twenty-first century than is the Pusslet, probably napping upon my keyboard now, hoping to be reprimanded and have her tail tweaked.

Life in Noank – that far and mist wrapped peninsula whose harbor lies at ten days sail from here – must go on without me. Boats must be prepped and varnished and launched without my guiding hand. And so they are, as they have been centuries past; and so they will be when I am long forgotten. We have such difficulty imagining life without our participation. Around the world, and one street over from ours, people awake and wash and eat and go about their business and have their doubts.

Herb Hilgenberg lived aboard his sailboat, *Southbound II*, at Bermuda for several years. Then the authorities deemed it best, in the interests of civilization, that Herb no longer remain independent of shore. We all know how insularity threatens the security of those who dwell ashore. Self-sufficiency, independence, and freedom of thought are all very well as ideals, but let them be put into practice, and they pose a threat to the sheep who live in the fold. And people who live aboard boats are as insular as they come.

Herb bade farewell to Bermuda and sailed for Nova Scotia. Now he resides near Halifax whence he broadcasts weather patterns and sage advice to mariners traipsing the North Atlantic. From 1600 to 1700 Herb takes shortwave calls at HF/SSB 12359.0 [*Southbound II*] from mariners reporting weather and currents, and dispenses wisdom on courses to steer to avoid the clashing of fronts. Check his website at www3.simpatico.ca/hehilgen/vax498.htm

What are the odds that one might discover the safest route, or course, or channel by which to steer the remainder of one's life? For adverse winds and currents are always with us: squalls during one's forties; cross currents during one's fifties; dangerous shoals during one's sixties; lee shores during one's seventies; staved planks during one's eighties; on the rocks at ninety and in danger of breaking up.

These are the sorts of thoughts one has at one o'clock in the morning at the wheel, when there's nothing ahead save ocean and more ocean, and, except for what's between your toes, you haven't seen terra firma for days and days.

An hour later *Wanderer* yaws while passing over a swell and the spinnaker has its chance to be in the spotlight. Its leeward edge collapses. *Wanderer* lifts with the swell, I spin the wheel, and, suddenly, the spinnaker is wrapped about the head stay. I roar down the companion-way and the skipper appears on deck. In a few minutes the spinnaker has been untangled, reprimanded, and put to work again.

I spend the remainder of my watch glaring at the spinnaker. Its vertical panels of white and aquamarine swell proudly; drive us toward Bermuda. But this is no sail for a dreamer of dreams to tend. The spinnaker tautens and lifts without a wrinkle, and bides its hour.

During the First Mate's watch in the afternoon, the spinnaker gets its chance.

The skipper has just laid aloft with a pan of oatmeal cookies hot from the oven. Just as the First Mate takes one hand from the wheel for a proffered cookie the wind changes, all at once, one hundred degrees, and increases from ten knots to twenty. The spinnaker collapses with a bang and wraps itself, oh, so lovingly, round and round the head stay.

The skipper and I dash forward, still chewing our cookies, to deal with it. To fight with a flogging sail of one-ounce material – material that's seen its share of weather – proves a lost cause. The more we unwind, the more sail for the wind to engage and lash both itself and us. One of the seams begins to part. When half the sail is free of the stay, it flogs itself into two pieces.

It takes us fifteen minutes to get the two pieces of spinnaker back in their bag. We unfurl the genny, trim our sails, and eat a few more cookies. We vote the skipper our pastry chef and award him a berth on our next voyage. We'll now expect cookies and milk each night at bedtime, and trust that he'll tuck in our covers and read us a story.

I have the next watch, from nine till midnight. I check our cross-track error on the GPS: we're four miles west of St. George's harbor with only eighty-three miles left to go.

Eighty-three miles! Why, Bermuda lies just beyond that cloudbank there! Eighty-three miles? We'll be there in time for supper! Dry land! Hot showers! Buildings ashore whose decks don't heave when you try to cross the room!

The mainsail flaps. I look down at the binnacle, and realize I'm twenty degrees off course...

Bermuda

3 June 2008

Twenty miles south of Bermuda and a pod of porpoises frisks about our bow. A greater shearwater circles the boat, her wingtips poised an inch above the water. A fleet of Portuguese men-of-war accompanies us, their nearly transparent, buoyant dorsals visible far off.

Now we can see the hazy shoreline spread the whole northwest quadrant. St. George's [the harbor] serves St. George [the town]. It took us a while to learn the distinction a little apostrophe makes. The harbor lies at the easternmost end of Bermuda; the town halfway up the harbor.

We've been in touch with the immigration authorities and given them an ETA of 1900. They tell us to make contact again when we round the large, black and orange channel marker labeled "SPIT." The wind dies, and we motor the final fifteen miles. The porpoises still leap about our bows, but I can't get a decent photo.

A huge cruise ship departs St. George's and heads due east. A few miles out she runs afoul of a rainbow and snags it on a foredeck cleat. Why would anyone leave a rainbow right in the shipping lane?

At 1800 we round the SPIT and renew contact with immigration and the harbormaster. As the pier at the Customs House is of modest proportions, each vessel must wait her turn. Fortunately, they direct us to proceed immediately. We bring the deflated dinghy on deck and inflate it with the foot pump. We tie it alongside and fix the 4 hp Mercury to it.

St. George's has two narrow channels connecting to the sea. These run close together, separated by Smith Island. Neither channel is wide enough for more than one large vessel. We need to receive clearance from the harbormaster to use a particular channel, even though Immigration has instructed us to proceed.

The harbor is a mile in length and half that in width, and besides having good anchorage, has immense wharfs to accommodate all but the largest vessels. Two huge cruise ships, ten decks high above their waterlines, dock here during our stay.

We secure to the pier at Immigration and take our papers inside. We leave a vociferous seagull to guard our vessel.

As the skipper's wife has faxed our documentation ahead from the States, we need only sign a few papers and pay our fees: US $35 per person.

"Well," says the affable and efficient young woman behind the counter, "you arrived just ahead of the weather."

"Weather?" we ask, and, just then, the heavens open. For fifteen minutes the rain sheets down so heavily, we can't see *Wanderer*, forty yards off, from the doorway.

The skipper smiles. "I believe I left the sliding hatch open," he says.

The young woman proves polite, expeditious, friendly, and considerate. Then she changes hats and becomes the Customs official. Lastly, she lets her hair down and plays the role of Purser. She persuades us to part with a bit of our well-traveled money. We men are always an easy mark for a young, good looking woman. We give her our wallets. In exchange for these she parts with a winsome smile and bids us good evening.

We promptly cast off, motor maybe half a mile, and set our hook in the anchorage known as Convicts' Bay. Then we dinghy ashore in search of supper.

Wanderer's dinghy is actually a bathtub toy the skipper bought for his kids. It holds two adults, if they're friendly, and perhaps two bags of groceries. With a foot of chop, you need foul weather gear, and one of you must bail. As the crew with the least displacement I am appointed Constant Ferryman. Shuttling the other two ashore takes about twenty minutes. At least the outboard motor proves reliable.

*   *   *   *

Tuesday night is festival night in St. George. King's Square, surrounded by the town hall, harbor, and shops, fills with live music and dancing and vendors and a small, appreciative crowd. People of every hue and nationality mingle and dance and shop. A few of the dancers have similar costumes and masks, but I'm not familiar with the characters or the theme. Were I alone I'd spend the evening dancing, then think about food. Instead I accompany two staid, elderly [one year older than I am] mariners who very much want their supper. Life is too precious not to dance at every opportunity.

This isn't a frivolous party town with discothèques and floor shows. This is a staid, small, British town where almost nothing happens. A crowd of one hundred watching two dozen people dance constitutes a happening. St George is a tiny, island town that hasn't changed much in the past four hundred years. The buildings boast only two stories; you won't see any neon lights or billboards; there's no fast food; no chain of coffee shops. Dogs sleep in the village square in the shade of the ancient pillory. Buildings are of brick or stucco, in white or muted colors; the roofs are of unglazed pantiles; the narrow streets of paving stones; the many fences and lamp posts of wrought iron.

The tour ships, moored a short walk away, provide their own amusement. There is music and dance and frivolity half the night, long after the locals have said their prayers and retired. The energy expended by a tour boat to keep her thousands of lights bulbs lit over twenty four hours would keep St. George illuminated for a month.

We enter the George and Dragon and go upstairs. The dining room is empty, but the balcony overlooking the festivities below is packed to overflowing with a dozen people. We sit within, marveling that the deck moves very little. We also remark how the dishes and glasses don't slide off the table. The fish and chips my shipmates have prove delicious. My curried shrimp is superb. Of course: the staff of the George and Dragon are all Indian.

By the time we finish supper it's nine o'clock. The festivities cease; the street lights come on; the square is deserted. Only the pubs stay open: all three of them. The two monstrous tour ships, a world apart, have just begun to ramp up for the night ahead. They seem some sort of anomaly – huge pale monsters intent on taking over this tiny community. Imagine two spaceships - acres across, taller than trees, glowing with millions of watts of incandescence, throbbing with air conditioners, generators, and multiple bands – sitting in your backyard month after month.

The staircase of the George and Dragon ripples only slightly as we make our way below. At the concrete town pier we descend the worn, tide lapped stair to our dinghy. I ferry each of my yawning mates the quarter mile to *Wanderer*. I have a flashlight in case I encounter another vessel, but the harbor is still. Most of the anchored vessels are dark. Sailors tend to rise early, retire early.

I secure the dinghy astern of *Wanderer* as the dark absorbs the dusk. We share a final cocktail liberally spiced with conversation. About us are anchored the vessels of a dozen nations. A breeze passes over the island and flutters the fronds of the palms. Our three hatches stand open, and the cabin below has cooled. At ten o'clock the three of us stumble below. I anticipate a sleep with no interruptions.

Should anyone wake me at three to take the wheel, I'll wring his neck.

4 June 2008

Took a deliciously lazy day and contrived, with assiduous perseverance, to accomplish nearly nothing.

I ferried the three of us into the village, wending among the few dozen sailboats tethered in Convict's Bay, and commented on their rigs and shear and seaworthiness and the number of socks drying on their life-lines. Once ashore we split up and wandered and shopped. I took enough pictures to get a sense of the Old World-ness of the village. Eventually we convened and returned to *Wanderer*.

*   *   *   *

The First Mate and I determined to do our laundry. The skipper, having been to Bermuda a couple of times before, suggested we go to the yacht club. We would also be able to take hot showers there. Hot showers! We sailors get excited about the most mundane of events. But when was the last time you went eight days without immersing your body in hot water? If you don't want to tell me, I completely understand. Is that your lovely ketch over there by the seawall? I believe there's a radish growing behind your ear...

The yacht club perches by the edge of the harbor away from the center of town. It boasts a tiny, enclosed basin having thirty slips and a dinghy dock. From that you climb a steel ladder to the top of the sea wall surrounding the basin and walk around to the shore.

The modest, two-story, new fashioned building consists of a dining facility surmounted by a recreation room and lounge with a small bar at one end. The showers and laundry room are at the ground level, accessible from without. Both levels have covered decks the length of the building. If you need to know more than this get in your boat and set a course for the most remote part of the North Atlantic and sail about until you fetch up at St George's. Bring your own dirty laundry.

Primed with the knowledge that the laundry machines required Bermudan dollars, and the showers required tokens available only at the bar, and the bar opened every afternoon at four, we went to the bank and exchanged our US dollars for an equal number of Bermudan one-dollar coins. Bermuda, though a British territory, accepted US dollars as their standard in 1972. The local currency still circulates, but is viable only in Bermuda: one nine billionth of the surface of this earth.

Despite this miniscule drawback, Bermudan paper currency is printed in cheery bright colors with the full-face portrait of Queen Elizabeth printed on their fronts. Denominations are two and five and ten and twenty and fifty and one hundred. The coinage is similar to ours, the largest being one dollar. All feature Queen Elizabeth's profile on their fronts; the dollar has a sailboat on its obverse.

We motored to the yacht club with our laundry and our dollars. Water is at a premium here, and washing our clothes proved only slightly less expensive than purchasing new outfits. Having gotten our washers started we went to the bar to purchase shower tokens. The barmaid wasn't sure how much hot water a two dollar token purchased. We bought two apiece and dove into the showers. Turns out a token supplies about five minutes of hot, hot water: more than enough to revel beneath the nozzle.

Clean and shining, we sat at the bar and sipped tall, cool drinks and awaited our clothes. The barmaid displayed Bermudan currency for us from the till. We watched a tennis match on TV and debated whether or not the game would ever be popular on sailboats in the under forty-foot range, and, if so, where would be best to convince the skipper of *Wanderer* to string the net.

I walked about and admired the plaques and pictures adorning the walls. Horrors! We'd been calling this organization "The St. George Yacht Club." The official name is "The St. George Dinghy and Sports Club." This being Bermuda, the sporting thing to do is to moor your dinghy, then row ashore in your yacht.

We walked about the veranda. This afforded a gull's eye view of *Wanderer* on her anchor, as well as a panorama of the harbor. We retrieved our clothes and motored aboard, clean beyond comprehension.

I should also note how enlightened we were, having left half pound of grime apiece in the clubhouse shower drains.

The skipper has been studying weather patterns and listening to Herb Hilgenberg on the shortwave. He avers that our best window for clement weather will open sooner than later. We had planned to stay in Bermuda between two and five days; now he plans to shove off by tomorrow evening. Our stay here will have been barely forty-eight hours.

He suggests I spend my final day at the far end of Bermuda at the Royal Naval Dockyards. This was an active naval base from the War of 1812 till World War II, and contains a museum, shops, an arsenal, gun emplacements, fortifications, and photo opportunities without end.

I've purchase a one-day transit pass that entitles me to use all ferry and bus services on the islands. The high-speed ferry departs St George's and returns at half past three. The skipper will clear our departure with immigration and meet me at the ferry slip. We should get underway by 1700.

This evening we share a final dinner at the White Horse Tavern, which fronts the harbor. We eat on the porch, the placid waters lapping along the wall beside our table. The hundred-foot-tall cruise ship obstructs most of our view, but on this side of it spreads a little park on Ordinance Island, connected to shore by a tiny bridge. A statue of Admiral Sir George Somers, inadvertent founder of Bermuda when his ship, *Sea Venture*, was driven ashore during a storm in 1609, dominates this park. Some canon and wrought iron lamp posts and swaying palm trees improve the view. Mothers with infants stroll about the island.

Between this park and the White Horse lies a small inlet housing a gaudily painted charter fishing boat. Farther along the sea wall by which we dine moors a forty-foot sloop. Half dozen people board her and she casts off for an elegant evening sail about the harbor.

This time tomorrow Bermuda will fall astern as we set a course for Portland, Maine.

*   *   *   *

5 June 2008

It's time to go ashore to catch the ferry. This is a high-speed catamaran that carries two hundred passengers, and makes the twelve mile trip along the north shore of Bermuda in half an hour, including getting in and out of two harbors. Once we round the old fortress at Tobacco bay, the northernmost point of land in all Bermuda, the ferry skipper gives his seahorses their heads. We tear along the northern shore with its colorful stuccoed houses.

On the outer side of King's Wharf of the Royal Naval Dockyard moors the inevitable huge white cruise ship. Within the fortified breakwaters two marinas provide slips and a few moorings to hundreds of yachts. Numerous tugs and working vessels and larger yachts share a basin, The Camber, deep within the harbor.

Massive walls and fortifications surround the entire harbor and building complex. The most conspicuous building now is known as the Clock Tower Mall, formerly the Great Eastern Storehouse. Built in 1856, it boasts a pair of 100' clock towers, one of which displays the time of high tide. The Keep, the highest and most defensible portion of this complex, now houses the Maritime Museum, and includes the huge Commissioners House, now filled with artifacts. This dockyard was built mostly by slaves and convicts, and much of this museum is dedicated to the deplorable labors and living conditions of these many unfortunates.

Nowadays, most of the shops that supplied or repaired wooden ships of war have been converted to artisans' workshops, restaurants, and emporiums. After trudging about with my camera, I stop at the Frog and Onion to have some lunch. The name derives from its founders: a Frenchman and a Bermudan. This pub fills a large stone apartment having a high ceiling and a fireplace large enough for two couples to dance in. On a chilly and damp Bermudan night, a cord of wood might take the chill from this room. The fish chowder I lunch upon has a rich, dark sherry base and tastes delicious.

I spend my time taking picture after picture. Arched gate, flowered embankment, tower, canon, tree, tugboat, architrave, stone dolphin pool.

For a fee you can swim with half tame dolphins and share their buoyant energy. After four hours I gladly collapse within the ferry, which whisks me back to St. George's. The skipper meets me, and we dinghy back to *Wanderer*. Sightseeing now gives way to piloting out of the crowded harbor.

We stow the dinghy and motor aboard, uncover the mainsail, start the diesel, and haul the anchor. I take the helm as we putter among anchored boats. The harbormaster gives us our final clearance and wishes us well.

I round the outermost channel marker and set a course of 060 to pass just seaward of the Northeast Breakers. We motor this first hour as we need to charge our batteries. When we round the lighthouse we raise our main, unfurl our genny, and set a course of 357 for Maine.

Farewell, Bermuda!

Neptune
Royal Naval Dockyards, Bermuda

En Route to Casco Bay, Maine

6 June 2008

Our first day out from Bermuda the wind and seas pick up a bit. By my second watch, 0300 to 0600, I find the helm a bit arduous. When the skipper lays aloft to relieve me we take a reef in the main, which helps considerably. We continue toward New England at a steady six knots.

By afternoon, the wind backs and blows straight out of the north, and we're forced to head four points off our course. It also calms till we make but three knots. The skipper decides to douse the jib, flatten the main, and motor dead upwind, directly on course.

At 1600 we tune in *Southbound II* and listen to Herb Hilgenberg discuss the weather patterns we're likely to meet. He speaks of easterly breezes north of Bermuda. After seven hours of motoring the wind veers enough to allow us to point within thirty degrees of our rhumb line. We shut down the diesel.

It has cooled off. We wear long sleeves and long trousers. After all, we've just passed 35 north. The sultry tropic isles recede, and the next land we'll see, or maybe not see, will be Cape Cod, Massachusetts. We log just over one hundred miles per day.

7 June 2008

During my morning watch, 0600 to 0900, I find I can steer a bit higher. The wind blows nearly northeast. Today, for me, proves memorable. It is warm and clear with gentle three foot swells that undulate and recede. And suddenly, a misty plume; and another. Then, just off the port bow, a sleek black back.

"Whale, ho, lads!" I whisper down the companionway, and the other two tumble up on deck, half dressed, clutching their cameras. The whale basks fifty yards abeam and totally ignores us. We never see more than fifteen or twenty feet of her gleaming back. I offer her coffee and biscuits if she'll come alongside and pose, but, like most women, she pays me no attention.

We leave her astern – the very first whale I've seen in the wild near to. Immediately, the breeze increases and veers a point in our favor – we're back on course! I send the whale my thanks and keep *Wanderer* as close to the wind as possible.

An hour later the wind blows foul; then doesn't blow at all. We need another whale. Again we furl the jib, flatten the main, and motor.

Five bottlenose dolphins come and cavort alongside. After ten minutes they arch their backs in tight formation to bid us farewell, and vanish. The sea remains calm – so very, very calm. Five porpoises have not the heft of one whale when it comes to wind.

Another day should bring us to the southern edge of the Gulf Stream where it turns to the east to clear the New England coast. At this point it will have a width of nearly eighty miles and the current will set us easterly at nearly a knot and a half. It will take us most of a day to cross it. We expect it to be slightly warmer; support more surface marine life; and attract more birds. All about us spreads this ceaseless sea: this ruffled carpet upon whose surface our little sailboat prances – putting one dainty forefoot after another.

8 – 9 June

Lots of Ocean, a bit of wind – not much else. Oh, for some rocks!

10-11 June 2008

Today we cross the Gulf Stream. I peep from the companionway, expecting to see meadow flowers; bird laden maples and sycamores; dappling shadows; a stream with a stony bottom; a shoeless lad with a fishing pole in search of the wily trout. There are only sullen rollers and the stony face of the sea.

"Another delusion," I mutter.

What sort of stream is this? It isn't the least like the cheerful stream that sped by the back of our barn when I was a boy; not the least little bit.

The Gulf Stream begins its peregrinations south of the Yucatan Peninsula. As it rounds the tip of Florida it narrows and accelerates. Between Florida and the Bahamas it runs at four knots or more. Off

Cape Hatteras it widens, slows, but contains twice as much water. It swings east, then divides. The north fork, The North Atlantic Drift, continues north to the Grand Banks east of Nova Scotia before it continues east to the British Isles. The southern fork, The Azores Current, heads southeastward to Africa. The North Equatorial Current, which flows from Africa west to the Caribbean, helps renew the Gulf Stream.

At its fullest the Gulf Stream carries 100 times the water of all of the rivers that feed the Atlantic Ocean. It varies from fifty to ninety miles in breadth; from 500 to 700 feet in depth. It conveys 100 times the world's demand for energy, as heat. When man has learned to harness the sun, the wind, the sea, there will be enough power to spare.

*   *   *   *

I take my trick at the helm and spot a whale. She basks on the surface, dead ahead, and I need to change course to avoid her. An hour later, the same thing occurs again. The whales here are lazy and lack motivation. They can't even be troubled to avoid us hapless tourists. You'd think the cooler water here would stimulate them to work. There's nothing so demoralizing as thick headed non-producers who obstruct progress. At least ashore they all tend to congregate in the nation's capital, and I know enough to plot my course around that.

The wind dies, and we start the motor again. After it runs a few minutes it, too, dies. At least we're beyond the dreaded Bermuda Triangle, but perhaps we are now in the clutches of the equally infamous New England Trapezoid.

As the skipper has added a jerry can of fresh fuel to the tank, we take a sample. It is filthy. Someone left the gate to the pasture open, and the cows have been wading in the fuel again. We change the fuel filter. The engine runs a few minutes then stops. We bleed the fuel line. The same thing happens. We break the fuel line and crank the engine. Little fuel comes out. The line and pickup are clogged with filth. There's no way to empty the tank or reach inside it. Blowing back through the fuel line to clear it allows the engine some fuel for only a couple of minutes Using the inflatable dinghy's foot pump to clear the line proves futile.

The wind has tired of waiting for us and returns to give us a lift. We surge northward toward Cape Cod at nearly six knots. The air grows decidedly cool. We keep on messing about with the engine – we'll need it sooner or later. I suggest we run the engine directly from another Jerry can. We hook this up, bleed the line, and, Voilá! We run the engine twenty minutes then tuck it in for its nap.

We pass between Cape Cod and George's Bank. Another twenty-four hours should bring us close to Casco Bay, our destination. We have a fair breeze and *Wanderer* will sail herself when close to the wind. I turn in wearing my safety harness as the skipper takes the helm.

I'm dreaming about a mermaid of my acquaintance when the skipper lays below to get his jacket. *Wanderer*, inexplicably, takes a notion to come about on her own. I'm thrown against the lee cloth and nearly crush the mermaid. The skipper flies up the companionway and I tumble up the ladder. I clip on my lanyard and scuttle about the cold deck in my underwear, helping put *Wanderer* to rights.

"She never does this," says the skipper.

I go below and apologize to the mermaid. I put on plenty of warm clothes and relieve the skipper at the helm. We now wear fleeces and coveralls and windbreakers and woolen watch caps and gloves when on deck. The temperature of the water is under fifty; the air not much warmer. I look about and can't see a single palm tree.

By morning we pass Massachusetts Bay, but fifty miles off shore. We won't see land until we get to Maine. All the next day we sail close reached on a healthy breeze out of the west. Someone leaves the cold water running. Some other inconsiderate person leaves the front door open. The sea grows chilly, and there's a decided draft. We bundle up as we pass Cape Ann.

I scan the sky for snowflakes. After all, it's only June eleventh. Hopefully, Casco Bay won't be iced in. We meet a flock of penguins flying south. We're only twelve hundred miles from the Arctic Circle. Can civilization flourish this far north?

Casco Bay, Maine

12 June 2008

Early in the morning, well before daybreak, we spot the light at Cape Elizabeth, Maine. We drag out our paper chart as our antique GPS hasn't a chart plotter. Now we need to pay attention and identify channel markers and lights ashore. We work our way in, all three of us on deck. By daybreak we pick out the old lighthouse at Portland Head and enter the channel leading to South Portland.

The skipper has a mooring just south of Spring Point. We short tack up the passage and through the mooring field until we find it. We head up and snag it just in time for breakfast. Up goes our yellow flag; off come our safety harnesses. We make a large pot of coffee and sit about the cockpit commending ourselves for the good time we've made this passage. After breakfast we prepare to motor to Portland to Immigration.

Just for fun we start up the diesel. It runs for a minute, then dies. We bleed the fuel system, then try again. We sacrifice two halibut and a pot of coffee to propitiate the god of internal combustion. We curse the injectors with epithets that we've brought all the way from the British Virgin Islands in a waterproof bag.

The breeze and the tide have turned against us. We call Immigration and ask if they make house calls. The best they can do is to meet us at Spring Point Marina in South Portland, just over a mile upwind against the tide. There's scarcely breeze enough and hardly room to tack upstream and make headway.

We inflate the dinghy and lash it alongside *Wanderer*. We strap on the four horse Mercury and hope it starts right up. It does. I clamber down into the dinghy as the first mate casts off our pendant and the skipper takes the wheel. It takes a few minutes for *Wanderer* to make any headway. The one-foot chop comes in over the bow of the inflatable. In minutes I am wet from the waist down. I need to give the motor all of its throttle to keep us going forward at half a knot. I call for a bailer.

One of my pontoons begins to lose air. If you want some fun, pump up

Thacher's Island Lights

your inflatable as cold water fills your pockets; steer the boat with your third hand and bail with your toes. We try to round the breakwater too soon, and lose steerageway. We fall off quickly as I continue to pump and bail. We slosh a tight circle and have at it once again. We clear the breakwater, barely, on the second attempt. Inside South Portland Harbor the sea subsides. I crank the little Mercury and keep bailing.

After an hour and a half, we make fast along a walkway at Spring Point Marina. I climb aboard, wring myself out, and, closing both eyes tight, visualize a hot shower. The two Immigration and Customs officials come by for a friendly visit and welcome us home. As soon as they leave, we douse our yellow flag and dash for the showers. The skipper makes arrangements for the local mechanic to commune with *Wanderer's* motor. The following day she'll return to her mooring for the summer.

Once I rinse Casco Bay out of my hair, I feel most lubberly. We convene at the pier head restaurant and stuff ourselves with hot grub. I'll take the bus from Portland to Providence, Rhode Island that leaves in a couple of hours. The first mate has found a flight back to Colorado. After we eat we return to *Wanderer* to pack our remaining gear. I have one bottle of Caribbean rum that I carefully swaddle in a hefty contingent of soiled clothes deep within my duffle. I manage to cram nearly everything within this bulging sack. All I need is a brawny stevedore to heft it up the gangway. Next time I'll pack a mermaid who isn't so plump. I also have a smaller bag that holds my camera and notebooks and binoculars.

As I squat alongside *Wanderer* at the walkway, cramming the last few items into my duffle, she suddenly surges against the pier and sloshes me one last time. The North Atlantic drizzles out one leg of my only pair of dry trousers. It will all evaporate in an hour or two. If the folks on the bus presume I have wet myself, that's their lookout. Maybe they'll leave me the pair of seats to myself. I fish the last bit of bladderwort from my pocket, shake hands with my mates, and kiss *Wanderer* farewell. I shoulder my bag and drip my way up the pier.

As Ratty was wont to say to Mole, "What's a little wet to a water rat?"

I'm home well in time for supper, which I eat standing up with one foot braced against the dining room window.

More Yarns from my Tapestry

I don't really recollect much of my purportedly formative years. Then someone totally irresponsible insisted I accompany him on a boat propelled by the wind. While I stood in the cockpit and expostulated on the foolishness of such a novel idea, he put the helm down, hard.

That was just the beginning of my notable sailing career. Since being struck on the head by that boom, I've owned fourteen different vessels, and have sailed as far as the wilds of Massachusetts. I would have picked up a mooring and maybe even ventured ashore, but the launch driver motored out to me and demanded I show him my passport. I presumed he was speaking English but at times I wasn't quite sure. Their language hasn't as many consonants in its alphabet as ours, and one of its vowels is pronounced in a way that the local sheep can't fail to understand it. I figured it was safer to remain aboard where I wouldn't be exposed to that local affliction the natives refer to as "chow-dah."

Nonetheless, I've had some memorable passages.

My very first sail single handed I took some very elemental precautions. As soon as I'd cleared the breakwater at our harbor, I secured the tiller so I couldn't get into trouble. I sheeted the main as tight as I could and secured the jib sheet as well. My boat fell off the wind a couple of points and the jib attempted to cross from port to starboard. "Ah hah!" said I. "You won't get away with that!" And so I remained hove to that whole afternoon, and slowly drifted with the tide until I wafted slowly into the harbor of the next town down the coast, where the natives proved friendly. I wafted gently up to a pier, put out my fenders and made fast for the night. I can't understand why people think sailing takes any particular skill. I dropped my sails and went ashore for a truly memorable meal at the local clam shack. The following day, I called a friend who helped me start my motor to clear the harbor. I hoisted my sails and made the four miles back to my mooring in just a bit less than two days.

Since then I've learned a lot about seamanship. I not only know how to splice the main brace, but I know how to reef before my mast starts dipping into the water. I can program my GPS all by myself and know not to trouble the Coast Guard on channel sixteen when I'm out of coffee. Why they don't consider this an emergency I haven't the faintest idea. Bridge tenders don't seem to know about coffee either. Aside from that, and the fact that they can't explain why the Red Sox didn't win the pennant this season, I've always found them polite and well informed.

In a few more years, I hope to have acquired the knowledge and skill to circumnavigate the entire state of Connecticut single handed. And after I have, I'll be sure to return and tell you all my adventures.

13 January

Sitting down to a breakfast of oatmeal and raisins aboard *MoonWind* at Shennecossett Yacht Club. It's 0812 and it remains foggy and misty. Forecast calls for sunbeams and fifty degrees, but what do they know?

I got under way from West Cove in Noank about 1130 yesterday only to find little of either wind or visibility. Well, what would you expect on a winter's day when the temperature is in the forties and the seals are basking shamelessly in the nude?

I motored out past Mouse Island and hauled up my larger genoa. My plan was to sail west to the Connecticut River – land of my mis-spent youth – ascend as far as Hadlyme where I grew up, and anchor for a couple of days of rest and elaboration.

I'd even brought my kayak to do some exploring. I had my wetsuit, plenty of grub, some reading material, my camera, and an empty notebook in which to record more lies for my doting readers.

What the forecast neglected to mention was visibility, or lack thereof. At noon time I could see about three miles, and as I almost made progress against the tide I thought I would probably see almost anything larger than a submarine before I ran it under.

Besides, thought I, I have my GPS. I switched it on and waited for it to greet all those handy satellites whirling about the earth. And waited. And waited. Meanwhile, I admired Groton Long Point for most of an hour while I debated raising my main and shaking out my winter's reef. Having both sails would assure me of making twice my forward progress – a half knot instead of a quarter. With both my sails, my long johns and my dish towel flying it shouldn't take me over a week to make the sixteen miles to the Breakwater Light at the mouth of the Connecticut.

Then the gale abated. My genoa slatted listlessly; my wind vane twirled carelessly at the mast head. With a sigh I started my motor. I dropped the genny and secured it with a bungee. The storm might resume momentarily, and I needed to be ready. Then I set a course due west and headed for… all that white stuff. I checked my non-cooperative GPS. It smiled at me and showed me its screen with a dozen satellites spinning merrily just above *MoonWind*'s mast. But none of them chose to come down to play with us. [Three weeks later I learned from an online chat room how to reboot my GPS so the satellites would cooperate.]

The visibility slowly diminished from three miles to two; then to one. I would need to hurry. I revved my motor till I was making six knots and set a course for nearby Pine Island Sound. At two miles I could nearly discern Pine Island – a darker mass disappearing beneath a dull white mantle. A misty rain descended, and I needed to wipe my glasses every few minutes. Fortunately, I'd chosen to wear my wetsuit.

At least I could see all the lobster pots and their tiny wakes in the tide. I soon could hear the bell at the harbor mouth, barely activated by the ebbing tide. Fishers Island Sound resembled the local mill pond. If you haven't seals in your local mill pond I can always ship you a couple.

By two o'clock – fourteen hundred to those of you who sail – I had shoved the dreary fog aside and snuck into Pine Island Sound. I found my summer slip at my friendly yacht club and tucked *MoonWind* into it. It was strangely quiet and deserted and eerie as the fog closed in about me - the only boat in the water. Pine Island, four hundred yards away, gradually disappeared. When the walkway lights came on I could just discern the end of the pier.

I gladly sat down to belated lunch and read a detective novel. I made a cup of hot coffee as my reward for not being stupid enough to continue into the fog without GPS. Ah, decadence! In no time at all, it was time for dinner. I took a constitutional up the pier between meals and watched a loon on her way back from the fish market.

The temperature dropped into the upper thirties. I put on my parka and read and ate and read and ate some more. I tucked into my sleeping bag in my long johns, sweater, and watch cap and read some more till all the mermaids came home.

18 March 2013

It's almost too chilly this morning to write with this ball point pen, but no ice in my whiskers, so a fair day looms ahead. Again I'm anchored behind little Gardener Island in Point Judith Pond. Yesterday's forecast declared mid-fifties with a gentle, westerly breeze, and an all afternoon ebb tide - both propitious for shoving *MoonWind* on her merry way eastward from West Cove in Noank to that wilderness known to us locals as Rhode Island.

Well, I bent on my larger genoa and shook out my winter reef. After all, spring was officially arrived with bushels of pert crocuses and bags of mild Zephyrs. In Fishers Island Sound all was indeed pleasant. I got underway at half past noon to catch the first of the ebb. My buxom genoa swelled in the six-knot breeze; my loosened mainsail filled; and I wafted eastward at a sedate three knots.

But Father Poseidon was basking on the reef by Wicopesset, a delighted gleam in his eye.

"Testing the waters so early, Lad?" said he. "Wouldn't you like a wee bit more excitement? I wouldn't want you to doze off at the helm."

Fortunately, it wasn't much more than a wee bit. As it was, it took me an hour to sand my finger imprints out of the tiller.

The breeze increased to fifteen knots and the tidal surge to five footers. The wind blew nearly dead astern and *MoonWind* thought it proper to fly her sails wing and wing. Already it was too late to try to reef. My preventer kept my mainsail close to the shrouds, while my booming jib shook the boat as it alternately collapsed then filled as *MoonWind* climbed the backs at five knots, then yawed down the fronts at eight. My cell phone, binoculars, and water bottle were flung about the cockpit.

Even steering as small as I could I verged on losing control. A few times the wind got behind my main and *MoonWind* skidded down the waves on her ear. My course on this tack brought me closer to shore; if I headed up four points, my jib behaved, but I had the sea on my beam. Plus this took me farther from Harbor of Refuge. After three hours of ardent plunging a little refuge seemed a worthy objective.

As I approached the sea wall round the harbor, I worried I might meet a Block Island ferry at the breach way and run her under. The water around the second breach way looked far less turbulent. I headed out to sea for a bit until I was nearly to it, came up a bit, removed my preventer, hardened both sails, then put the helm down, hard. *MoonWind* came into irons, stalled, and the wind and sea forced her back in a trice.

"Well, then Lass, let's see how you like to jibe," said I, and spun her round on her heel. *MoonWind* adores jibing; it's as close to pirouetting as makes no nevermind.

Round she went, and I set a beam reach toward the windward edge of the breach way. I had let go the genny when I jibed her, having both hands full of other matters, and the jib had turned wrong side out. I fell off the wind and attempted to haul the jib back where it belonged. The knotted loop where my jib sheets met snagged on the head stay, of course. With every second the wind and tide, though somewhat abated, swept me past my mark.

I headed back up and left the pounding jib to fend for itself. In ten minutes time I tucked behind the seawall. Here was only a two foot chop. I could actually stand without holding on to something. I motor sailed across the harbor, wrestled with my genoa, and dropped my mainsail into her lazy jacks. I went below and replenished my water bottle. My mouth was parched, and my arms ached, but here we were, safe and dry. My standing rigging and sails were still intact.

I motored up the placid channel between the jetties and up the pond - past the docked ferries and the fishing fleet to starboard; past the empty pleasure boat piers to port. I traipsed my way up to uninhabited Gardiner Island, overlooked by vacant summer houses; rounded it; coasted to a halt; then let down my anchor. The tide had now turned and carried me up the pond. I let out ninety feet of roding then snubbed it on the cleat. *MoonWind* set her anchor, then cast a longing glance at a weedy boulder astern. I've learned, during the past ten years, to respect her glances. I rigged my anchor sentinel with a twenty-pound lead weight.

The sun was low as I stowed my jib, secured my main, made things all-a-taut-o, and thought about lunch.

28 April 2013

I approached Connecticut's Stonington Point about 1600 yesterday to find myself amid a regatta of little sailboats. I had passed the outer breakwater, and just doused *MoonWind*'s sails, and started her motor, as the breeze would be blowing from dead ahead as I followed the channel toward Watch Hill. As soon as the regatta jibed for the mouth of

Stonington Harbor, I gave *MoonWind* some throttle, and sprinted toward Sandy Point.

I'm now anchored behind Napatree Point beside Watch Hill Harbor. Napatree is a mile-long neck of land fronting the sea with a shallow, sheltered cove, Little Narragansett Bay, behind it. The name Napatree came from "nape of trees" – a wooded neck. Now there is scarcely shrubbery, let alone a tree, the length of this neck. The Great Gale of 1815 destroyed the trees. The numerous summer houses built here later were swept away by the Hurricane of 1938 – now remembered by none save ancient folk.

That same hurricane cleared a half mile breach between the end of Napatree and that shoreward pointing isle whose northern tip is Sandy Point. As this breach way is shoal, most of us boaters must wend the mile-long channel that begins at Sandy Point, and parallels the Stonington shore until it reaches the mouth of the Pawcatuck River. If you turn due south and run along the Rhode Island shore for half a mile, you'll fetch up at Watch Hill Harbor.

The channel also ascends the Pawcatuck River for a few miles. Both along the shore and up the river you must not extravagate – in many places the water beside the channel is shoal, and you shouldn't disturb the egrets who are stalking beside your boat.

Along the backside of Napatree Point is an anchorage sufficient for hundreds of boats – at least they think so. One hundred boats can anchor comfortably there with room to swing. Two hundred vessels ensure you will stay awake half the night to see whose anchoring scope is greater than yours. Three hundred boats ensure you will have more company in your cockpit than you ever bargained for.

Actually, the bottom holds anchors well. Were it not for three or more rafting boats attempting to share one anchor... but that's another story. I trust that wasn't you I roused at five AM in the center sloop as your boat and her two companions dragged into *MoonWind*.

Yesterday afternoon when I traipsed in here there were but three power boats anchored. Only one spent the night. I dropped my hook in nine feet of water and paid out lots of scope. Fortunately, the tide hereabouts seldom exceeds three feet. I let out 100' of roding with a 20 lb sentinel.

My neighbor anchored a quarter mile away. A five-knot gale was forecast for the evening.

The harbor at Watch Hill, bereft of boats, proved quiet. During boating season, an active fleet of "Watch Hill 15's" moors here. These are Herreshoff sloops with a fifteen-foot waterline, a variation of the "Buzzards Bay 15:" a slim, tender, open, centerboard racing craft with plenty of sail; 24' 6" overall length with a modest 6' 8" beam.

Another fixture of Watch Hill Harbor is the beautiful "*Aphrodite*," our lovely goddess of these local waters. A 74' motor cruiser with a deep blue whaleback hull and magnificent bright work deckhouse, she was built in 1937 as a commuter yacht, and both rebuilt and renovated just a few years ago. She was relaunched by Maine's Brooklin Boatyard in 2005 following 45,000 hours of restoration. She graces nearby Mystic Seaport's Wooden Boat Show each summer. You are welcome aboard to admire her if you first remove your shoes.

Watch Hill is a village that comes alive in warm weather. Its swank hotels and stately houses stand quiet this time of year. Its high end boutiques and restaurants await the bloom of summer. The antique carousel at the foot of the village is closed; the little horses remain in their stalls awaiting fresh paint, and a chance to flaunt their luxurious, horsehair manes.

Only the lighthouse stays busy this time of year, alternating her red and white lights to keep sailors from her shoals. From where *MoonWind* lies placidly tethered I can also see the lighthouse at Latimer Reef beyond the breach way. The air being still, I can hear the automated, double bell from this tower, and the single horns from both the breakwater light and Watch Hill Lighthouse. Off Napatree Point a bell buoy adds her random voice to the mix.

Despite this muted clamor I sleep quite well. The nearly full moon shimmers on the rippled bay. I snuggle into my sleeping bag in *MoonWind*'s quarter berth, pull my watch cap over my ears, and readily forget the shore where landsmen work and worry.

6 May

It's time *MoonWind* and I had a little talk. The last two times we went out sailing I wanted to ascend the Connecticut River to visit my former

Lighthouse - Watch Hill, Rhode Island

haunts. Somehow, we wound up both times in Rhode Island, which lies in the opposite direction. Despite having lived in Rhode Island for seven years I'm still not accepted as a native son. Every time I request they serve me cream in my clam chowdah they demand to see my visa.

MoonWind, being more a cosmopolite than I, isn't so assertive about her diet. A helping of breeze and a cupful of brine suffice her. Consequently, we spent two overnights in Rhode Island this April.

"It has to do with the tides," *MoonWind* explained to me.

Apparently, it's beneficial to have the tide behind you both going and coming. When the wind blows only four knots this makes a difference. When it blows fifteen, *MoonWind* wants to go as fast as she's able. It seems sensible as *MoonWind* explains it to me. Perhaps I shouldn't leave those tide tables aboard where she can peruse them.

One of these weeks the tide must surely run in my direction, that is to say, westerly. Last weekend we spent in Westerly, Rhode Island, which, from here, lies easterly. It sometimes grows confusing. I have one of my senior moments and *MoonWind* nudges the tiller the other way, and, anyway, Watch Hill, in Westerly, proved a very good place to visit. This time of year there was plenty of room to swing on our hook behind Napatree Beach. That is to say, only one other boat anchored there over-night. We were so far apart that *MoonWind* couldn't be bothered to drag her anchor.

It's only twelve miles from the mouth of the Thames, where *MoonWind* summers, to the mouth of the Connecticut. I think we may make it there before the snow flies. Then we can ascend amid the wooded islands and shouldering hills; pass the reedy salt marshes startling with redwings; traipse by the mouths of gorging estuaries; watch the osprey linger aloft while she waits to commune with a fish.

I grew up by the Connecticut and hadn't dry feet until I was thirty years old. I fished and foraged, paddled and rafted, sailed and bathed in this river. I thought I might live on my island forever and ever. This is the idyll I've striven for in my stories. I've actually come to believe in it myself. The last time we passed Whalebone Cove, I saw Ratty and Mole in their little boat, languidly rowing down river to stately Toad Hall in time for tea.

That's another matter on my agenda. I mean to demand of *MoonWind* that tea be served at 1600 hours, no matter what. A six foot chop is no excuse for not receiving sustenance at the helm. Lapsang Souchong and hot ginger scones would be preferable, but *MoonWind* argues that baking scones can be problematic seeing as she hasn't an oven. She suggests I chase another raisin about the cockpit, and anticipate a lovely, hot lunch about nightfall.

Another item on my agenda is neatness. *MoonWind* is not the tidiest lady I know. Her fenders lie about her deck in abandoned poses, their naked bellies visible through the rents in their shabby covers. Her spinnaker halyard, unused these many years, has grown nearly as green as *MoonWind*'s hull. The shackle on her anchor chain is rusty. There are splotches of epoxy on the lids of her cockpit lockers. And her cabin!

If I didn't love *MoonWind* as I do, I'd never cohabit with her. Her galley is a disgrace. Her dining table needs a good wash. There are dirty mugs in the sink. Whenever I bring these to her attention, *MoonWind* just shrugs and responds, "If you don't like the mess do something about it, and quit your infernal whining!" So, sometimes, I do. I dab at the galley with her weary sponge, wipe down the table and the cutting board, and, occasionally, even roll up the sleeping bag. After a night with *MoonWind* I'm fortunate if the sleeping bag isn't wrong side out. We do share good times together.

Especially when the ripe breeze heals, and the tame waves slake, and we fly across the sun warmed sea for mile after mile; when *MoonWind* breasts the brunt of the tide, and her sails swell voluptuously, and her smooth and gleaming flank glistens with spray; when we agree that a muddy anchor detracts so very little from the thrill of sailing; when, as dusk descends, we wend a familiar channel to our favorite anchorage. Wherever that is.

17 July 2013

The moon was green, and the sea was yellow as Captain Salty Whiskahs and I cast off our lines and gentled *MoonWind* out of her slip and motored out to the sound.

"Salty," sez I, "we must set a course for lobstah rolls and milkshakes."

"Avast, ye lubbah," sez Salty. "Doan *MoonWind* know her way to Noank by now?"

"No where? sez I.

"That place you can't drop yer hook in the mud," sez Salty.

"Oh, that place," sez I. "Where boats sleep peacefully at their piers, and the lobstahs eat any children what wades in the Cove?"

This is the way me an' Salty Whiskahs converses, but then we ain't but in our fourth or maybe our fifth childhoods.

If I had to write, let alone, think, like this all the time, I'd never get anything published whatsoever. And *MoonWind* most probably wouldn't allow me aboard. She has her standards, you see. Sparkman and Stephens educated their boats before they launched them. Grammar, diction, orthography, and punctuation are mandatory for every boat before she even learns to compute her hull speed. Of course, living with an author has allowed *MoonWind* a certain latitude in sentence construction. I've been told that longitude is entirely different.

MoonWind and I have a relationship loosely based on syntactical divagation. Not that we don't employ impeccable English the while we sail from over there to about here. Aside from sentence fragments, which *MoonWind* deigns to accept, our conversation would satisfy Mister Strunk, Mister White, Mister Fowler, and, especially, our great uncle Noah Webstah. No need to be alarmed by sentence fragments. What's good enough for Walt Kelly is good enough for *MoonWind*.

Now that her autobiography has been published, *MoonWind* feels a confidence that heretofore eluded her, except for those afternoons she chooses to bestow her affections on local rocks. She now knows herself capable of ridding West Cove of any boulders audacious enough to avoid being on the chart.

But Salty Whiskahs was right for once in a while. Of course *MoonWind* knew her way to Noank. She lived there most of her forty years and still spends winters there if I can help it. Just point her at a lobstah roll and whisper, "Get 'em, Girl!" Nothing *MoonWind* prefers to lobstah rolls. Especially with potato chips and a view of Mystic Hahbah.

We'd a sailed up to the pier at Noank Shipyard only the wind died away to a less than a fitful whisper before we'd even rounded the nun by the hahbah mouth. I dropped the mainsail into her lazy jacks, doused the genny, and started the motor. The last half mile we puttered up the channel. We pirouetted into the wind and laid *MoonWind* alongside the pier what belongs to Abbot's Restaurant. After securing, we stretched our legs the quarter mile to Abbots. If this sounds like an excursion for unrequited lubbahs, you got that right. After a four mile sail we deserved not only a lobstah roll, but the cole slaw and chips as well.

Salty Whiskahs also indulged in a milkshake, but only, I fear, for the privilege of flirting with the young lady at the concession. It don't need twenty minutes to make a milkshake. Nonetheless he enjoyed his lunch and even picked up the tab, which he paid in Euro's. *MoonWind* was much impressed when I told her this. It ain't every crew what picks up the tab and knows how to twiddle the tiller into the bargain.

On the way home the breeze ramped up to a satisfying eight knots and heeled us over. Salty hooked his ankles over the leeward lifeline and rinsed the excess butter out of his beard. We eventually wafted into slip B forty-four behind Pine Island, and secured in time for aperitifs and supper. These included smoked bluefish and local ale. We then proceeded to praise *MoonWind* until she blushed, praise each other until we guffawed, and praise the day until it faded and the moon intruded herself.

Over the crackers and cheese, we nearly waxed serious. 'Nearly' being the operative word as we ain't waxed all that serious in nearly half a century. The crackers and cheese sustained us, nonetheless, and the moon indulged us after her pearly fashion. We made up our bunks and turned in early, exhausted by a surfeit of conversation.

Needless to say, which is why I especially need to say it to you, Salty Whiskahs and I enjoyed our sail, and reminisced most shamelessly about our continuing boyhoods. We ain't but knowed one another forty-odd years, and this gives us liberties unbeknownst to those whom Age ain't mellowed.

For those of you what's known one another for years beyond recall, I wish you the utmost pleasure in this world. There aren't but diminishing years to share such love, so if you have a friend what loves you as a sister or bonds as a brother, be especially good to each other for ever and for always.

For the tide flows in and the tide ebbs out, but friendship contrives to remain on course, notwithstanding.

*   *   *   *

One pristine September morning I bail my Whitehall pulling boat, grease the leathers, and load my day bag with digital camera, spare batteries, water, granola bar, apricots, bandana, sailing gloves, sunglasses, and mermaid identification cards. I keep the Whitehall at West Cove — wherever that is — a quarter mile from where *MoonWind* swings, oh, so indolently, on her mooring. I need to be able to row out and fondle her on occasion, and maybe take her out to sluice the marine growth from her bottom.

But today I need to straighten out some of my lumbar vertebrae with applied leverage: bend, reach, dip, straighten, pull; lift and breathe. Bend, reach, dip, straighten, pull; lift and breathe. Do it maybe six or eight times a minute for an hour or so and you maybe get to the next place. Depending on the tide and current and breeze and that blister on your fourth finger. You may have noticed my body's not in the shape it was about forty years ago. Why is that, I wonder?

Still, I make it as far as the piers. The launch driver is lazing in the yard's Halsey Herreshoff launch alongside the walkway in case someone wants to quit his mooring to enjoy some lubrication and calamari at the café. Being a sailor, he has a weather eye for a pretty boat.

"Love your Whitehall," he says. "Is she for sale?"

"Don't know that she is," I say. "But you're welcome to scratch her ears."

He kicks off his sandals and hands me his VHF.

"Anyone calls, you can tell 'em I've eloped," he says.

He adjusts the footrest, and rows her out to the breakwater and back.

"What a sweetheart!" he exclaims.

"And she's house broken," I tell him. "Nearly. And she's had all of her shots."

Finally, I'm off to row up to Mystic Seaport. I wend past most of the moorings, behind Mouse Island, past Morgan Point Light, and into Mystic Harbor. The tide is slack; the current not oppressive; the mildest breeze presumes. I make good way considering my state of decrepitude. By the time I pass the shipyard, the two lobster pounds, and the tiny public beach I'm feeling easy: the Whitehall glides glibly through the water, and avoids the spate of yachts that returns from across the sparkling waters.

Mystic Harbor is filled with pretty sailboats on moorings. The slips are filled with cruisers of every description. Stately Colonials flank the shores. Then I have to round Six Penny Island – a mere salt marsh of a sandpit that shoves itself athwart the harbor. Then things spread out, and posh marine facilities indulge the overtly fortunate. On the eastern

MoonWind and Whitehall

shore a large marina accommodates a 100' yacht from the Cayman Islands at a tee-head pier. It takes me several strokes to leave her astern.

Eventually, I reach the railroad bridge. A forty-something foot, lovely wooden sloop awaits its opening. I scoot ahead and pass beneath the trestle, sitting upright. A few hundred yards, two more marinas, and then I approach the venerable bascule bridge in downtown Mystic. The tide being full, I need to hunker down to avoid decapitation. I emerge to find Mystic Seaport just where I'd left it – a mere quarter mile upstream.

I meander about the Shipyard taking photos of the steam launch *Sabino* and the fishing smack *Emma C. Berry* to convert to pen and ink drawings for my forthcoming book of local landmarks. I play touch last with the little catboat, *Breck Marshall*, which wafts about the Seaport with her mere handful of visitors. The tide turns in my favor. Downstream at the Schooner Wharf I find the three-master, *Mystic*, is abroad. The charter schooner, *Argia*, is out in the Sound. An old salt enjoys his lunch aboard his pretty little wooden launch alongside the pier. I back the *Whitehall* up to him and we swap a few threadbare yarns. He peers at my transom.

"How do you call your Whitehall?" He inquires.

"I don't have to call her," I say. "She comes to me when I whistle."

"You ought to name her," he says to me. "Boat ought to have a name."

"Still haven't thought of a name for my son," I say, "and he turns thirty-eight in a couple of weeks."

"Boat ought to have a name," he says again.

"I sometimes call her *"Esmeralda,"* I tell him. "Not that she listens."

I drift away and splash a bit as I back water.

"Where did you learn to row a boat?" he asks me.

"If I knew how to row a boat," I say, "I'd be up the River annoying old men at lunch."

"You'd be better off safe at home where it's dry, writing one of your foolish stories," he says.

"I may just try that," I tell him.

*   *   *   *

Life without *MoonWind*

From the Journals of Constant Waterman - November 2014

Will this be the last time I get to wet *MoonWind*'s anchor? It has come to selling my beloved boat in order to pay our bills, as our Colonial Cape in Mystic hasn't sold. We are both unemployed and eking but a precarious existence from our respective crafts.

So here I swing on a cool November morning between Old Lyme and Old Saybrook up the mouth of the Connecticut. I took a photo of the full moonrise last night and a photo of this pink, striated sunrise; took the Whitehall for a row about the marshes a couple of miles; and now enjoy some French roast and my notebook here in my cabin.

Were I to indulge my fantasies, my dreams, I should ever thus rise to a dreamy dawn with none but birds to embrace me. You hear the poet in me, so long submerged, surface to express my inmost yearnings.

And you, my friend – what are your inmost yearnings? Does your spirit crave love, or expression, or immortality? Are you satisfied with, or resigned to seventy summers? How many, how few remain? Will your ultimate sun go down in the sea with a stirring display of color, or will some grim mist glide up and over your soul?

Do not expend a moment in contemplating your grace or lack thereof. Exult! Create! Share! Shout your amazement of this world! Though you be bound by a wheelchair forever, pick up a plume and share your passion; pick up a brush and portray the force of life; pick up your flute and cause the world to cry. Cast up your music to the god and goddess; offer your soul to Heaven!

The marshes behind Great Island spread stilly this morning. I wiped the dew from the Whitehall's thwart, greased my leathers, and shoved off into the nearly bird deprived dawn. The estuary behind Great Island lay a hundred scant yards abeam. I made the turn into the broad stream lined with tall phragmites. I saw one osprey during the course of an hour. Few little birds were abroad – it was eerily quiet.

Muse, Polyhymnia, Serenades Olympus

No fish jumped, no boats went by, no revelation leapt from the whispering reeds. I explored some narrow cul-de-sacs, poling with one oar. I straggled amid the yellow grass; I stretched to embrace the sky. I glided upon the ebb tide to return.

MoonWind awaited me patiently, as always. She understands my moods, and seldom objects to my forays and divagations. I made a pot of oatmeal and put some raisins into it. I made a second cup of coffee and scribbled in this journal. I stowed as much as I could in my quarter berth and washed my dishes.

Being but twenty miles from home – *MoonWind*'s home I should say – there was no need to look at a chart or plot a course or confer with

Uncle Aeolus. I started my motor, hoisted my main, and unemployed my anchor. I headed into the wind and hoisted my jib. The six-knot breeze and the running tide took me back out to sea. I patted the Jetty Lighthouse a fond farewell and set a course for old number eight – that tall red bell that lies beyond Long Sand Shoals. Once around that it's sixteen miles due east to downtown Noank – and the wind was out of the west and the tide would abet me another couple of hours.

I had but to twiddle the helm and muse on mortality.

We are sentient beings, you and I, with receptors designed to fulfill our every desire. We are generative, in the physical sense; we must attempt to prove our spiritual genius. "Dust to dust, ashes to ashes," mouth the Lord's many ministers. Lo! We are all ministers after our fashion, and the dust we become shall nurture those plants that sustain some future spirit; and the ash we become shall cradle another ember to warm this world.

My genoa slatted, and I needed to pay attention lest I jibe. I scuttled forward and set my preventer. I headed up a few degrees and sheeted my genoa snugly. I revived myself with water and a mealy apple. I wandered half way out to the Race where the tide and current were having an altercation, but left them to it, and jibed and headed back toward the mouth of the Thames. Off Pine Island I reset my preventer and wung out my rags. I traipsed my last few miles wreathed in beauty.

The melted sun had drooped halfway to the sea when I fetched West Cove. I started my motor, dropped my mainsail into her lazy jacks, unhanked my jib, and kicked my basking fenders over the side. I pulled the Whitehall alongside and told her she'd been a good girl. I puttered around the end of Pier 'D' and whispered into my slip.

Life should be this easy.

*   *   *   *

Sailing is much like playing the piano. I should know, because, although I can sail, I have no ability with a piano, except to stack non-fiction books, matted prints, and the cat's breakfast upon it. My very best friend died after playing the piano for merely sixty years, and I'm still here, so I guess sailing my boat is a healthier pastime.

Those of you who both sail and perform on the piano might consider stepping a mast on your Steinway to spend your weekends sailing her around the Elizabeth Islands off Cape Cod. There used to be a couple of old, cutter-rigged Steinways that moored at Cuttyhunk after the summer people had all fled back to the mainland of Massachusetts. In the evening you would hear Chopin or maybe Rachmaninov wafting across the water. It was most delightful. I've also heard a string quartet employing a jib halyard, a backstay, a topping lift, and a lazy jack, but there was really no comparison. The topping lift was invariably out of tune.

Speaking of Cuttyhunk, I've spent a few pleasant weekends there. By October, the cottontails outnumber the winter residents six to one. The little schoolhouse has so few students that they're obliged to teach horticulture and herblore to twenty-three bright-eyed bunnies, otherwise they'd be in grave danger of losing their state accreditation.

After class lets out at three o'clock, the bunnies all troop next door to the little library, and read from the extensive "Mother West Wind Stories" until their mothers get off blossom culling at five o'clock and pick them up. The older bunnies from the fourth form generally prefer the Doctor Doolittle books. The two librarians invariably serve lavender cookies and chamomile tea promptly at four o'clock.

For those of you surfeited with the least doings of the admirable Doctor Doolittle, the library also carries the journals of May Sarton and Henry Thoreau to stimulate your mind. Neither of these will help you much if you've previously succumbed to sixty years of playing a piano, no matter how grand. Even George Gershwin and Scott Joplin may not suffice to keep you among the living for more than a century, though I've heard that lavender cookies may make you immortal. As eating merely one lavender cookie assures you of living until tomorrow, it follows that one daily cookie will keep you alive forever.

So can sailing. No one has ever contested this except for one curmudgeonly salt who traded in his Alberg sloop for a trawler. She promptly found the only rock for forty miles around, and sank in merely forty minutes in forty fathoms of forty-degree water. His body was never recovered, but they say that a number of local crabs complained of serious colic not too long after.

Aside from him, all sailors live forever. I know this for a fact, and my elderly friend, Odysseus, confirms it. Despite the wiles of Calypso, Circe, Polyphemus, and Poseidon, Odysseus survived to be reunited with his wife, Penelope, and their son, Telemachus. Although Odysseus had been away from Ithaca for twenty years and Telemachus was only eighteen, Penelope convinced Odysseus that their son had been born prematurely. Some men will believe anything their wives tell them. Sailors' wives, especially, have cultivated the art of storytelling. Musicians' wives not only are unconvincing storytellers, but are lucky if they can differentiate between a day-sailer and a Dobro. And we all know how poorly a Dobro sails, especially close hauled. Any sailor who can get his Dobro to hold her course within five points of the wind deserves to live forever – and to own a Herreshoff boat after his Dobro spews her caulking.

Given the choice between a Steinway piano and a Dobro, I'd take a week on Cuttyhunk every time.

*   *   *   *

28 Dec 2014

Jeremiah Mason House

Limerick, Maine

Before me in this parlor is a modest black marble fireplace – dormant and cold – surmounted by an ornately gold framed mirror five feet wide that rises nearly to the foot-wide molding surrounding this twelve foot ceiling.

All I can see in this mirror is my boat, though *MoonWind* lies forlorn in her slip two hundred miles to the south. The Whitehall hugs the opposite pier six cormorant lengths away. I choose to think they console one another in a sisterly fashion and await my infrequent ministrations during this inclement season.

Most of this week it has rained – a chill and dis-consoling procession of raindrops from the gloomy heavens. But Christmas day arrived in dryer fettle. By mid-morning we had an unwonted glimpse of the sun, and it grew unaccountably mild – near sixty degrees. I lashed my slim spruce oars in my truck and trundled off to the boatyard.

I should have liked to go sailing one last time. Had I left at an earlier hour, I should now be able to brag that I went sailing on Christmas day. I might even have returned in time to partake of Christmas dinner. I resigned myself to merely messing about.

Cormorant and Mummichog

The Whitehall held a mere forty gallons of sweet water. I should start *MoonWind*'s motor and let it run while I bailed her tender. I tilted the outboard into the drink, primed the carburetor and pressed the starter.

The silence was impressive. I checked to be sure my thumb was on the button. I checked the main power switch that supplies the panel and discovered that I had neglected to turn it off my previous trip. All my little electrons had snuck off for the holidays. How thoroughly thoughtless of them.

I discovered my pristine starter cord among my effects and removed the motor cowl and flywheel cover. She started on the third pull and ran smoothly. I should row about for a while and let the whirling motor charge my battery. I hopped down and walked round the slip to the Whitehall and bailed her dry. I wiped the seat, stowed the oars and set the footrest in place. I cast off and clambered aboard.

MoonWind lazed in her slip as I passed her astern. On my way to the fairway I also passed *Endeavor*, *Galadriel*, and *Rapture*. Rapture, indeed!

Hearing voices, I pulled to Pier A where a local skiff departed with a handful of joyous travelers to nearby Fishers Island. I pulled partway into a slip to let her pass and exchanged waves with her skipper. In moments she was on her way to the Sound, leaving the boatyard still as I'd ever known it. Neither yard crew, mechanic, nor sailor could be seen or heard. The seagulls were on sabbatical; the five hundred boats were free to dream of sunshine and breeze and birdsong.

I rowed across the inlet, and past the piers stacked high with lobster pots. The lobster boats lay fast in their slips; the four by four mooring markers glistened in the pale sun. The inner cove, sheltered by Mouse Island, the point, and the breakwater, placidly rippled. The breeze refrained from any undue exertion. The tide sloshed quietly 'gainst the retaining walls. My easy fisherman's stroke sufficed to part the supple water.

This was my Christmas present to myself and I unwrapped it moment by moment.

I let the breeze spin me slowly back toward the piers. With a few choice strokes I scooted between piers C and D and returned to check on *MoonWind*. There she lay, with her motor purring contentedly and peeing unashamedly into her slip.

I secured the Whitehall fore and aft, adjusted her fenders, unshipped her Shaw and Tenneys, and scuttled ashore. Back aboard *MoonWind*, I turned off her motor and started it with the button. I turned it off, tipped it out of the water, and replaced the cowl. I gathered up bits of my gear from below: my Leatherman pliers, a wet bandana, a 12-volt converter, a near empty bottle of tincture of myrrh, my registration certificate. I checked the bilge, the head, my chafing gear. I shut down my 12-volt panel, replaced my drop boards, and slid home my hatch.

I carried my oars and my bucket of gear to my truck, who ruminated in the shade of two tall sloops asleep in their poppets. It was now nearly noon and I needed to return and prepare for Christmas dinner.

Why are there never hours enough to mess about with our boats? Those hours we borrow to mess about we must treasure as rubies and pearls.

The present is all we have or shall ever have, and though gift wrapped with care must be opened with eager fingers and squandered with joy.

Season's greetings to all, and remember to tell your boats how much you love them.

*   *   *   *

It was near freezing this February morning but threatened a balmy fifty degrees by afternoon — not bad for February the first. I believe global warming was designed with us boaters in mind: we not only get more days to play in our temperate zone, but shall soon have a new coastline to explore with more and expanded tidal marshes. All the rivers will be backed up by the rising sea and will spread out. All the little, previously un-navigable streams will become deep and wide. The sale of canoes and kayaks will multiply enormously — especially as many of the roads will be under water and people will be forced to paddle to work.

So I took advantage of this balmy winter day to explore a reach of the Pachaug River with which I wasn't familiar. Having been corrupted by sailboats the past ten or fifteen years, I hadn't done much exploring of our local streams. My bright yellow kayak, *Goldfinch*, lay in my yard and whimpered.

"Today, Lass," I whispered, and slid her into the back of my old Ford van. I tugged on my wetsuit and booties, donned my floppy sailing hat, kissed my cat and petted my wife farewell.

"If I'm not back by Thursday," I told her, "send the other kayak out to find me."

I grabbed my camera, gloves and water bottle, jumped in the van, and galumphed on over to the landing in nearby Voluntown, Connecticut. As expected, there was still a bit of ice verging the river. I bumped *Goldfinch* across it and slid into the water. Ah, Freedom! For some reason there weren't any other paddlers on the river this sunny morning. Between two dams, I had about four miles of quiet water. Beachdale Pond, downstream, lay mostly iced in, so I couldn't go messing about in the shallows. The muskrats were busily sleeping the winter away; the kingfisher was still away on vacation. The pines greenly adorned the hill; the little grey alders clung tightly to their cones; the sere phragmites, cattails, and flag whispered palely with the breeze.

I paddled down to the dam, parked *Goldfinch* between the yellow stripes, and got out to look around. This dam backs up about fifty acres of placid pond. Below the dam a thirty-foot-wide, shallow rapids looked not the least inviting. There seemed more stones than water, and no one had cut away the trees fallen across the stream. I paddled back to the landing and proceeded upstream. The Pachaug here in its upper reach is seldom more than fifty feet broad, and sometimes half of that. A few summer cottages hunker along one brief stretch of bank, just above high water. Most of the land about the river is part of Pachaug State Forest, and remains delightfully wild. "Pachaug," in Native American denotes, "bend in the river." There proved no shortage of bends. The current was scarcely discernable, but we haven't had much precipitation lately.

Boaters had sawed or hacked off limbs that leaned across the stream, but there wasn't much leeway for sneaking by at the narrowest portions of the river. This is mostly a swampy stretch without any rocks – except, of course, one five-foot, water smoothed boulder just in front of the cabin with the blue canoe. On this particular day this rock's broad mossy crown lay only two inches below the surface, and the current scarcely produced a revealing ripple.

Goldfinch decided she needed a rest and climbed atop this boulder. We each admired the view for a minute and then I pushed off the rock and got us afloat.

The water ran silkily, the sun shone brightly, the adverbs remained eminently employed. I found reflections galore and photographed the best after allowing my tiny wake to subside. I may begin a new career in photography one day soon, as my urges to illustrate in black and white leave something to be desired. Someday I may publish a book entitled "Reflections," to glorify the sun and water and trees and small stone bridges.

Aside from a few mallards, I saw nothing that moved – not even the Pachaug. I picked my way upstream another mile or so until I met a twin maple that lay athwart the river. Even with my wetsuit it didn't seem worthwhile to slosh about waist deep in the frigid water. Besides, it was half past lunch. I turned *Goldfinch* around and tapped the 'home' key - and here I am.

Later in Feb 2016

Well, I have to write something, don't you know? Today I figured would be a good day to go out and wet a paddle. It was crowding 60 degrees, at least at NOAA. It wasn't nearly that on Hopeville Pond, but it was quite mild. I had on my wetsuit and a wooly hat knitted by some thoughtful person in Nepal. I understand the winters can get quite brisk in the Himalayas, though the sailing is problematic.

I took my camera, extra gloves, a length of line – I'll explain about this in the next paragraph – and a bag of organic trail mix sent to me by my organic son who lives organically in San Francisco. What more could you possibly need save a water bottle – which I forgot – and a two-piece double paddle – which I didn't. Fortunately, I was out on the water only for an hour. My patient wife was in our van reading her book and hoping I wouldn't drown. Well, I paddled down to the modern dam that spans the Pachaug River in Griswold, Connecticut, and messed about watching a hawk whom I disturbed, and who circled several times while I ineffectually tried to extricate my camera from the bottom of my kit bag.

This is the next paragraph. For those of you not in the know, or maybe, not in the no, a length of line is a handy thing for walking your kayak, or even your canoe, either up or downstream where it isn't practical to paddle it. If you tie a long length of line – maybe thirty or forty feet – between your bow and your stern, you can walk your canoe along the bank. Depending how you hold this bridle, you can guide your boat either with or against the current. To walk upstream, keep the bow away from the bank; downstream, keep the stern away from the bank. This is a handy maneuver when the water is too shallow or stony to allow you to stay inside your boat. If the bank is littered with fallen trees, boulders, ravines, or ravenous beasts, you may have to wade in the water to lead your canoe. If you get your feet wet, you can tell your mother it was solely my idea.

I'd actually scouted out this dam yesterday afternoon. I'd driven up Edmund Road till I crossed the river. Just across the bridge, on the upstream side, lay a most respectable farm house on the river bank with two respectable, elderly canoes basking on the riverbank in the pale sunshine. I parked in the drive, knocked at the door, and explained to the amiable lady there my concerns about the dam – just down river two hundred yards. She called her husband in from the barn and he patiently explained to me the way to portage the dam.

"Why don't you drive down the access road as though you were inspecting the dam, and park up against the barrier? The folks in the yeller house won't give you any trouble."

So I did, and, of course, they didn't. I walked down the sward beyond the dam and checked out possible put-ins. This modern concrete dam is constructed with two separate falls with an earthwork between. There's a sturdy bridge below the near dam by which one can access the farther dam and the stream proceeding below it, which seemed far friendlier and less lumpy. The two streams merge a few hundred feet down stream. I didn't think I could buck the current to return to where I would park.

A mile downstream the Pachaug spreads to fill up Ashland Pond, which provided the power for Ashland Cotton Mill – a concern that employed some 400 souls engaged to produce cloth. Hopeville Mills, Ashland Mills, and Slater Mills – below the Ashland dam – kept this town productive into the early twentieth century. Ashland Mills and Hopeville Mills have long since burned to the ground. Slater mills now houses a huge flea market. Hopeville Pond is now a state park with a lovely camping area and a pristine beach. You can read about it in "Quiet Water" by Alex Wilson and John Hayes – a guide for paddle boaters in Connecticut, Massachusetts, and Rhode Island.

Around this part of the world we haven't hundred-foot waterfalls to tempt the dare devil kayakers you may know. We take a leisurely jaunt with binoculars and cameras, then slop into local diners, swill coffee, and regale one another with our lies. Those of us who can't get a word in edgeways go home and write these stories for magazines. This has a distinct advantage, as readers will believe anything.

November 2016

Now that the muskrat has chosen his winter lair, and the night heron enjoys the longer nights, I thought I might take a moment to attend to the rites of autumn.

I'm now fast approaching my biblical three score and ten. I've squandered a score or more lightweight years wedded to a thirteen-foot, lightweight Grumman canoe with which I wended the lower reaches –

Black Crowned Night Heron

mostly – of the mostly languid, lovely Connecticut River. For those of you who don't know me, I grew up a mile from this lissome river, and walked or crawled or galumphed my way down to its waters most of my life. I fished and swam and sailed and rowed and paddled my first thirty years. Then I settled in to be a father, a husband, a businessman, and a disgruntled boat-less boater for the following twenty.

At fifty I had my midlife crisis. I divorced my first wife, embarked on a second, bought my first sailboat in twenty years, and proceeded to dub myself "Constant Waterman." I now wonder if this phase of my multifarious life has come to an end. I've sold my second spouse, "*MoonWind*." [The woman I wedded in 1999 still considers herself my second spouse, but what does she know?] It seems there is some subtle difference between a spouse and a boat. I'm not sure I'm the one to resolve this difference, lest my connubial privileges be revoked.

If you have both a boat and a spouse, I suggest they resemble each other in more ways than one. A spouse should be there to regale you and relieve you of your cares. A boat should be there to regale you and relieve you of your cares The yellow perch, the snapping turtle, the twist of the tide, the waning moon should regale your lease on life. The setting sun, the sibilant breeze should relieve you of your ultimate care – who's going to feed the cat while you're out sailing?

There are not months, nay, years enough, to try the riffle, to test the wave, to stem the current, to reeve the breeze through your sail. We are not here merely to work, to strive, to justify, to merely witness the wind. We are here to glide, to illustrate, to examine. The river is wide, is narrow, is only ourselves. Ply your paddle, your sail, your only proprium. Today is but one of your not-too-many morrows – be thankful for every one of them.

And here am I – stuck in this furrow I've plowed for myself – repairing houses and selling books and illustrations and mending boats that haven't a competent owner to do it for them. The years stream by and my kayaks and Whitehall pulling boat bask in my nigh backyard where I can watch them and weep. *MoonWind* has gone to a family in Westport, Mass. My wetsuit is in the back of my closet, somewhere. My paddle is in the back of my tool shed, relating tales of estuarine adventure to the mice.

Meanwhile, I ply this electronic paddle, this internet narrative of my dependence on the river, the stream, the raindrop. You catch me at my most lyrical, most reflective. Does not the pool in the forest reflect as well or better than any tidal pool? I never forget the large tidal pool amid a granite outcrop of Rockport, Massachusetts. It was there I learned to sail my 20-inch sloop; to gather periwinkles; test the tide.

Come February I count myself an elder of this human race. Hopefully not a race around those marks that many of you consider a measure of competence. Booming home on a broad reach, though it may be fun, is merely a measure of time; and time, to one of my years, is merely a measure of competition and not a love of the sea, the sky, the breeze. Let your sails bear you to oblivion; let your journey neither begin nor end by a steel marker. I hope to see you extravagating across the extravagant waters; hope to hale you in the lee of that island.

Eight Mile River, Old Hamburg, CT

A Final Digression

I have now nearly finished another book; poured the requisite words and pictures onto these pages; tried to balance inspiration with editing; drawn on my funds of creativity.

Now nearly destitute of any inspiration. I shall have to renew my resources by living as opposed to recording. It is not enough to think. One must act as well. My energy to strut and fret may wane with each passing decade, but I must assure myself of my capabilities. I must sail my boat, or, at the least, paddle my smaller vessels; and illustrate; and mingle with authors and painters and musicians; and love my wife and my friends.

I must spend as little time as possible looking in my innermost windows. Though the view be fine, yet it is merely three dimensional. One needs as many dimensions as exist to be complete. The dimension of Time has most relevance to us mortals: knowing the limitations of our lives, we strive for assurance; flout mortality; wrestle with ill health; deplore the commitments that keep us from creating. We are but as our Creator made us: stubborn and reluctant; fragile yet resilient. We must cultivate resolve; simulate strength, if we mean to accomplish much.

*   *   *   *

Distractions are rife. Communication is now so prevalent that one can spend hours and hours on social networking. People text and telephone while walking through the woods, and return, having neither heard nor seen the life, the beauty, about them. People listen to music as they sail. Watching television is so compulsive that people turn it on as soon as they wake for fear of missing - what? Life? Open your window and listen. Even reading is but a substitute: a set of vicarious thrills. Don't read a murder mystery. Go out and kill a friend.

Much of my joy of sailing is the relative quietude. I refuse to listen to the VHF, the radio, or my cell phone. I may listen to music in the evening when I'm at anchor, but to sail is to sail is to sail. I wish my every fiber to be strung; my senses to be acute; my mind receptive. I cannot record the words of the wind, the heave of the sea, the distain of the gull, the urge of my spreading sail. But I can enjoy them. For the merest moment, occasionally, I can be the wind, the sea, the gull, my sail. But not often. And not for long. I need to practice. The greatest art of all may be to Be Here Now, as Ram Dass maintained.

The words in my head interfere enough as it is. I have no need of electronic distractions. To be as one with this world is a lifelong challenge. To record and interpret that challenge the aim of my creativity.

My humorous interludes only record my awareness that life is precious, that life is short, that time and possessions get in our way. Humor is an outlet for frustration. For a writer it is also a chance to play with our marvelous language. For play is underrated. Pure laughter is underrated. True love is underrated. Good food and drink are sometimes underrated. These are the consolations of our less than perfect lives, and we shouldn't ignore them. Ask any handicapped person. Such as yourself. If you are exemplary in body, mind, and spirit, you needn't read any further. Heaven help us.

My handicap is taking myself seriously. I've tried to give up this immature habit, but every so often I falter in my efforts.

Every mystery I encounter leads to another realm of realization – coming to know, if not accept, another mode of madness. For that is what propels our need to know: our mad denial of the obvious; to have this world other than we perceive it.

Our prophets and our sages tell us this: to be at one with this world, this life, this time; to live; to respect all life; to attempt to learn. Of speculation little do we know; of the machinations of our minds, less still. Is deduction truer, more relevant than induction? Who can tell, or prove it to one of contrary opinion? To convert the unwilling world detracts from what little time is ours to enjoy.

Rather, learn to accept all philosophies; live discreetly; waste no judiciousness on trivialities. Choose from lofty ethics; be sincere. Your love, your loss, your longing are your own.

Here is your world – see to it when you can. It is full of miracles – some explainable, but miracles nonetheless. If your life stales, look to another, a fresher. What fresher than nature, who renews herself continually; whose every year and day and moment should astound you. Only learn to be sentient without judgment. Forget the rest of the world for a little while. Take a camera and notebook, but leave your cell phone behind. Be careful not to fall into your microscope, lest you become as significant as the microbe on your slide.

Nature has authored the arch and the steeple; wind and water power, cosmic lighting. Astronomy is grand, but never confuse your awe with astrophysics. Read Walt Whitman's marvelous poem, "When I Heard the Learned Astronomer." If you study most diligently you may in time learn something of yourself. Then you may be able to deal with other people.

Most of us cultivate rage out of frustration. As our culture, schools, churches, leaders, and media mostly foster frustration, what should they expect save greed, violence, and hatred to result? These haven't solved the world's problems the past ten thousand years, and now that we can broadcast greed, violence, and hatred more efficiently than ever, we can expect dignity, respect, and understanding to lose their influence on civilization.

Dignify, respect, and understand! Learn and teach! Create, exult! Differ and dare! Share your wonder! Life is precious, but, fortunately, not permanent. Not in our present form, anyway. We weren't designed to love this world too long. Nor to abuse it. We have enough bad habits.

This Universe may be eternal. Then again it may not be. I won't be here nearly long enough to dispute it with any authority. Nor shall I presume to teach the gods their job, let alone provide them entertainment. My little bit of the Universe at this Midpoint of Eternity more than suffices my simple needs. It's fortunate that energy and matter, though interchangeable, are mutually indestructible. I'm glad to know that, ultimately, my body may serve to fertilize a tree, and that you may live to breathe that tree's exhalations.

Now I shall leave you to ponder that most imperative question: what do you mean to do with yourself today?

St. Stephen's Episcopal Church
East Haddam, Connecticut

One Last Lament

There used to be a good-sized river running down to the sea. Perhaps it's there even now, but there's no guarantee.

I grew up a mile away and used to carry my lightweight, thirteen-foot, Grumman canoe over the hill by our upper orchard, and down to the ferry landing. Returning, I had to trudge up that long, long hill. Then I got friendly with the couple in that big, yellow colonial on the riverbank – you know the place I mean. Somebody used to build good size boats out back of it by the Cove, but that was before I cut my teeth on an old, Shaw and Tenney paddle.

That four-room wing on the downstream side had been fished from the River after a flood, and spliced onto the house. Folks didn't shirk improbable projects back then. That house was full of fireplaces, and wide board floors that the River had warped on occasion. You know how it is – every half century or so they send us a bit of low pressure from the Caribbean, and the River ramps up maybe fifteen feet and kindly sands our floors for us.

We had a good storm in '54 when I was just a mere tadpole. I recollect there was water way past the fork in the road and over Cove Cemetery. The river road back to the bridge across the Creek was under water. The old man who lived across from Dutchman's Point declared he could fish for pickerel in his well that following autumn, but when he invited me to try, I caught nothing but perch. You can't believe everything folks from our village tell you.

I was going to say, before you diverted me, that I came to be friends with the couple in the yellow colonial and kept my canoe with theirs on the riverbank. They had an old seventeen-footer. Before science came up with all these modern, fancy plastics, somebody had the bright idea you could build a canoe of fiberglass. Well, you could. You just couldn't lift the darn thing up to put it into the water. Besides the fact that she weighed as much as a maple log and swam like a gravid cow, she was quite impressive. You could turn her around with only two people paddling in just a little bit under twenty minutes.

We kept our canoes on the riverbank beside all those rotten pilings. There'd been a commercial pier out front for the riverboats to tie up to when they made their daily trip on up to the Capitol. Used to be, you could ride that boat all the way to New York City, though I can't see why you'd want to. After the Second World War they discontinued that service, and let the pier return to the Powers of the Earth. Now there were maybe thirty, slimy, carious fangs just above or just below the surface, depending on the tide, and possible hazards to navigation – presuming you neglected to duck behind the silver maples that trailed their twigs in the River.

When we wanted hazards to navigation, we'd choose a small river: one with rocks and logs and dams and frothy water headed downhill in a hurry. This river I'm trying to tell you about was old and rather lethargic. It had tides and salt marshes and ospreys and swans and big, old, primitive things with beaks that lived in holes about water level and hissed and would take your fingers off were you fool enough to pet them.

Occasionally, you might see a deer in the River, or maybe a sturgeon. I used to hear all sorts of stories, growing up, about the things that used get snagged in shad nets. Anything small as a Packard got caught in a drift net they'd toss it back, but anything decent size, well, they'd likely slice it into steaks and drive it down to the city, then come home and lie to their wives how it took them all night to wrestle it into their boat.

Me, I was more interested in exploring the estuaries and backwaters and watching birds and catching small fish and petting the random mermaid who'd swum up the River to soak those pesky barnacles off her bottom. You salt water boaters know what I'm talking about.

In the summer months there were wild flowers and wild rice and ducks and herons and bushels of fish: everything you'd ever need to make you shirk your chores at home and sneak off through the woods to play on the River. I owned a few acres upstream on an island so, naturally, I built a cabin out there. That way I could delude myself I hadn't any chores at all.

I had a bundle of tongue and groove boards lashed alongside my canoe one day, down by the Landing, when here came a zealous man in green with an attitude, and a hat and a badge to go with it.

"Where you taking that lumber, Son?" he demanded.

I wasn't his son. At least I hoped I wasn't.

"Just up to my island, Pappy," I said. "Need to get my cabin closed in before you people pass any more regulations."

And off I paddled. After all, I had a building permit. Didn't much care that he jumped up and down and flailed the breeze and got water in his shoes. Wasn't my problem. I needed to catch the tide.

Seems as though things have speeded up considerably since then. They started allowing cigarette boats on the River. Then they had to go and post a speed limit: forty-five knots. How can you see anything at forty-five knots? You know how large a paddle you'd need to canoe at forty-five knots? At supersonic speeds like that, you'd never hear the wind rattle the cottonwood leaves. At speeds like that, you'd never hear that big bass jump midst the cattails. At speeds like that, if you looked up to watch Orion fling his spear at Leo, you'd likely run down that oil tanker crossing below the island.

I don't suppose there are many people do that anymore – canoe by moonlight. Now that I've been corrupted by the sea and sailing boats I no longer do it myself, these days. I don't even live within a long day's paddle of that river, those coves, those islands.

As I said, there's no guarantee that river of mine still makes its way down to the sea. There's no guarantee it still laps the Landing just down the hill beyond our upper orchard. There's no guarantee that Grandfather Bass and his lovely mate even now patrol the Cove. Maybe, if you swing by that way, you might take a look, and break it to me gently.

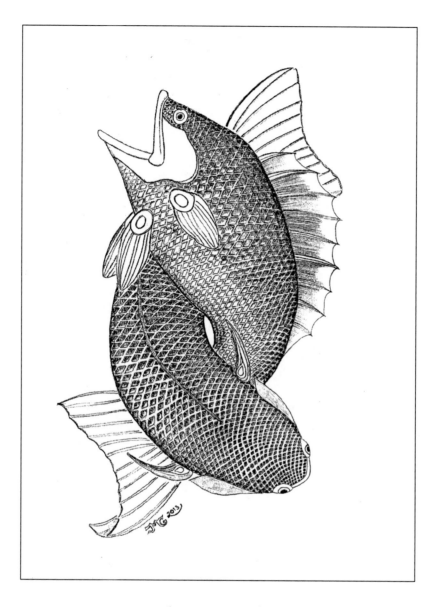

… and His Lovely Mate

Epilogue

As I am again arrived at the Midpoint of Eternity, I must bid you here a deferential farewell. My final shaft is sped, my quill is dry, my bowl is nearly empty. When next I overtake this Here and Now, my quiver and quill and bowl may again be full. I shall nock a shaft and take aim at the Infinite.

Time roars by at a furious pace, and threatens to leave me, shipwrecked upon an unsubstantial dream. As oft before, I shall swim to another island, clamber ashore, and waste another half century writing books and drawing pictures.

I scarcely comprehend the extent of time. I scarcely follow the sun's radiant passage across the sky. I scarcely notice the gravid moon as she rocks the ocean to sleep. I am busy in my little world of words. Thus it behooves me to sail my boat upon the heaving sea at every occasion; to reach my outspread fingers to touch the heavens; to sleep with my head upon the breast of the night.

I hope to return to be with you sometime soon; to continue my quest for the Midpoint of Eternity. The raindrop, the stream, the river, the sea; all champion continuation. The tall tree stoops to tell the earth, again, of his boundless love. The flower resolves that tomorrow will find her more beautiful than she is today.

Perhaps it will.

Constant Waterman

Griswold, Connecticut

May 6, 2018

… and take aim at the Infinite.

CPSIA information can be obtained
at www.ICGtesting.com
Printed in the USA
FFOW01n1615030618
46983010-49257FF